BORDERS AMONG ACTIVISTS

Borders among Activists

International NGOs in the United States, Britain, and France

Sarah S. Stroup

Cornell University Press

Ithaca and London

Cornell University Press gratefully acknowledges receipt of a grant from
the Scholarly Publication Subvention Fund of Middlebury College, which
aided in the publication of this book.

First published 2012 by Cornell University Press
Printed in the United States of America

Library of Congress Cataloging-in-Publication Data

Stroup, Sarah S. (Sarah Snip), 1978–
  Borders among activists : international NGOs in the United States,
Britain, and France / Sarah S. Stroup.
    p. cm.
  Includes bibliographical references and index.
  ISBN 978-0-8014-5073-0 (cloth : alk. paper)
  1. Non-governmental organizations—United States.   2. Non-
governmental organizations—Great Britain.   3. Non-governmental
organizations—France.   I. Title.
  JZ4841.S79   2012
  341.2—dc23   2011042190

Cloth printing   10 9 8 7 6 5 4 3 2 1

Contents

Acknowledgments

My words of thanks are insufficient payment to the many people who have made this book possible. Most immediately, my work was made possible by generous and honest activists and analysts in the humanitarian and human rights fields. They remain anonymous, and I remain grateful for their time and help.

Colleagues at many institutions helped move this project from concept to book. At Berkeley, particular thanks go to Steve Weber for getting me thinking about nonstate actors in international relations and to Steve Vogel for a careful eye and always generous advice. Ann Swidler, Chris Ansell, and Vinnie Aggarwal each offered thoughtful attention and insight. At Middlebury, many people have been wonderfully helpful. Thanks to the college, especially Jim Ralph for research funding, and to Kyle Hunter, Michal Micner, and Xiaoxue Weng for their able research assistance. I am also grateful to the following people who read part or all of the manuscript: Michael Barnett, Peter Bell, Erik Bleich, Kateri Carmola, Maggie Clinton, Orion Lewis, Joyce Mao, Sidney Tarrow, Jessica Teets, and Wendy

Wong. Parts of this project have been presented at the College of William and Mary, Colgate University, UC Berkeley, and the 2008 and 2009 annual meetings of the International Studies Association; I very much benefited from the comments of those in attendance. In Britain, Stephen Hopgood was particularly generous with his time and helped facilitate several key interviews. Other colleagues have improved my thinking at various stages of this project. Thanks especially to: Naazneen Barma (my evil rival), Jennifer Bussell, Tim Büthe, Thad Dunning, Martha Finnemore, Michael Goldstein, Ken Haig (who suggested the term "varieties of activism"), Rebecca Hamlin, David Kang, Jeffrey Legro, James Morrison, Amanda Murdie, Kim Reimann, Kaja Sehrt, David Stoll, and Amy Yuen. Finally, I am grateful for the support and careful attention of Roger Haydon and two anonymous reviewers at Cornell University Press, who were instrumental in helping me build a more robust argument.

Family and friends have given love, encouragement, and much-needed perspective. My parents, Robert and Virginia Snip, are incredible role models—brilliant, fun, and loving. Many thanks to Katherine Snip, Gerrit Snip, Kathleen and Stephen Stroup, Jason and Sarah Provonsha, Elizabeth Stroup, Sunny Bowles, Kim Keith Berglund, Betsy Querna Cliff, Leslie Plaisted, Amanda Trause Manger, Lucy Buford Ricca, Harrison and Michaela Grubbs, Sean and Jill Walsh, Sarah and Chris Hale, and Nan and Nate Guilmette.

My last words are for those who enrich every one of my days. To John, Madeleine, and Henry—thank you for this joyful life.

ABBREVIATIONS

ACF	Action contre la Faim
AI	Amnesty International
ATD Quart Monde	Aide à toute détresse Quart Monde
BOND	British Overseas NGOs for Development
CAFOD	Catholic Overseas Development Agency (Britain)
CARE	Cooperative for Assistance and Relief Everywhere
CCFD	Comité catholique contre la faim et pour le développement
CI	CARE International
DFID	Department for International Development (Britain)
ECHO	European Commission's Humanitarian Aid and Civil Protection department (formerly European Community Humanitarian Aid Office)
ESC rights	Economic, social, and cultural rights
FCO	Foreign and Commonwealth Office (Britain)
FIDH	Fédération Internationale des ligues des Droits de l'Homme
HRF	Human Rights First

HRW	Human Rights Watch
ICRC	International Committee of the Red Cross
INGO	international nongovernmental organization
IRC	International Rescue Committee
IS	International Secretariat (Amnesty International)
LDH	Ligue des Droits de l'Homme
MSF	Médecins Sans Frontières
MSF-I	MSF International
NGO	Nongovernmental organization
OI	Oxfam International
Oxfam	Oxford Committee for Famine Relief
RSF	Reporters sans frontières
SC-UK	Save the Children UK
USAID	United States Agency for International Development
WVI	World Vision International

Introduction

Where Have All the Borders Gone?

On January 12, 2010, Haiti was hit by a magnitude 7.0 earthquake that killed over 200,000 people, opening a devastating new chapter in the troubled nation's history. As often happens after such tragedies, developed nations and international organizations convened a donor conference a few months later to discuss Haiti's reconstruction and development. Among those that sought to shape the debates were major private relief and development organizations that had long experience in fragile states like Haiti. But they did not all say the same thing, nor did they say it in similar ways. The medical relief organization Médecins Sans Frontières (MSF) argued that access to health care must remain free, and pressured donors to provide direct financial support to the Haitian government to build the capacity of the state. Oxfam International focused on holding international donors accountable. Oxfam spokesman Philippe Mathieu pointed out that victims of natural disasters have often been promised money that has never materialized, and provocatively argued that this donor conference "cannot be a VIP pageant of half promises." Another prominent organization,

CARE, emphasized instead the shared goals of private and public agencies. In a series of private meetings in the United States and Europe, CARE diplomatically stated that the global community must make a long-term commitment to Haiti aimed at creating "good governance and a more just and egalitarian society."[1]

These three charitable groups had decades of experience in Haiti and all faced the same situation, but throughout the year following the earthquake, each organization focused on distinct aspects of the crisis and used different tactics to make its point. Even as short-term medical care improved through 2010, MSF's reports and field worker testimonies focused on the problems with the earthquake response and continued to demand that the international community provide funding to the Haitian government to support long-term health care for the Haitian people.[2] Meanwhile, Oxfam published a half-dozen research reports in which it made specific and ambitious policy recommendations, including the full disbursement of aid, the cancellation of Haiti's $890 million in foreign debt, and the opening of American markets to Haitian agriculture.[3] By contrast, CARE's reports and press releases played up the positive contributions being made on the ground in Haiti, and when new challenges like the October cholera outbreak emerged, CARE delicately called for a "joint and long-term effort" involving the Haitian government, international donors, and NGOs.[4]

1. Jonathan Katz, "Donors Pledge $9.9 Billion for Haiti," Associated Press, April 1, 2010; "UN Donor Conference: Given the Immense Needs, Haitians Must Have Continued Access to Medical Care," Doctors Without Borders/Médecins Sans Frontières press release, March 30, 2010; "CARE Announces Key Recommendations for Haiti's Recovery, Reconstruction, and Development Needs," CARE press release, March 22, 2010.

2. *Emergency Response after the Haiti Earthquake: Choices, Obstacles, Activities, and Finance,* MSF report, July 2010; *Haiti One Year After: A Review of Medécins Sans Frontières' Humanitarian Aid Operations,* MSF report, January 10, 2011; "Frontline: One Year after the Haiti Earthquake," MSF Frontline podcast, January 19, 2011.

3. *Haiti: A Once-in-a-Century Chance for Change, Oxfam Briefing Paper 136* (March 2010); *Planting Now: Agricultural Challenges and Opportunities for Haiti's Reconstruction, Oxfam Briefing Paper 140* (October 2010); *From Relief to Recovery: Supporting Good Governance in Post-earthquake Haiti, Oxfam Briefing Paper 142* (January 6, 2011); "Oxfam Urges Quick Action on Haiti Trade Bill," Oxfam America press release, February 2, 2010.

4. *The Way Forward: Haiti Three Months after the Earthquake, April 2010; CARE, A Long Journey: Haiti One Year after the Earthquake,* CARE report, January 2011; "CARE: Addressing Haiti's Vulnerability beyond the Current Epidemic," CARE press release, November 22, 2010.

How can we explain the differences in these policy prescriptions and political strategies? Unfortunately, the expansive literature on these international non-governmental organizations (INGOs) offers little help. In fact, the hopeful tone of both *sans frontières* activists and INGO scholars suggests that we should actually see increasing cohesion and similarity among these organizations.

This book takes a detailed look at organizational life at many of the world's leading INGOs in order to understand the causes and consequences of this variation in organizational practices. While many INGOs are increasingly active in *international* arenas, I find that actual organizational structures and strategies are deeply tied to *national* environments. Enabled by changes in communications technology and travel, many INGOs have tried to "go global" over the past decade or two by creating more offices in developed countries and increasing the number of projects abroad (Lindenberg and Bryant 2001). The main goal of this internationalization has been to create truly global structures that will reflect a more cosmopolitan identity. Despite these efforts, central organizational practices are driven by resources, institutions, and norms within their home countries.

The effects of those national settings can help explain the actions of these INGOs in Haiti and elsewhere. Medécins Sans Frontières has its roots in France, Oxfam in Britain, and CARE in the United States. These three countries all house vast numbers of INGOs, and each country has tremendous wealth and a vibrant civil society that offer support to private groups interested in international assistance. Yet ideas of "charity" and "activism" are quite different in each country, manifested in distinct opportunities and constraints for charitable organizations. French INGOs work in the shadow of a powerful welfare state and face a public that gives relatively little to charitable causes. British INGOs benefit from a generous public interested in international affairs and a state that can be quite open to INGOs while still allowing them their independence. American INGOs have a home government that is generous but demanding and a public that generally gives generously to charities but not to international causes. INGOs adopt strategies well suited to each of these quite different environments, and the result is the sort of variation among INGO responses seen in Haiti.

In the following chapters, I explore these national environments and the specific organizational practices at home and abroad of some of the world's largest and most transnationally active INGOs in two sectors, humanitarian relief and human rights. The continued divergences in organizational practices that I find suggest the existence of enduring national patterns. These differences are most marked in the humanitarian relief sector and less stark, though still apparent, among human rights organizations. Ultimately, I argue, CARE, Oxfam, and MSF resemble other charities from their home countries more than they do humanitarian relief groups around the world. Put simply, CARE is an American organization first, and only then a relief and development organization.

This argument might sound familiar to those interested in multinational corporations, another type of private transnational organization. In the 1980s and early 1990s, some analysts claimed that multinational corporations were so powerful that they challenged the very core of an international system based on states (e.g., Strange 1996). In response to these claims, comparative political economists examined the practices of specific corporations and found instead that, even while globally active, they were fundamentally shaped by factors in their home country environments (Doremus et al. 1998; Hall and Soskice 2001; Berger and Dore 1996; Harzing and Sorge 2003). For example, Paul Doremus and his colleagues (1998) found that for American, German, and Japanese multinational corporations, organizational practices in core areas—including financing, research and development, and internal governance—are shaped by political structures and ideologies at home. If the country of origin influences for-profit organizations subject to the impersonal forces of the market, it seems reasonable that national origin could affect organizations with political goals operating across national boundaries (for a similar argument, see Sell and Prakash 2004). In parallel with the "varieties of capitalism" literature in comparative political economy, I suggest that scholars of nongovernmental organizations need to better understand the "varieties of activism" that inform the interests and identities of INGOs and activists.

In this introductory chapter I describe what we know, and don't know, about the strategic choices of INGOs from existing scholarship. I then explain why an argument for the importance of national origin matters to academics and practitioners. The third section details the causal logic of the "national origin" argument, offering more precise elaborations of the concepts of nationality and organizational practice. In the fourth section, I explain the research method and plan of the book.

The How and Why of International NGOs

The study of global politics has seen an exploding interest in nonstate actors, a broad category that includes INGOs, individuals, firms, domestic
NGOs, and terrorist networks. The term "international nongovernmental organization" describes those groups that have an explicitly international focus and have members in three or more countries.[5] INGOs are
useful objects of analysis for scholars interested in transnational politics:
they have an identifiable structure, they are primarily active at the international rather than national level, and they are often important nodes of
transnational communication and coordination for global activists. Drawing upon past scholarship on interdependence and the role of ideas in international politics, a vibrant INGO literature has emerged.

Several decades of research have demonstrated that INGOs have successfully achieved social and political change across many issue areas.
INGOs have changed how states pursue security, conduct war, use weapons, and engage in torture (Risse-Kappen 1994, Finnemore 1996a, Price
1998, Clark 2001; see also Khagram et al. 2002, Smith and Bandy 2005,
Korey 1998, Welch 2001). Keck and Sikkink's (1998) *Activists beyond Borders* offered a useful focal point for much of this literature; they argued
that INGOs and other activists have formed "transnational advocacy networks" in order to campaign to protect human rights, end deforestation,
and stop violence against women. While not exhaustive, these examples
demonstrate that INGOs are central to the processes and outcomes of
global politics.

Not only do INGOs shape policy outcomes, some even argue that their
growing size and strength is changing the very nature of world politics.
The editors of the *Global Civil Society Yearbook* at the London School of
Economics argue that what we observed in the 1990s was "the emergence
of a supranational sphere of social and political participation" (Anheier,
Glasius, and Kaldor 2001). In an early discussion of this "global civil society," Paul Wapner (1995, 313) posits that "the interpenetration of markets, the intermeshing of symbolic meaning systems, and the proliferation

---

5. These frequently used criteria come from the authoritative data source on INGOs, the
Union of International Associations. For an extensive discussion and critique of the UIA, see
Sikkink and Smith 2002.

of transnational collective endeavors signal the formation of a thin, but nevertheless present, public sphere where private individuals and groups interact for common purposes."

Outside this small but vocal group of proponents of the global civil society idea, many analysts of INGOs make a more measured argument that these potent networks transcend national borders but do so in a fragmented and uneven way. Most INGO analysts recognize a clear North-South divide in the level and type of participation in global associative life (e.g. Khagram et al. 2002). Jackie Smith and Dawn Wiest (2005) find that national-level factors, including economic development, polity type, and links to international institutions, matter tremendously in shaping the possibility for individuals to join these transnational associations. Still, while they may be more cautious about proclaiming the existence of a civil society without borders, INGO scholars generally focus on the cross-border activities of these groups, and most appear to work under the assumption that transnational associative life is progressively expanding over time. Even Sidney Tarrow, who has challenged the idea of an emergent transnational civil society, has recently argued that transnational activism may be fairly rare but also may be growing (Tarrow 2010).

Two decades of vibrant scholarship have indisputably demonstrated that INGOs matter. But exactly when and how do they shape global politics? In order to answer this question, we need a much better understanding of what INGOs do and why they do it.

Putting the Organization Back into INGO

This book focuses on a little-discussed but critical point: INGOs are not amorphous agglomerations of international activists but formal *organizations* with defined structures and strategies (though see Johnson and Prakash 2007). As organizations, and particularly as charitable nonprofit organizations, INGOs have offices, budgets, staff, boards of directors, mission statements, and guiding principles. They create organizational structures to serve their goals, and they choose issues and strategies in the face of limited resources. These choices directly impact the substantive work of service delivery and advocacy. Stephen Hopgood makes this point well in his excellent study of Amnesty International, arguing that a foundational understanding of human rights organizations is critical for understanding human rights activism and the social origin and evolution of human rights norms (Hopgood 2006, vii). Across many issue areas, an organizational perspective helps explain what INGOs do, and don't do, in the important day-to-day of charitable work.

Instead of studying INGOs as passive carriers of transnational norms, we need to examine INGOs as purposive actors with their own identities and interests. Some scholars have embraced this approach (Hopgood 2006, Redfield 2006, Ebrahim 2005, Johnson and Prakash 2007). Still, the theoretical dominance of the constructivist paradigm in INGO research and its project of demonstrating how norms shape state interests may have ironically kept scholars from focusing on the construction of INGO identity and interests. This book shares many constructivist assumptions but treats INGOs as an object of inquiry rather than as an intervening variable between norms and policy change.

Explaining INGO Strategies

Beyond describing what INGOs do, a deep and difficult question is how to explain those practices. Why do INGOs choose some strategies and structures and not others? Several different scholars who have tackled this question have argued that INGO practices are determined primarily by forces in the international environment—forces that are driving them to adopt similar strategies, structures, and values. More formally, the international environment may be creating isomorphism among INGOs. We can identify at least three paths by which INGOs worldwide might converge upon shared norms and practices—exposure to the same world culture, reliance on the same financial resources, and work on the same problems.[6]

The first variant of the isomorphism argument comes from the world culture school. Drawing upon the theoretical insights of sociological institutionalism, this approach argues that an expanding world culture, based largely on a Western Enlightenment ideal, is driving organizations

---

6. A fourth possible factor that might drive convergence in organizational practice is the emergence of international institutions that offer new political opportunities to INGOs (see, e.g., Reimann 2006). In chapters 2 and 3, I argue that the effects of these global political opportunities are weak in relation to the domestic political environments of INGOs.

to converge upon a narrow set of values and organizational practices. For the world culture school, local and national environments are in fact embedded within a global system, making this global environment the primary determinant of actors' behavior (Finnemore 1996b, 330). While the world culture approach has spent most of its energy focusing on convergence in state structures and strategies, with INGOs as a sort of transmission belt for world culture, INGOs are not immune to the effects of growing global integration (Boli and Thomas 1999, Sikkink and Smith 2002). Jackie Smith has argued that global market integration and the increasing importance of interdependence among nations have substantially transformed the organizational field in which these organizations operate. According to Smith (2005), globalization has pushed INGOs to grow in number, become more professional and formalized, create governance structures that are more transnational, expand into more issue areas, and develop a greater awareness of global activism and interdependence (see also Clark 2003). In sum, these scholars argue that globalization and world culture have affected both how INGOs work and how they think about their work.

Another possible driver of isomorphism is money. In an important essay, Alexander Cooley and James Ron (2002) argue that the endless scramble for international funding and government contracts creates a competitive dynamic among INGOs—competition that encourages the adoption of similar (and dysfunctional) strategies, including the withholding of information from donors and a focus on securing contracts instead of delivering assistance. This argument has important parallels with the resource dependence approach to the study of organizations (Pfeffer and Salancik 1978), but Cooley and Ron view the available pool of INGO resources as a particularly global one.

A third reason that has been offered for INGO convergence is that NGOs work on similar issues. In both humanitarian relief and human rights, activists and analysts often refer to a global sector or field. In the area of human rights, Amnesty International talks about a global "human rights community," while a major study of human rights INGOs argues that "the strategies NGOs adopt are not isolated but interactive" (Welch 2001, 7; see also Risse et al. 1999, Dunne and Wheeler 1999). In the humanitarian realm, INGOs have developed global codes of conduct for the provision of relief; these and other developments have led scholars like Michael

Barnett to argue that global humanitarianism became an "institutionalized field" in the 1990s, "increasingly rationalized, standardizing basic codes of conduct for intervention, developing accountability mechanisms, and calculating the consequences of actions" (2005, 725; see also Chabbott 1999, Hoffman and Weiss 2006). According to Antonio Donini (2010), these institutionalized fields can cross the North-South divide, as Southern humanitarian NGOs mimic the language and strategies of their Northern counterparts. Overall, while the general argument for isomorphism is not always made explicitly, INGO watchers who speak about a global "community" or "sector" are suggesting that these groups regularly look to the international environment for information, resources, partners, and even values. In short, the international environment plays a constitutive role in defining the basic meaning of human rights or humanitarianism.

These three arguments for isomorphism describe different causal chains but the same outcome—increasing similarity among INGOs. There are others, however, who note continued diversity. Tarrow (2005) argues that most of those groups engaged in contentious politics at the global level are "rooted cosmopolitans," firmly based in diverse national environments. There is also an extensive case study literature on human rights and humanitarian NGOs that documents incredible diversity among INGOs, but most of these are either descriptive histories of single organizations or attempts to create typologies of INGO strategies and structures (Welch 2001, Korey 1998, Lindenberg and Bryant 2001). Within the relief and development field, several important works have explicitly argued that national origin creates divergent INGO practices. The Organization for Economic Cooperation and Development sponsored two reports in the 1990s that described wide variation in government-NGO relations among member countries (Smillie and Helmich 1993, Smillie and Helmich 1999). In a study of Norwegian development INGOs, Tvedt (1998) found that major donor governments are a powerful national force in an international social system of INGOs. A fascinating recent project sponsored by the Social Science Research Council examines how philanthropic organizations form organizational norms and practices in one national environment and then project those models into other contexts (Hammack and Heydemann 2009).

Altogether, there is comparatively little research on why INGOs choose particular practices. Among those explanations offered, the dominant one has been that INGOs are becoming more globalized and uniform over time. However, most of these groups were not actually created as international NGOs, but rather began as domestic charities with international interests.[7] Today, even as they are active around the globe and have offices in many countries, INGOs remain legally, materially and normatively grounded in these national environments. For example, the humanitarian organizations CARE, Oxfam, and MSF receive 55% to 75% of their income from their home countries, not from international institutions or other global sources of income. The rights groups Human Rights Watch and FIDH also are heavily dependent on home country resources, while over 40% of Amnesty's global income comes from just the United States and Britain (Hopgood 2006, 197). Normatively, the ways in which these groups conceive of what it means to be a charity is fundamentally shaped by values in their home countries. American nonprofits speak of a "businesslike" approach to their public benefit activities, and they tend to value professionalism and efficiency much like their for-profit counterparts. In France, by contrast, *la vie associative* is understood as a special calling separate from the corporate world, and charities emphasize their voluntary spirit and solidarity with those in need. Britain, perhaps unsurprisingly, is somewhere between its transatlantic and continental peers, mixing professionalism with voluntarism and efficiency with solidarity.

There are other reasons to focus on the national origins of INGOs. First, there appear to be strong parallels between the targets and methods of INGOs and the foreign policy priorities of their home governments (Koch et al. 2009, Berkovitch and Gordon 2008).[8] Additionally, other types of private transnational organizations are deeply shaped by their home environments, as the "varieties of capitalism" literature makes clear. Finally, the growing comparative literature on nonprofits and civil society offers a

---

7. There are a few obvious exceptions. Amnesty International (which was explicitly created as an international movement) is discussed in chapter 3. Another prominent exception is the International Federation of the Red Cross, which brings together the many national Red Cross chapters around the world. David Forsythe (2005) has demonstrated that the federation is quite fragmented; some national sections work very closely with their home governments, and coordination among different national chapters is inconsistent.

8. While state-level factors continue to shape nonstate actors, I do not go so far as to argue that transnational organizations are merely manipulated by calculating and capable home country governments.

wealth of information for understanding which dimensions of the national environment might influence international charities.[9]

Implications

The argument that national origin plays a significant role in shaping INGO practice is important for at least three reasons. It helps explain variation in transnational advocacy networks, it predicts that future convergence among INGOs is unlikely, and it offers practitioners an alternative explanation for the frequently lamented failures of INGOs in the field.

Variations in Transnational Advocacy Networks

While I examine more than just advocacy in the following pages, my findings do speak directly to the literature on INGOs as activists. The case studies of humanitarian and human rights groups offer insight into at least three issues: who participates in transnational campaigns, which tactics they choose, and how frequently transnational campaigns happen. On the first issue, the existing literature suggests that transnational civil society is composed of confrontational and vocal campaigning organizations, but in fact many large and important INGOs like CARE do very little campaigning. Thus, while campaigns may aspire to be global, participation in those campaigns may be far from universal. On the second issue, my research reveals patterned variation in the advocacy tactics used by INGOs. Keck and Sikkink (1998) highlighted the politics of information, symbolism, leverage, and accountability as four tactics frequently used by INGOs. But while all four might in theory be available to all INGOs, each INGO is likely to use a smaller range of tactics appropriate to its home country environment. For example, all INGOs may engage in information politics by providing data to state officials, but American organizations are less likely than their French or British counterparts to engage in symbolic politics,

---

9. I deliberately use the term "charity" here. Scholars of American nonprofit organizations have taken a leading role in this literature, but the term "nonprofit" is a legal one and is rarely used elsewhere. I use "charity" to refer to those organizations that are both nonprofit and aim to serve some public benefit; "charity" is a legal category but also a conceptual one.

which target public audiences and thus are used by groups involved in out-sider campaigning.

Finally, the evidence presented here implies that transnational cam-paigns actually happen fairly infrequently. This requires further ex-amination, as few scholars study failed transnational campaigns or the difficulties encountered in successful campaigns (though see Bob 2005, Ron et al. 2005, Carpenter 2007, Carpenter 2010). Yet the substantial di-vergence in advocacy strategies among American, British, and French INGOs suggests that bridging these differences to create durable trans-national campaigns can be quite difficult.[10] Leading INGOs have very different understandings of the usefulness of political action and the ap-propriateness of particular advocacy strategies, yet "organizations with similar institutional logics and repertoires of contention work together more easily than those who do not" (Pieck and Moog 2009, 420). Large and successful global campaigns like the International Campaign to Ban Landmines may be the exception rather than the rule among INGOs; the landmines campaign may have been so successful because it involved a very narrow focus that offered few contentious claims.[11] Successful global campaigning on broad issues like poverty or globalization may be much more difficult.

Divergence, Not Convergence

This book also speaks to scholars interested in the power and reach of glo-balization, among whom the question of "divergence or convergence" is a central point of contention (Guillén 2001). The charitable organizations discussed here are a new source of evidence for the globalization debate, as the past and current practices of the world's leading human rights and humanitarian relief organizations have been substantially consistent over time. In addition, the discrete American, British, and French charitable

---

10. Keck and Sikkink (1998) recognized this point, arguing that the creation of a common frame of meaning for a transnational campaign can be quite difficult, and they carefully included examinations of failed campaigns such as the attempt to end female circumcision. Subsequent scholarship on transnational campaigns has been less concerned with how these differences might impede global advocacy.

11. My thanks to Roger Haydon for pointing to the importance of the narrow scope of the campaign.

models discussed in the next chapter have remained resilient in the face of globalization and continue to shape INGO behavior.

The diversity of INGO practices in the face of several decades of globalization suggests that the idea of a "transnational" or "global" civil society is misleading both as a description of existing conditions and as a predictor of future patterns. The seemingly modest claim of transnational civil society scholars, that the international realm is a key arena for INGOs, has had not so modest implications for how INGOs have been studied. For example, INGOs are often used as a proxy to measure the growth of transnational civil society without any investigation into whether these groups are really transnational actors. There is no global civil society, but rather a set of national civil societies coming into more frequent contact with one another. That interaction may create changes in each environment: for example, the British government has tried to create new tax incentives for charitable giving in ways informed by "American-style" regulations. Nevertheless, national polity types are durable and act powerfully upon the charitable organizations within their borders. Global civil society proponents might respond that INGOs might increasingly share broad norms like cosmopolitanism and individualism even as micro-level practices of INGOs diverge, but this robs those norms of any explanatory power in understanding the identities and interests of actors.

Let me qualify this argument with two caveats. First, saying that national origin is important does not equate with a deterministic argument for national uniformity. As any INGO watcher knows, there is substantial variation among INGOs from the same country, and the challenge here is to separate within-country variation from cross-country variation. My research design helps in sorting out national effects from organizational singularities, but there other factors that might shape organizational strategies and structures, including powerful leaders and the competitive pressure to differentiate oneself from one's peer organizations (Barman 2002). Still, among humanitarian relief INGOs, though perhaps less so among human rights INGOs, groups from the same country look quite similar in cross-national perspective. This problem of explaining variation and similarity is a recurring one in both organizational studies and comparative politics and ultimately requires more comparative work.

Second, these groups are internationally active, and the international environment may create convergence in some limited areas; I simply argue that attention to these international forces has come at the costs of an understanding of INGOs' domestic environments. A few factors in the international environment are worth noting. Worldwide, INGOs encounter the "CNN effect," in which media coverage substantially influences both their agenda and their ability to raise private donations (Randal and German 2002). At the micro level of program design, most governmental and intergovernmental donors require INGOs to use some variant of a bureaucratic tool called a "logframe," or logical framework, to plan and manage their projects in the field (OECD 2000). Additionally, because humanitarians and human rights groups tend to respond to the same international crises, they often draw the same lessons afterward. For example, after the Rwandan genocide of 1994, many INGOs concluded that they needed to develop their learning capacities to avoid making the same mistakes in future crises.[12]

Ultimately, INGOs are active in multiple environments, and an explanation for INGO practice may remain unsatisfying without an analysis of each environment. But if other factors—including individual leadership, domestic competition, and international pressures—all might inform the practices of any one particular INGO, national origin *limits the range of possible responses* to any one of these factors. INGOs are governed by national laws; they receive the majority of their funding from nationally based donors; they have developed advocacy strategies in response to domestic political opportunities; and they are shaped by powerful sets of social norms at home. As Sandra Moog (2009, 260) writes in an insightful examination of environmental groups, "Though their lines of communication and political activities may cross many borders, most of the NGOs and social movement groups that engage in new forms of transnational activism are still essentially nationally based phenomena." If the global humanitarian sector has become more uniform, or if human rights activists are increasingly part of a global community, these fields are at best weakly institutionalized in comparison to the national environments whence INGOs originate. As an example, consider the role of media coverage: while the ability of media appeals to generate private charitable donations may be a global phenomenon, the need to attract private donations varies based on the availability

---

12. See, for example, the Active Learning Network for Accountability and Performance in Humanitarian Action (ALNAP) which was formed after the Rwandan genocide and publishes evaluations of relief and development efforts.

of funds in the home environment—French humanitarian organizations are much more dependent on these private, and perhaps fickle, donors, than their American counterparts. The pressures of the international environment are refracted through a national lens.

Explaining Organizational Failure

The evidence presented here has important consequences for how practitioners understand INGO failures in the field. As INGOs have played an increasing role in providing basic services, distributing foreign aid, and publicizing human rights abuses, questions have been raised about their effectiveness. Some critics argue that the failures of INGOs should ultimately be attributed to the states and international institutions that ask INGOs to perform tasks beyond their capacities, but others respond that INGOs are fundamentally dysfunctional organizations unable either to form effective partnerships or to accurately assess the needs of those they are trying to help (Edwards and Hulme 1996, Smillie 1995, Fowler 1991, Darcy and Hoffman 2003).

My findings suggest an alternative explanation for the failures of INGOs in the field. Instead of some core dysfunction in the INGO sector due to resource scarcity or organizational incapacity, I suggest instead that there is a core disconnect among INGOs as a result of their different ideas of what a charity is and what it should do. As with advocacy coalitions, the creation of meaningful and effective mechanisms for coordination can be very difficult when such distinctive organizational practices are involved. In addition, given the strong and continued presence of INGOs in their home countries, it is unsurprising that they find it a struggle to respond to the needs or demands of other environments in which they operate. It follows that more effective coordination among INGOs may occur through national umbrella organizations like InterAction in the United States or British Overseas NGOs for Development (BOND) than through global offices like the UN's Office for the Coordination of Humanitarian Affairs. The national origin argument also helps explain why INGOs have been able to assemble a few codes of conduct but have had relatively little success in achieving compliance with these codes. Convergence upon a single set of universal best practices is unlikely when INGOs differ in the very ways they think about their work.

These implications—the relative infrequency of successful transnational campaigns, the continued diversity of organizational practice, and the possibility that INGOs are not dysfunctional but rather disconnected—speak to central concerns of both practitioners and scholars. International charities face enormous obstacles in serving their altruistic aims, and a better understanding of transnational associational life should contribute meaningfully to the success of these charities. Importantly, I do not see national origin as an obstacle to be overcome, though cosmopolitan proponents of global civil society might see it otherwise. As long as different state institutional arrangements persist, reflecting different models of associational life, INGOs will need to adopt strategies and structures tailored to those environments in order to succeed. As Jordan and van Tuijl (2000, 2063) write, "The iron law of transnational advocacy is that a firm relationship with one's own political arena is an essential condition for working in one or more other political arenas." The myth that INGOs are global rather than national creatures encourages these organizations to shed the very practices that have made them financially and politically successful at home. Instead of trying to transform from national groups to transnational associations (a process that has thus far been largely unsuccessful for the INGOs profiled here, with the possible exception of Amnesty International), INGOs might instead look to boost their chances of success by better delegating responsibility abroad to partners more likely to succeed in these different environments.

National Origin and INGO Practice

INGO practices are shaped by incentives, constraints, and social standards of legitimacy in their environment. These strategies and structures, adopted in reference to national institutions and resources, remain resilient even as INGOs attempt to make the transformation from internationally oriented national NGOs to truly global organizations. In fact, most INGOs keep their headquarters in their home countries, thereby reinforcing these national effects over time.

In order to understand the relationship between an organization and its environment, I employ a sociological institutionalist approach. In an early analysis of nonprofit organizations, Dimaggio and Powell (1983) argued that, for organizations operating in highly uncertain environments, three sets of isomorphic pressures—coercive, mimetic, and normative—encourage organizations to adopt similar structures and strategies. Coercive pressures—rewards and sanctions for certain behaviors—can emanate from the legal environment, donors, or coordinating philanthropic groups. Mimetic isomorphism is a function of the uncertainty or ambiguity of organizational goals, driving organizations to consciously imitate the practices of other organizations in the charitable field that they perceive to be successful. Normative pressures for isomorphism stem from the educational background and professional networks of members within an organizational field; as the field becomes professionalized, members struggle to collectively establish the legitimacy of their occupation through explicit statement of shared principles and values. Thus, nonprofits functioning in institutionalized fields are shaped not by a logic of consequences ("What are the costs and benefits of this choice?") but rather by a logic of appropriateness ("Is this choice appropriate for the situation I face?") (March and Olsen 1998). Sociological institutionalism offers a theoretical handle on the complex material and ideational pressures that shape INGO practices. The institutionalist lens has been used fruitfully by international relations scholars before, particularly by constructivists concerned with the construction of state identity and interest, but it has been infrequently used to examine INGOs.

Of course, sociological institutionalism is one of several possible ways of understanding the practices of organizations interested in social change. Yet both organization studies and social movement scholarship have seen converging interest in the role of the surrounding environment, with particular attention to available organizational models, belief systems, and political opportunities (McAdam and Scott 2005). Among the different ways of understanding the surrounding environment, sociological institutionalism is uniquely helpful for two reasons: it draws attention to patterned organizational behavior over time, and it incorporates both normative and material factors.

National Origin

Which parts of a nation's institutions might be relevant to a study of INGO practices? While the North-South divide among INGOs has long been recognized, regime type and resource availability are not the only ways in which countries differ. Dieter Rucht (1996) describes how social movements in the North have been shaped by a national "context structure" with cultural, social, and political dimensions. Schofer and Gourinchas (2001) have found that different patterns of state-society relations create substantial variation in voluntary association membership in developed countries.

Drawing guidance from sociological institutionalism and social movement studies, I focus on four identifiable and narrow dimensions of the national environment: the regulatory framework, the political opportunity structure (including both formal and informal opportunities for interaction), the availability of resources, and social networks. Together, these four factors create distinct environments in the United States, Britain, and France for charities in general and for international charities in particular. In combination, they reflect different social conceptions of what is appropriate and legitimate action for charities and generate distinctly American, British, or French ways of working on humanitarian relief or human rights.

There are at least two potential problems in arguing that national origin affects INGOs. First, how do you identify an INGO's nationality when the organization claims to represent cosmopolitan concerns of individuals around the globe? Much of the publicly available material from INGOs highlights international, rather than national, components of INGO activities. At the same time, a few INGOs change the location of their central headquarters or, more frequently, establish an international umbrella organization in Geneva or New York, which means that their "legal" nationality may not be the same as their national origin. This problem has been successfully confronted in studies of multinational corporations, however (Doremus et al. 1998, 9). Rich knowledge of each INGO's history allows for an accurate assignment of national origin.

A second problem is that INGOs are active in more than one country. We can separate these national environments into three types: home country, host country, and field office country. The home country is, of course, the organization's country of origin. A host country is one (usually another developed democracy) in which an INGO has an operational or fundraising office; CARE, for example, was started in the United States, but CARE France might also be affected by its French context. Finally, nationality might matter in field offices; CARE's operations in Thailand, for example, may be affected by Thai culture and institutions. This last context is widely addressed by many practitioners, who increasingly recognize the importance of local knowledge and contacts in order to achieve INGO goals, and many case studies talk about translating INGO concepts into meaningful local program activity.

Both home and host country effects are interesting for understanding how INGOs operate across national boundaries, but this book focuses on home country effects, for several reasons. First, host country effects may not meaningfully influence an INGO's international activities. Many host country offices were set up by outsiders, lack operational authority, and have less power in the INGO's international confederation. Thus, there is an interesting intersection of French and American practices at CARE France, but this doesn't drive the major decisions of CARE's international confederation. A second reason to focus on home country effects is that host country offices vary in size, age, and locale (not every INGO has a French host country office, for example). My research suggests that many INGOs have established host country offices only in the past decade or so in response to pressures to address a global rather than national constituency. Given the recent establishment of many of these host country offices, organizational practices may be unsettled. For example, Oxfam formally incorporated a preexisting French NGO as Oxfam France, but this happened only in 2003. Finally, and perhaps most important, a focus on home country effects allows us to trace what Hammack and Heydemann (2009) refer to as the projection of institutional logics abroad. The counterintuitive finding that CARE France acts like an American organization, despite the heavy influence of French national laws and French culture, suggests that INGOs may be agents of home country cultural diffusion rather than empty vessels waiting to be filled by altruistic individuals in various national settings.

Organizational Practices

National origin thus may affect INGOs, but which aspects of INGOs deserve attention? I examine three practices across humanitarian relief and human rights INGOs—professionalization and management; fundraising; and advocacy and research—as well as two sector-specific strategies—government relations for humanitarian INGOs and issue selection for human rights INGOs. Because so much of the INGO literature investigates INGO practices out in the field, I explicitly focus on the patterned behavior of the home country office of each INGO (though see Young et al. 1999). Thus, instead of considering a single human rights campaign or the response to a particular humanitarian crisis, I focus on the broad strategies at INGO headquarters in order to discern patterned practice over time and perhaps around the world. In the final chapter, I examine how these broad patterns translate into specific strategies in a single situation, Iraq.

Professionalization is an important aspect of organizational structure that affects overall management. Organizations become professionalized as part of a broader move toward what Hwang and Powell (2009) call the "rationalization of charity," seen in hiring practices but also in the use of strategic planning, independent audits, quantitative program evaluation, and outside consultants (see also Karl 1998). In this study, I look at several key indicators of professionalization. First, I consider the balance between paid professionals and volunteers, and the location of professionals in major positions of authority. Importantly, there is no one-to-one tradeoff in the staff/volunteer balance: an ethos of volunteerism can coexist with a paid staff, and an ethos of professionalism can pervade a volunteer community. In addition, I provide when possible the credentials of those who work for each INGO as well as evidence of the standardization of internal management procedures. Professionalization and rationalized management are important dimensions of INGO practice, as they reflect the INGO's understanding of what it means to be a humanitarian or a human rights activist based on the relative importance of various goals, including efficiency, solidarity with partners and victims, and principled activism.[13] Research on other nonprofit organizations suggests that professionalization can lead to shifts in both mission and structure; for example, professionalization may reduce experimentation in programming or encourage advocacy groups to adopt more moderate tactics (Hwang and Powell 2009).

INGOs obviously need to engage in *fundraising* to survive and thrive, but fundraising strategies vary significantly. INGOs not only go to various

---

13. Professionalization can be both cause and consequence of isomorphism: professionals can bring in particular values and skills that then change organizational practices, but organizations may also choose to professionalize themselves based on a socially constructed understanding of what is appropriate action by a charity.

sources for funding (home government, private donors, private founda-tions, international organizations) but also vary in how heavily they rely on any particular source. As the resource dependency school has made clear, financial pressures affect a wide range of organizational practices, including management (how much money is available to hire a profes-sional accountant, for example) and projects in the field (how much money is earmarked for a particular issue, for example) (Pfeffer and Salancik 1978). The concentration of funding sources in an INGO's home country is also a direct measure of how embedded that INGO is in its national environment.

Advocacy is an organizational strategy generally orchestrated by the central office of an INGO (though some advocacy happens in host country and field offices). Advocacy is a general term used by practitioners and analysts to denote the strategic use of information to shape politics, in-cluding both public policy and social practice, though not all INGOs use the term advocacy to describe their political actions (Jordan and van Tuijl 2000). Advocacy can involve private lobbying of public officials (an insider strategy), public campaigning to mobilize grassroots interest or support (an outsider strategy), or public education to broadly raise awareness.[14] Any of these strategies can involve the specific tactics identified by Keck and Sik-kink (1998)—providing information, using powerful symbols, exercising leverage, and holding others accountable. As part of their advocacy work, INGOs also use *research* in various ways, and that research can be highly technical or policy-directed. Advocacy and research strategies are central to the success or failure of INGO projects. For example, if global policy change is necessary in a specific issue area, those organizations whose strat-egies are best adapted to global advocacy have the highest chance of suc-cess. Alternatively, INGOs with confrontational advocacy strategies may fail to achieve policy change in closed political systems or where INGOs tend to collaborate with government.

In the humanitarian relief sector, INGOs make different choices regard-ing their *relationships with government.* The frequency of interaction can be high or low, and the relationship not only affects the financial well-being of an organization but also the ultimate success of projects in the field. For

---

14.   There are innumerable typologies of advocacy strategies; see also Nelson 2004. In a dis-cussion of social movements, Meyer (2004) identifies four advocacy tactics that largely echo those discussed here: public education, protest, lobbying, and research.

example, INGOs active in a country that has a hostile relationship with the INGO's home government may see their access or success affected if the INGO has a pattern of working closely with its home government.

Finally, in the human rights sector, *issue selection* is an important strategic choice for INGOs. First, within the broad field of human rights, INGOs make choices about the balance of domestic and international human rights work within their portfolios. In addition, given the limited availability of resources, INGOs must choose specific issues, including whether to work primarily on civil and political rights (the so-called "first generation" rights covered by the Universal Declaration on Human Rights) or on economic, social, and cultural rights. The selection of issues has mixed effects on the success of human rights INGOs. On the one hand, INGOs dependent on home country funders must address human rights issues that resonate with their supporters; on the other hand, INGOs risk becoming irrelevant if they work on human rights issues abroad that fail to address the central needs of their intended beneficiaries.

By comparing leading INGOs in these dimensions, I show that each INGO has a core set of practices, and that these practices vary by national setting, creating distinct varieties of activism. These core practices shape the very identity of INGOs; for example, the heavily professionalized CARE and Human Rights Watch see themselves as skilled specialists that excel at a particular task, while the less professionalized Amnesty and MSF see themselves as voluntary embodiments of a particular ethos. I thus address a central constructivist concern—the formation of identity—but advance the constructivist project by looking at the identities of nonstate actors. In addition, an understanding of core practices is a necessary precondition for exploring how organizational practices are transferred to INGO offices and projects. While core practices should in theory shape all the activities that INGOs undertake, the particular manifestations of national influence may vary based on the situation in which an INGO is involved.

One of the key determinants of the transfer of organizational practices is the global structure of each INGO. For each of the organizations profiled in this book, I begin with an examination of its history, focusing on the process of internationalization. INGOs have faced pressure from donors and their peers to create more internationalized governance structures and a more cosmopolitan identity. INGOs have responded to those pressures in fairly idiosyncratic ways; some, like Oxfam, have created decentralized international networks while others, like Amnesty, have centralized important functions. This next point is critical: the structure of these international confederations determines how practices get transferred beyond the home offices of the INGOs concerned. The less centralized an INGO is, the less we would expect to see strong national origin effects in an INGO's host country or field offices. Moreover, centralization is defined not simply by formal structure but by informal processes as well. CARE International, for example, is formally a very decentralized INGO, but the center of gravity for the global CARE confederation is firmly based at CARE USA.

Sociological institutionalists might object to my focus on INGO practices at headquarters by pointing out that, though an organization may adopt particular structures in response to its environment, these structures do not necessarily determine its work activities (Meyer and Rowan 1977). This objection has some merit, particularly when it comes to the discussion of professionalization, but it is still worth investigating whether this structural convergence has actually occurred. A decoupling of strategy and structure is actually one of several possible outcomes for organizations in institutionalized environments; other analysts have found that changes in structure can instead produce socialization, standardization, or an indirect drift toward socially legitimate practice (Goodman and Jinks 2004, Loya and Boli 1999, Schofer and Hironaka 2005). I test this relationship by including both formal structure (board of directors, membership, the structure of decision making) and actual strategy (particularly advocacy and issue selection). Finally, the case study of Iraq offers an opportunity to examine how broad patterns in professionalization, fundraising, advocacy, and programming reveal themselves in a particular instance.

The organizational practices examined here are not the activities of INGOs, but they provide a manageable and meaningful way to systematically compare organizations. Of course, these practices are not wholly separate. An organization that focuses on civil and political rights may have access to particular funders interested in those issues; organizations that want access to government grants may hire fundraising professionals capable of completing complex applications; organizations that hire more professionals may be better able to form the long-term relationships necessary for insider advocacy. Still, if these three practices are tied to national-level factors, these interrelationships should reinforce the national roots of an INGO even as it becomes more globally active.

Research Method and Plan of the Study

There are many ways of exploring the role of national origin in transnational life, but a comparative case study approach is useful in elucidating the process by which organizational practices are established and evolve. International sociologists have used large-scale survey data to chart the varied landscape of global civil society. Unfortunately, the data on specific INGOs and their practices are sparse and incomplete.

I adopt a critical case approach to the selection of both particular home countries and organizations, examining cases where it is least likely that evidence of enduring national effects will be found. I chose home countries that are all Western developed democracies with large populations of INGOs—the United States, Britain, and France. Likewise, I selected the most transnationally active and largest INGOs, which work in dozens of countries and cultures and are active in the international arena through their work with international organizations and their interest in international law. These INGOs are most likely to have lost their nationally shaped identities and formed cosmopolitan identities and interests. More detail on the case selection method is available in Appendix A.

This book includes three different types of organizations. The primary focus is on six major INGOs drawn from the humanitarian relief and human rights sectors. These organizations—CARE and Human Rights Watch from the United States; Oxfam and Amnesty from Britain; and Médecins Sans Frontières and the Fédération Internationale des ligues des Droits de l'Homme (FIDH) from France—are the largest and most transnationally active INGOs in their particular fields. Second, I have included all the host country offices of these six INGOs in the United States, Britain, and France.[15] Thus, I look not only at MSF France but at MSF UK and MSF USA. These host country offices are where the national rubber meets the international road, and they offer a fascinating look into how established organizational practices fare in a different environment. Third, I offer a dozen other smaller case studies for comparison with the

---

15. Importantly, many human rights INGOs do not have host country offices of this kind. The notable exception is Amnesty International, an issue addressed in chapter 3.

primary cases. In order to show that national origin matters, it is necessary to demonstrate that organizations from the same country share similar practices; in more formal language, to demonstrate that cross-country variation is greater than within-country variation. The primary case studies do the heavy lifting of demonstrating how features in the national environment translate into particular INGO practices, but because those cases draw from two different sectors, it is hard to sort out sectoral effects from national effects. Thus, for each country, four additional "mini-cases" are presented—two from the humanitarian relief sector, and two from the human rights sector. Table 1 displays the INGOs included in this study.

Since most studies of INGOs are either deeply descriptive single case studies or broad generalizations about the INGO community, the systematic comparisons of six INGOs offered here are valuable even without the national origin argument. Despite a growing literature on INGOs, we still

TABLE 1. INGO case selection

	Humanitarian relief	Human rights
United States		
Primary Cases	CARE USA	Human Rights Watch (HRW)
Outposts	MSF USA Oxfam America	Amnesty USA
Mini-Cases	World Vision (WVI) Intl Rescue Committee (IRC)	Human Rights First (HRF) Global Rights
Britain		
Primary Cases	Oxfam GB	Amnesty International
Outposts	CARE UK MSF UK	Amnesty UK
Mini-Cases	Christian Aid Save the Children	Interights Article 19
France		
Primary Cases	MSF France	Fédération Internationale des ligues des Droits de l'Homme (FIDH)
Outposts	CARE France Oxfam France	Amnesty France
Mini-Cases	Action Contre la Faim (ACF) Comité catholique contre la faim et pour le développement (CCFD)	Reporters sans frontières (RSF) ATD Quart-Monde

know surprisingly little about what these transnational actors do and why, even as scholars make predictions about the future of global activism. As Thomas Risse (2002) has argued, scholars who study transnational actors need to stop focusing on how these actors shape state institutions and policy and instead examine how state-level processes influence them. I take a first step toward reversing that causal arrow, but much more work is needed to understand the identities and interests of those organizations dominant in transnational associational life.

By including multiple branches of the same INGO, I reveal what happens when different varieties of activism meet up. For example, in chapter 2 I show that when the Oxfam model was transferred to the United States, Oxfam America had to farm out its advocacy work to a taxable entity and, facing a donor government that was less tolerant than its UK counterpart of an INGO's desire to maintain its independence, adjust its fundraising strategies by refusing U.S. government funding. These INGO "outposts" offer fascinating insight into the interaction of intra-organizational processes, global pressures, and national environments.

Yet while the cases are important in and of themselves, it is implied that national effects should be evident at other INGOs as well. The smaller comparative cases in chapters 2 and 3 reveal substantial consistency in organizational practice among INGOs from the same country, despite the idiosyncrasies of any one INGO.[16] For example, the British humanitarian INGOs Oxfam, Save the Children UK, and Christian Aid are strikingly similar in their approaches to fundraising and advocacy. These similarities enable and reinforce cooperation among these groups, whether in fundraising at the national Disasters Emergency Committee or in meeting with officials through the very selective British Overseas Aid Group. The evidence from these cases supports the claim that the national patterns revealed here should be found at many other INGOs in the United States, Britain, and France.

To construct these case studies, I use a wide variety of sources. First, I conducted almost seventy-five interviews with staff and partners of the

---

16. This consistency across organizations makes alternative explanations for organizational practices suspect. For example, several analysts explain the practices of Human Rights Watch by pointing to its powerful leaders—Aryeh Neier and Kenneth Roth—but this neglects the fact that, in global perspective, Human Rights Watch shares many organizational practices with other American human rights groups.

INGOs. Most of these were conducted between February 2006 and May 2007 in the United States, Britain, and France (see Appendix B). Most subjects agreed to being identified simply as "staff member" of the INGO concerned, and all were assured anonymity. A few subjects elected to have their name used, and they are identified in the text. Second, I supplemented these interviews with data drawn from internal reports, member newsletters, and publicly available documents such as annual reports and external reviews. Finally, to construct profiles of the charitable environment in each country, I drew heavily on the growing comparative literature on civil society and nonprofits.

Chapter 1 provides the foundation for the case studies by describing the national environment for international charities in the United States, Britain, and France. These profiles focus on four dimensions in each country: the regulatory environment, relations with political authorities, material resources, and social networks. While charities may be broadly engaged in similar types of work, they face very different constraints and incentives in their home environments.

Humanitarian and human rights INGOs are the foci of chapters 2 and 3. Chapter 2 describes humanitarian relief INGOs in the United States, Britain, and France, with a focus on CARE, Oxfam, and MSF. The chapter offers a side-by-side comparison of the practices at the three major INGOs and then compares CARE, Oxfam, and MSF with other organizations from their home countries. Chapter 3 considers human rights INGOs. As in the previous chapter, I explore American, British, and then French INGOs, with a focus on Human Rights Watch, Amnesty International, and FIDH. Because human rights INGOs are structured differently from their humanitarian counterparts, there are no cases of human rights INGO "outposts" in chapter 3, with the notable exception of Amnesty International. The effects of national origin are somewhat less marked for human rights INGOs than for those in humanitarian relief, but national origin effects are observable in human rights INGOs' advocacy, fundraising, and internal management.

Chapter 4 offers a synthesis and extension of the national origin argument. The chapter first compares humanitarian and human rights groups side by side. This allows an exploration of the role of national origin compared to other factors that shape organizational practice. Next, the role of national origin is made concrete through an exploration of the response of the six major INGOs in the months immediately before and after the

U.S.-led invasion of Iraq in 2003, showing that scholars of transnational activism ignore the role of national origin at their own peril. The last few pages offer some thoughts for practitioners involved in transnational activism.

The number of organizations "without borders" has exploded: today, there are organizations for architects, lawyers, veterinarians, acupuncturists, and even mothers that claim to be *sans frontières*. Yet much of the literature on these INGOs has failed to question whether this expression of solidarity translates into substantively different practice. While a focus on the global dimension of INGO activities has persuasively demonstrated that INGOs matter to global politics, only a closer examination of INGOs as organizations active in both global and local environments will reveal *how* and *when* they matter. International charities may face more political opportunities, participate in more international networks, and access more international resources than in the past, but INGOs remain products of highly institutionalized national environments that shape their interests and identities.

1

Varieties of Activism in Three Countries

Upon arriving in Paris in early 2007, I was greeted by a vivid illustration of French civil society in action. Blocks away from my apartment, lining the canal Saint-Martin, two neat columns of bright red tents had been set up by an organization calling itself "the Children of Don Quixote." The organization had created this "sleep-in" in to demonstrate solidarity with France's homeless population. Given the relatively small number of homeless in France relative to the United States, I was struck by the vibrancy of this public protest and by the fact that it was an INGO, Médecins du Monde, that had initiated the idea of giving tents to the French homeless.[1] These protests in early 2007 had practical consequences—homelessness became a substantive issue in the 2007 presidential election—but also embodied a particular variety of activism.

In this chapter, I explore the different "varieties of activism" in France, the United States, and Britain so that in later chapters we can examine

---

1. "Middle-class French Join Sleep-in over Homelessness," *New York Times,* January 2, 2007.

how each national environment shapes the specific practices of the world's leading humanitarian and human rights INGOs. The domestic environments of INGOs are highly institutionalized settings where INGOs encounter resource flows, regulations, and values that are firmly established and have remained resilient in the face of globalization. I pay particular attention to these national environments since the early 1990s, as this is the period during which greater global integration should have transformed the operations of internationally active organizations, but this chapter also draws upon historical detail to show the deep roots of national institutions. National environments are of course neither static nor isolated. Still, while it is important to understand how national environments evolve over time, it is also important to recognize that, in cross-national perspective, these environments remain quite different.

There are several layers of the national environment that together create an institutionalized field. First, there are broad national political institutions and cultures that define the appropriate roles of state and society. Second, each country has a narrower charitable sector that has its own particular regulations and customs. Last, there is the even finer category of internationally oriented charities. These organizations are governed by charity law but are also shaped by other factors, including national foreign policy institutions, particular social networks of internationally interested citizens, and even a country's colonial history. Together, these layers create for INGOs an institutionalized field in which organizations "participate in the same meaning systems, are defined by similar symbolic processes, and are subject to common regulatory processes" (Scott 1994, 71).

The United States, Britain, and France are home to many of the world's richest, largest, and most internationally active INGOs. And while all three are Western industrialized democracies with vibrant civil societies, INGOs in each country encounter vastly different settings. To understand the "varieties of activism" in the three countries, I utilize several existing literatures that have been largely neglected by NGO analysts. Valuable information comes from cross-national studies of nonprofit organizations, such as the Johns Hopkins University Comparative Nonprofit Sector project led by Lester Salamon. This ambitious undertaking has all the normal frustrations of gathering comparable data but offers rich and explicitly comparative country studies of the resource base and regulatory environment for the nonprofit sector. Another useful source for information on charities comes from the comparative civil society literature, which may have many touchstones but none more important than the work of Robert Putnam. If the Johns Hopkins project offers information on charities as organizations, the civil society literature provides insight into the underlying social values through comparative explorations of political culture, trust, and social capital.

In each country, there is a distinct subfield of international charities, but this is firmly embedded in a larger charitable sector. This is an important point for understanding the relationship between an INGO and its environment. Institutionalists of many stripes have long recognized that an organization's early entry into a new field may carry with it certain "first mover" advantages that allow the organization a very wide array of choices, while latecomers enter into a fairly rigid environment.[2] Thus, one might argue that the earliest INGOs like Amnesty International or CARE were innovators in the new fields of transnational human rights activism and international development and may have themselves defined what these fields would look like. While this may be true at the global level, it is not true at the national level. Amnesty International and CARE entered well-established charitable fields in their home countries when they were created; they may have been transnational first movers, but they were most definitely not the first American or British charities.

The present chapter fleshes out the fascinating differences among the national charitable sectors in the United States, Britain, and France. Following sociological institutionalism, I argue that both regulative material pressures and constitutive normative pressures are important for understanding an organization's environment. Thus, I examine four dimensions of the charitable sector in each country: the regulatory environment, the political opportunity structure, material resources, and the way in which social networks locate international charities within society. I then explain how these four dimensions are both product and producer of different logics of appropriateness for charities. In sum, "doing good" for others has fundamentally different meanings in the United States, Britain, and France—meanings that internationally oriented charities carry with them when they move around the globe.

---

2. I am grateful to an anonymous reviewer for reminding me of this insight.

United States: INGOs Doing the Job Right

The United States is a natural place to start to understand nonprofit organizations and charitable work. The fascination with the American charitable sector, which is alternately called the "voluntary," "nonprofit," "third,"
or "independent" sector, is expressed not only in popular discourse but in
scholarship, as there are arguably more studies of nonprofit organizations
in the United States than in any other country worldwide. The American
nonprofit sector is also the world's largest: the combined income of nonprofits accounts for about 8% of the American economy, larger than the
gross national product of all but ten nations worldwide (Salamon 1999b;
Hammack 2002). The state-society relationship in the United States has
informed the popular conception of civil society as an autonomously organized sphere that both solves social problems and checks the power
of the state. The popular myth of American civil society as independent
and antistate is actually somewhat disconnected from real practice. Despite a deep-seated suspicion of government in the United States, the "autonomous" charitable sector relies heavily on government support (Watt
1991; Hammack 2002). In addition, the idea that nonprofits operate as
a third sector separate from the market and the state is also inaccurate:
the government has increasingly relied on nonprofits for service delivery,
and nonprofits compete with and incorporate management tools from the
commercial world (Light 2000; Ott 2001).

Internationally oriented charities are only a fraction of the vast American charitable sector, though they make up a large proportion of the global
INGO community. International charities account for only 1.5% of the total
expenses of all American charities, but this was the fastest growing subsector between 1992 and 2005 with an increase in revenues of over 240%.[3] A
2006 study from the Urban Institute uses Internal Revenue Service data to
construct a detailed profile of the American INGO sector. Authors Elizabeth Reid and Janelle Kerlin (2006) report that nearly 5,600 nonprofits
work in international affairs, three-quarters of which are INGOs that actively work abroad in development and assistance.[4] Of these, 1,200 work

---

3. Kenneth Wing et al., *The Nonprofit Almanac 2008* (Washington: Urban Institute, 2008),
4, 131.
4. The remaining organizations are think tanks or cultural exchange programs.

in international relief, while another 300 organizations work on human rights and democracy. The behavior and identity of these INGOs are to a large extent determined by the fact that the United States offers a friendly regulatory environment, a fragmented government willing to work with charities, a wealth of material resources, and social networks that reach into the corporate world.

Regulatory Environment

In the United States, private charitable enterprises have received protection from the state since Daniel Webster famously argued *Dartmouth College v. Woodward* (1819) before the Supreme Court. Over the past century, the relative ease of establishing a nonprofit organization and the accompanying legal protections have encouraged substantial growth in the nonprofit sector (Hammack 2002; Hall and Burke 2002). In the United States, "charity" is a legal definition encompassing groups with tax status as 501(c)3 organizations, a much narrower category than nonprofit organizations in general. American charities are required to file detailed annual reports with federal authorities (per the 1969 Tax Reform Act) and to provide three years of annual returns to individuals upon request (per the 1996 Taxpayer Bill of Rights). Still, charity oversight is weak in the United States. The subdivision of the Internal Revenue Service in charge of charity oversight has not been well funded by Congress.[5]

American charities benefit from two tax advantages that have been in place since the late nineteenth century. Like most charities around the world, they are exempt from income tax, but they also benefit from a generous tax exemption for donors on contributions.[6] While the United States and the Britain both have tax regimes that encourage individual charitable giving, the United States is unique in several respects. First, American tax exemptions on charitable giving have existed for a century, whereas in

---

5. U.S. Senate, Committee on Finance, *Written Statement of Mark Everson, Commissioner of the IRS, Hearing on Charity Oversight and Reform,* 108th Cong., 2d session, June 22, 2004.

6. Donors who itemize their contributions can receive tax exemption on up to 50% of their adjusted gross income. Nonitemizers give at levels often exceeding those of the very wealthy (Hall and Burke 2002, 13). See also Congressional Budget Office, *Effects of Allowing Nonitemizers to Deduct Charitable Contributions* (December 2002).

Britain tax relief is relatively recent. Also, American donors can receive tax relief on noncash donations (including automobiles, computers, and cell phones) as well as on cash contributions. Finally, most charitable contributions in the United States are planned donations at the end of the year rather than spontaneous ones, which may help explain why the average size of donations in the United States is much larger than in Britain (Charities Aid Foundation 1994).

There is one important restriction on American charities, in the realm of political activity. According to federal law, "no substantial part" of a charity's activities can involve "carrying on propaganda, or otherwise attempting, to influence legislation," though charities may engage in limited lobbying activities (Joint Committee on Taxation 2005).[7] In addition, charities cannot use federal funds for lobbying and political activities. The restrictions surrounding political activities by charities have been tightened since the mid-1990s, and although some of the most restrictive legislation has failed to pass, the battle "has put a chill on at least some nonprofit engagement in policy deliberations and has left nonprofits that choose to engage in policy advocacy with considerably expanded paperwork burdens" (Grønbjerg and Salamon 2002, 465).

There have been several responses to these restrictions. Organizations like Independent Sector and the Center for Lobbying in the Public Interest were expressly created to support political activity by charities. They argue that the tight restrictions prevent these organizations from fulfilling their missions as public benefit organizations (Salamon 1999b, 20). Other charities have asserted their independence by refusing to seek or accept government funds. The most common response, however, has been to avoid political action. The exact effects of these restrictions are difficult to discern, as there are few comparative studies that offer insight into the levels of advocacy work across all nonprofits or among charities (though see Child and Grønbjerg 2007). In a study of national and local nonprofits, Chaves et al. (2004, 297) find that "it is common for nonprofit executives and board members to *believe* that accepting government funding legally restricts their political activity more than it actually does," even though some organizations receive

---

7. Many charities elect to become 501(h) organizations—a provision that allows large groups to spend up to $1 million on lobbying. Only 25% of that sum may be spent on "grassroots lobbying,"—direct communication with the public as opposed to legislators.

government funding and still engage in political activity. Cumulative statistics on lobbying by 501(c)3 organizations reveal that no more than 2% of all American charities reported any spending on lobbying in the 1990s (Boris and Krehely 2002, 303–4). Lobbying is not the only form of advocacy, but it is difficult to find sector-wide statistics on other advocacy activities. A few sectors—environment, civil rights, social action—show high levels of political activism, but some of the most famous advocacy groups like Greenpeace and the Sierra Club are 501(c)4 organizations and thus cannot offer donors tax relief on their contributions. Ultimately, the limitations on charities' political activities are much more severe than in either Britain or France. In sum, the legal environment makes it easy to establish a charity and raise money but discourages political activism.

Political Opportunities

American political culture supports a vision of government and civil society working side by side to solve social problems, and these values are reflected in the formal policy structure and the informal patterns of collaboration. Political power is dispersed, both at the macro level (for example, the federal division of power) and at the micro level (within particular government agencies). This fragmented political structure creates incentives for charities to focus on incremental policy change achieved through personal interaction with policymakers.

Internationally oriented charities see this substantial fragmentation of authority in the foreign policy realm. There are multiple points of contact at the many federal agencies involved in the provision of international assistance or the making of foreign policy. At the State Department alone, there are various offices with competing agendas. One former State Department official referred to the Bureau of Democracy, Human Rights, and Labor as the "NGO inside the building"—an office frequently willing to work with NGOs and advance the "NGO agenda" vis-à-vis other bureaus within State.[8]

These many points of contact place high demands on INGOs for advocacy and fundraising. As the head of government relations at one NGO stated, "some people think this is just very chaotic. The government has

---

8. Personal interview, April 19, 2006.

to make sure that the left and the right hand know what's going on, and they want to make sure they are moving in the same direction, that they are pushing for the same results, the same object."[9] In other words, the structure of political opportunities offers many channels through which charities can gain access to policymakers but also makes effective advocacy work costly.

Beyond the formal structure, informal foreign policymaking patterns affect the INGO-government relationship. The American government views the private sector as a partner and ally in the projection of American power and interests abroad. This support for private international assistance has been an explicit part of American foreign policy since the 1973 Foreign Assistance Act, which identified charities as effective mechanisms for grassroots development and urged greater government subsidies for these groups (Smith 1990, 67–68). More recently, the United States Agency for International Development (USAID) has defended the relatively low amounts of U.S. official development assistance as a share of gross national income by highlighting the privatization of foreign assistance, arguing that international spending by American NGOs rivals official government foreign aid (Hudson Institute 2006, 14).[10] While in practice some INGOs might complain that they are treated more like subcontractors than partners, the U.S. government generally accords private organizations much higher status than Britain and especially France. Consider a 2006 comment by President Bush on the subject of global development: "The generosity of our nation is reflected in the private sector.... I think that's what makes us such a unique country. You know, government helps, and government does a lot...but what our private sectors do is—it's unbelievable, when you think about it.... This is a collaborative effort. Some of the best work in fighting poverty is accomplished in partnership with private institutions."[11]

Similarly, in a statement that was received with some apprehension in the NGO community, Colin Powell referred to NGOs as "force multipliers"

---

9. Personal interview, April 26, 2006.

10. Earlier versions of this study were commissioned by Andrew Natsios, director of USAID.

11. "President Attends Initiative for Global Development's 2006 National Summit," White House Office of the Press Secretary press release, Washington, D.C., June 15, 2006.

of the U.S. government's efforts abroad.[12] This statement was perhaps only a more extreme version of a long-held sentiment in government *and* the private sector: American NGOs and American foreign policy are, separately and together, generally positive forces in the world.

Material Resources

American charities enjoy an embarrassment of riches. Not only is the U.S. government a major source of financial support, but the United States also has the most generous private donors worldwide. Finally, the American foundation sector is the world's largest and is a global leader in international grant-making.

The fragmentation of political power is evident also in the foreign aid spending of the U.S. government. In absolute terms, the United States is the world's largest donor in both development assistance and humanitarian aid (Hudson Institute 2006; Stoddard 2002). This aid is distributed through a multitude of government offices. USAID and the State Department are the primary donor agencies, but together they account for only about half of American official development assistance (OECD DAC 2006b, 45). Although there have been multiple efforts over the past several decades to streamline foreign assistance, there are today at least twenty-six government agencies that spend money on foreign aid. Some type of foreign assistance exists at nearly every executive department and agency, with sizeable programs at the departments of Defense, Treasury, and Agriculture (Congressional Research Service 2006; OECD DAC 2006b).

In dispensing this international aid, the government relies heavily upon what USAID calls "private voluntary organizations," a group that includes INGOs as well as for-profit contractors like Development Alternatives and Deloitte Touche Tohmatsu. In 2000, $4 billion of USAID's program budget of $7.2 billion was marked as contracts and grants for private organizations (General Accounting Office 2002). It is estimated that as much as 30 percent of American official development assistance goes through

---

12. "Remarks to the National Foreign Policy Conference for Leaders of Nongovernmental Organizations," U.S. Department of State press release, Washington, D.C., October 26, 2001.

private organizations, though the government does not report exact figures on its support to INGOs (OECD DAC 1998, 34). This heavy reliance on private organizations is good politics, as American public opinion polls demonstrate substantial support for dispensing foreign assistance through such organizations.[13]

In comparison to other donor agencies, USAID does not require that its INGO partners receive substantial private funding. From 1986 to 2005, Congress maintained required that partner agencies had to obtain at least 20% of their annual revenue from non-U.S. government sources, and since 2005, USAID has simply required that its partners maintain an undefined "private nature."[14] The comprehensive survey of the Urban Institute found that American INGOs receive an average 20% of their income from the American government (Reid and Kerlin 2006, 7), and while this may sound fairly low, it is an enormous amount of money given the size of the INGO sector. This figure used to be much higher: in the late 1970s, government contributions may have accounted for as much as 40% of the revenue of all INGOs.[15]

This support does not come without strings, however. Among Northern donor agencies, USAID "has been one that has placed great emphasis in assessing its aid effectiveness, measuring and evaluating program performance... and using this information to 'manage for results'" (OECD DAC 1998, 13). USAID was the first donor agency to use the "logical framework approach," or "logframe," as a mechanism for evaluating project outputs. USAID's focus on the micro level of projects has long put heavy reporting requirements on its private partners, though in the mid-1990s USAID began incorporating more qualitative metrics into its historically

---

13. In 2001, 58% of respondents to a PIPA poll favored the idea of channeling aid through private charitable organizations. Program on International Policy Attitudes, *Americans on Foreign Aid and World Hunger* (University of Maryland, February 2001).

14. At the project level, USAID also has relaxed requirements for private contributions, abolishing cost-sharing requirements in 1994 (McCleary 2009).

15. This is a conservative estimate; the only figures available are for those organizations registered with USAID, which may not accurately represent the entire American INGO sector. According to USAID's annual report on private voluntary organizations, from 1979 to 1981, all sources of U.S. government support accounted for an average 40% of such organizations' income; the same report indicates that the share of U.S. government support for these organizations has been falling somewhat steadily since then, to about 15% in 2007. US Agency for International Development, *VOLAG: Report on Voluntary Agencies* (various years).

quantitative methods of evaluating project impact. Much of this pressure to demonstrate results originates outside of USAID, which has been subject to Congressional criticism since its creation. Still, USAID's use of performance-based financing mechanisms has led INGOs to complain that they are being treated as service contractors rather than partners in international assistance (Brinkerhoff and Brinkerhoff 2004, 259).

In addition to government support, American INGOs benefit from a large pool of private donors. American individual donors are the most generous worldwide, giving the equivalent of 1.67% of gross domestic product (GDP) to charities in 2006 (Charities Aid Foundation 2006).[16] Not only do many Americans give to charities—an estimated 70% of American households—but these donations are relatively large (Wright 2001).[17] For the international charitable subsector, two trends in private giving are important. First, religion plays an important role in patterns of charitable giving. Church attendees are more likely to donate, and religious organizations are the most popular recipient of charitable donations (receiving 35.8% of all donations in 2006).[18] Second, foreign assistance is not very popular in the United States. One study by Giving USA found that international affairs nonprofits received about 4% of all charitable contributions in 2006, while the Urban Institute put the figure somewhat lower, at 2.5%.[19] Private contributions to international causes appear to have tripled in absolute terms since 1992, but international affairs still remain marginal. Thus, American INGOs might in theory have access to more private funding than their international peers, but in reality international charities actually

16. In this survey, the UK was next at 0.73%, and France was last at 0.14%. The Johns Hopkins comparative nonprofit sector research project offers slightly older but comparable figures, putting giving as a share of GDP in the late 1990s as 1.85% in the U.S., 0.84% in the UK, and 0.32% in France (Salamon et al. 1999, table 5).

17. Cross-national comparisons are complicated by the fact that Americans tend to count households who give, while the British count individuals. See Charities Aid Foundation 1994; National Council for Voluntary Organizations, "Charitable Giving in 2002," http://www.ncvo-vol.org.uk/policy/index.asp?id=1203.

18. *The Nonprofit Sector in Brief: Facts and Figures from the Nonprofit Almanac 2007* (Washington, D.C.: Urban Institute, 2006), table 4, p. 5.

19. Giving USA Foundation, "US charitable giving reaches $295.02 billion in 2006," press release; Urban Institute, "The Nonprofit Sector in Brief," 5. In 2001, 84% of Americans agreed that taking care of problems at home is more important than giving aid to foreign countries. Program on International Policy Attitudes, *Americans on Foreign Aid and World Hunger* (University of Maryland, February 2001.)

receive relatively little from the otherwise generous American public. The relatively small size of the subsector is reflected in employment figures: 0.3% of all American nonprofit employees work for international charities, compared to 2.4% in both Britain and France (Salamon 1999a, table B.2).

Finally, American INGOs are fortunate to have access to the largest foundation sector in the world. Helmut Anheier calls the U.S. foundation sector "the engine of transnational philanthropy," giving generously to both American and foreign NGOs (Anheier and Daly 2005, 158). In 2006, international grants accounted for 22% of total grants by all American foundations.[20] Foundation funding may thus compensate to some extent for low public attention to international causes. International giving by foundations has been increasing, from $1.6 billion in 1998 to $5.4 billion in 2007.[21] Importantly, most of these international grants are directed not to foreign groups but to U.S.-based INGOs operating abroad (Anheier and Daly 2005).[22]

Foundation support for charities has also encouraged professionalization. Peter Frumkin (1998) describes an increasing homogeneity across the American foundation sector, particularly as foundations adopted multidivisional structures and oversight procedures in response to hostile legislation in 1969. In one study of grant-making, Sada Aksartova (2003) argues that American foundations prefer to give to professional and elite NGOs rather than to social movements, since the former are "organizationally isomorphic" with foundations (see also Vogel 2006). Foundation support pushes charities to hire specialists, adopt uniform management principles, and develop fundraising capacities.

Social Networks

Geographic factors, sector-wide umbrella organizations, and patterns of staff and volunteer recruitment affect the place of international charities in American society. Geographically, internationally oriented charities are

---

20. Foundation Center, *International Grant-making IV* (New York: Council on Foundations, December 2008). From 1990 to 2002, international grant-making accounted for 12–14% of total grants.

21. Ibid.

22. In 1998, 59.9% of international grants went to U.S.-based recipients; in 2005, the figure was 64.4%, measured by dollar value of grants. Foundation Center, "Summary of Domestic and International Grant Dollars" (various years).

spread throughout the United States. Washington and New York are of course central bases for INGOs, but so are Atlanta, Los Angeles, and San Francisco.[23] This dispersion makes effective networking among INGO staff more difficult than in Britain or France, where INGOs are geographically concentrated in London and Paris. One way in which INGOs have worked to overcome this is by establishing umbrella groups through which INGOs can gather and discuss common problems. In the humanitarian relief and human rights sectors, two major networks link INGOs. InterAction is an umbrella NGO that brings together American relief and development organizations. Created in 1984 and headquartered in Washington, InterAction aims to facilitate coordination and cooperation among members and provide a forum for discussing issues like the foreign assistance budget and quality control. Outside the United States, InterAction is known for its emphasis on building consensus among members and its close ties to the U.S. government.[24] In the human rights sphere, cooperation among INGOs has historically been less formal. In the mid-1990s, the director of Amnesty International USA took the lead in coordinating an email listserv and regular meetings among the executive directors of leading human rights groups in the United States.[25] More recently, cooperation has been formalized through the creation of the U.S. Human Rights Network, whose substantive work is organized into issue-area caucuses.

Beyond these formal organizations, the social networks of INGOs are often built upon the connections of their boards of directors, and in the United States many of the leaders of charities come from the corporate world. In a nation where elite authority is largely based on wealth and financial success, elite participation in nonprofit governance boosts the profile and enhances the legitimacy of nonprofits.[26] Although the literature on elite networks in the charitable sector is small, a few important studies suggest that nonprofit board members have strong ties to the corporate and government sectors as well as to other nonprofits (Grønbjerg 1998).

---

23. 16% of INGOs are headquartered in the New York/New Jersey area, 15% in Washington, and 13% in California (Reid and Kerlin 2006).

24. Personal interview, Article 19 staffer, November 9, 2006; personal interview, Médecins du monde staffer, February 28, 2007.

25. Mohan Seneviratne, "A New Morning," *Amnesty International Magazine* [AI-USA] (Spring 2006).

26. For attitudes toward wealth in France and Britain, see Lamont 1992 and Wright 2001.

These interlocking networks of elites serve as conduits by which organizations share information, compare strategies, and develop standards for best practices, all processes that create and maintain an organizational field. Such networks are particularly important inasmuch as they reflect and further attenuate the weak divide between the nonprofit and corporate worlds (Useem 1986; Moore et al. 2002).

Finally, but perhaps most importantly, the social networks of the international charitable sector are affected by those who work for these organizations. As Robert Putnam (2000) and Theda Skocpol (2004) have noted, American civic associations have since the 1960s become increasingly professionalized and have provided fewer opportunities for citizen participation. InterAction reports that only a small number of American INGOs rely heavily on volunteers, and most "take a business-like approach to accomplishing their tasks," resulting in highly professionalized organizations.[27] As early as 1980, one study of American INGOs found that, relative to other American nonprofits, INGOs tended to be younger, slightly better staffed, and more frequently were nonmembership organizations (Smith et al. 1980, 174). At large INGOs, executive salaries are relatively high. Many leaders throughout the American charitable sector assume that, "in an economy that offers an increasing array of opportunities for executives, charities must offer to top executives wages and benefits that are comparable with those in the for-profit sector."[28] The emphasis on efficiency, particularly for the international assistance subsector, has reinforced the professionalization of nonprofit staff over the past three decades (Frumkin and Kim 2001).

Volunteers thus play a different and more limited role in international charities than in Britain and France. For the charitable sector as a whole, the cross-national differences may appear limited, with 22% of the American adult population volunteering, compared to 30% in Britain (and 14% in France; see Salamon 1999a, table 2).[29] Yet as with charitable donations, volunteer time in the United States is concentrated in religious

---

27. InterAction, *Nongovernmental Organizations in Overseas Assistance,* Occasional Paper September 2004, 6.

28. Eric Twombly and Marie Gantz, "Executive Compensation in the Nonprofit Sector," *Charting Civil Society* 11 (November 2001): 1.

29. The Department of Labor offers a slightly higher figure, a range of 26.7% to 28.8% between 2002–2006. Bureau of Labor Statistics, *Volunteering in the United States 2006.*

and educational activities, not in internationally oriented causes. A 2006 report on volunteering in America found that volunteering in general was at a thirty-year high, but that volunteering for political and international causes had dropped. In 1989, about 13% of volunteers worked for an organization whose focus was civic, political, professional, or international; by 2005, that figure was around 7%.[30] A survey by Independent Sector found that only 1% of volunteers reported any volunteering for international charities in 2006, the lowest figure among over a dozen causes.[31] Internships are one popular method for community participation, where college students and graduates work for a limited period of time in an intense fashion. These internship programs are often a way for nonprofits to attract young, educated people for eventual employment.

The American Environment for INGOs

The four dimensions discussed above together create a unique environment for internationally oriented charities. INGOs based in the United States operate in a resource-rich environment in a large country with no single geographic hub. The legal environment encourages charitable giving by individuals, but international assistance is not a popular charitable cause, so INGOs rely more heavily than other American charities on government agencies and foundations. While government agencies embrace cooperation with private agencies, charities regulations discourage political action.

In general, two broad norms define what is considered appropriate charitable action in the United States. The first is efficiency. Resource dependence scholars might argue that low spending on overhead is a strategic choice that charities make to maintain donor support, and there is some truth to this. For American INGOs, which enjoy less unrestricted funding from private donors than British and French INGOs, heavy

---

30. Corporation for National and Community Service, *Volunteer Growth in America: A Review of Trends since 1974* (Washington: CNCS, December 2006),3.

31. *Giving and Volunteering in the United States, 2001* (Washington: Independent Sector, 2002), 39. Americans also volunteer overseas but these numbers are hard to get. One study puts the number at 38,000. Lex Rieffel, *Reaching Out: Americans Serving Overseas, Brookings Institution Working Paper* (December 2005).

reliance on government agencies and private foundations means that they must demonstrate their efficiency and effectiveness. But the commitment to efficiency comes from other sources besides donor pressure. Given the American aversion to big government and the Tocquevillian tendency to self-organize to solve social problems (Lipset 1996), there is no real social consensus in the United States over whether government, corporations, or nonprofits are the best way to address social problems, including poverty and rights abuses abroad. Instead, these three sectors compete for resources and support, a phenomenon unseen in France or Britain. Thus, it is not just USAID and foundations that push INGOs to demonstrate their professionalism and efficiency. The American fear of big government is also an aversion toward bureaucracy (Wilson 1989), and all organizations, including INGOs, face pressures to minimize "wasteful" spending.

Broader social norms inform the preferences of all U.S. donors. Even individual private donors use efficiency as a yardstick for evaluating charities. The popular ratings systems at large watchdog groups like Charity Navigator and the Better Business Bureau punish charities for high spending on either management or fundraising, as these are considered wasteful overhead.[32] A similar ratings system exists at the world's largest annual workplace giving campaign, the Combined Federal Campaign (CFC), which provides only two pieces of information to potential donors: a charity's date of founding and the percentage of expenses directed toward overhead.[33] Also troubling for a resource dependence explanation are several recent studies that find that charities with low administrative costs are not rewarded with greater financial support (Frumkin and Kim 2001; Prakash and Szper 2011; for a contrasting view, see Tinkelman and Mankaney 2007). If spending little on overhead does not attract greater support, why would organizations do it? One possible answer is that efficiency is a constitutive norm that helps define good charitable work in America, and

---

32. For example, at Charity Navigator, which has a four-star ratings system, charities lose a star if they spend more than 20% of functional expenses on management or more than 15% on fundraising. "Our Ratings Tables," www.charitynavigator.org, accessed September 7, 2007 (on file with author).

33. "Combined Federal Campaign," U.S. Office of Personal Management. http://www.opm. gov/cfc/ (accessed May 23, 2006); "Defense Department Sets Record with Charitable Giving," *Global News Wire,* January 24, 2006.

that while efficiency is also a concern for British and French charities it is substantially less important.

These pressures to maximize efficiency are present across the charitable landscape in the United States, though they may manifest themselves in different ways according to the nature of an organization's work. For humanitarian relief and human rights organizations donor pressures and social norms both encourage INGOs to get the most "bang for their buck." For humanitarian groups, this might mean maximizing the amount of supplies delivered in the field to relieve suffering, while for human rights groups, this might mean maximizing the amount of pressure placed on states to change the treatment of individuals. While all INGOs around the world may feel some pressure to demonstrate efficacy, INGOs in the United States are much more focused on results than they are on process.

A second important norm present in American society and in the sub-sector of American international charities is pragmatism. This is less evident from the above profile but becomes clearer in comparison with the British and French environments. If there is no hierarchy of state, market, and civil society in the United States, it may be cause or consequence of an outcome-oriented focus upon which sector can best perform any particular task. Private watchdog agencies are again a place where this norm shows up for charities: in a list of questions for donors to ask before giving, Charity Navigator suggests that donors ask "what are the results?" because "being concerned with a problem" and having "good intentions" is not enough when "the marketplace is too crowded."[34] With few volunteers and many board members from the corporate world, INGOs understand their role as getting a job done rather than serving as a voice for the disempowered or acting as representatives of a particular philosophical position.

Pragmatism and efficiency are long-standing norms that govern appropriate charitable action for American INGOs. Consider the words of a 1975 report from the Senate Appropriations Committee: "The Committee again applauds the outstanding contributions to development made by...Private and Voluntary Organizations....They exhibit the finest qualities which may be inspired by a tradition of voluntarism and a sense of mission. Their *Spartan-like expenses,* and *their ability to get things done*

---

34. "6 Questions to Ask Charities before Donating," http://www.charitynavigator.org/index.cfm?bay=content.view&cpid=28 (accessed August 24, 2010).

stand in marked contrast to other, larger national and multinational organizations" (quoted in Sommer 1977, 95; emphasis added). As the cases of Britain and France will demonstrate, being "Spartan-like" and "getting things done" are distinctly American preoccupations.

Britain: INGOs, Activism, and Change

The charitable sector in the United Kingdom has a long and venerable history. From the Young Men's Christian Association to mutual aid "friendly societies," many of Britain's oldest charitable organizations trace their history to the nineteenth century, when charitable action was understood as a moral responsibility for the wealthy (Alvey 1995). Like the United States, Britain "has long had some of the densest networks of civic engagement in the world" (Hall 1999, 419). Yet the British charitable sector has enjoyed less independence from the state than its American counterpart. Civil society is firmly in the British Establishment, as the history of the major cultural and philanthropic institutions "has tended to link them with the state either by royal charter and patronage or by the network of elite kinship" (Beckford 1991, 32). While British charities have historically worked in concert with the state, the sometimes competitive relationship with the state may make the British voluntary sector resemble its American cousin more than its European neighbors (Halfpenny and Reid 2002, 538; Kendall and Almond 1999).

While long an important feature of British life, charities have not always been understood as a coherent sector that deserved separate analysis (Kendall 2000, 545). Attention to what Britons refer to as the "voluntary" or "third" sector has increased since the 1980s, particularly as Conservative governments promoted voluntary associations as alternatives to the state for social welfare provision (Halfpenny and Reid 2002, 534). The sector got an additional boost from the New Labour's 1998 Compact with the voluntary sector, which represented "an unparalleled step" in bringing charities into public policy discussions (Kendall 2000, 542). A decade later, the British charitable sector continues to grow in size and prominence. Expenditures in the nonprofit sector account for almost 7% of the total British economy (Kendall and Almond 1999).

British INGOs see themselves as capable agents of broad and meaningful change at all levels of the politics of international assistance. Humanitarian affairs scholar Hugo Slim (2006) refers to British INGOs as "Establishment radicals," a determined and energetic group drawn from the political, academic, and commercial elite. The subsector of internationally oriented charities is much larger in Britain than in the United States, as British INGOs build upon a long tradition of concern for international causes. With a population one-fifth the size of the United States, Britain supports the same number of INGOs. According to the Johns Hopkins Comparative Nonprofit Sector project, the size of the British international affairs charitable subsector is three times the Western European average, and this subsector "is the single area in which the UK's third sector is significantly larger, compared to other fields, than that of any other country on which data for this field are available" (Kendall and Almond 1999, 193–94). Many of these numerous INGOs are also large—out of the three largest INGOs in Western Europe, two are British, and the combined income of the top five organizations makes up 50% of the country's development sector (Sunderland 2004, 20).[35]

Regulatory Environment

Britain offers a hospitable regulatory environment to charities, though not to the degree found in the United States. While it is fairly easy to establish a charity, British law has historically offered a more narrow definition of charitable purposes than in the United States. This has resulted, for example, in the classification of Amnesty International as a political group rather than a charitable organization, which makes donors to Amnesty ineligible for tax relief and challenges Amnesty's identity as a public benefit organization.[36] The responsibility for oversight of charities lies with the Charity Commission, which also offers guidance and advice to charities.

Charities in Britain enjoy several tax advantages. They are exempt from income and corporation taxes and enjoy several other tax exemptions or

---

35. Those five organizations are Oxfam, Save the Children, Christian Aid, ActionAid, and the Catholic Overseas Development Agency (CAFOD).

36. Guidance from the Charity Commission in 2005 expanded the definition of charitable purpose to include human rights promotion. Future changes are likely to allow Amnesty to become a fully charitable organization (it currently has its activities split into charitable and noncharitable organizations). See Charity Commission, *RR12: The Promotion of Human Rights* (January 2005).

reductions.[37] In addition, private donors can take advantage of tax relief on their charitable gifts through one of two schemes, Gift Aid and payroll giving. Gift Aid was introduced in 1990 and allows a charity to receive what would have been the tax on a donation, increasing the effective size of any donor's gift. Gift Aid donations now account for about a third of all individual charitable donations.[38] Payroll giving was introduced in 1987 and more closely approximately the American system where the tax benefit accrues to the donor, but giving through this system accounts for only 4% of total household donations.[39] These giving schemes, which were reformed in 2000 to encourage even more giving, has had some success, but the Charities Aid Foundation finds that growth in each scheme is leveling off.[40] In sum, British regulations encourage charitable giving by private donors but the system is less well established and more complex than in the United States.

Compared to the United States, British law allows for more political activity by charities. Historically, political activity has been acceptable as long as it does not constitute the primary focus of a charity's work. The Charity Commission actively investigates complaints and has actually penalized large charities like Oxfam and Christian Aid, but it has also endorsed most of the political activities of charities (Burnell 1992). In 2004, the Charity Commission wrote in its revised guidance on campaigning and political activities: "We want charities to be in no doubt about this point. Campaigning, advocacy, and lobbying are all legitimate and valuable activities for charities to undertake. In fact the strong links charities have in their communities, the high levels of public trust and confidence they command, and the diversity of causes they represent, mean that charities are often uniquely placed to campaign and advocate on behalf of their representatives."[41] Thus, while political action must be "ancillary" to an organization's activities, this action is understood as both acceptable

---

37. Charities are subject to a value-added tax if involved in the delivery of goods and services.

38. Charities Aid Foundation, *Analysis of Giving through Gift Aid: CAF Briefing Paper* (January 2006), 3–4.

39. Charities Aid Foundation, *Analysis of UK Payroll Giving: CAF Briefing Paper* (July 2005).

40. Ibid. Tax-effective giving accounted for 13% of all donations in 1999. *Taxation of Charities, House of Commons Library Research Paper 01/46* (April 12, 2001), 13.

41. Charity Commission, "Campaigning and Political Activities by Charities—Some Questions and Answers" (April 2007), at www.charity-commission.gov.uk.

and important. Interestingly, charities' heightened advocacy efforts have often preceded, rather than followed, changes in charity legislation (Burnell 1992).

The British Charity Commission is more active in penalizing British charities than the American IRS, but this has not slowed the political activities of British INGOs. As early as 1993, Michael Edwards wrote that "most UK development NGOs accept that significant improvements in the lives of poor people around the globe are unlikely to be achieved solely by funding 'projects' at the grassroots level" (163). One leading guide to NGO advocacy by the British umbrella organization BOND suggests that successful advocacy involves public awareness, realistic objectives, and lobbying strategies that are employed at multiple levels and directed toward multiple audiences.[42]

Political Opportunities

The political opportunities available to British INGOs are shaped by both formal political structures and informal patterns of interaction. In the postcolonial era, the foreign policymaking process has been highly centralized in Britain, though perhaps less so over the past decade, and the legislature plays a much more subordinate role than in the United States (Clarke 1988; Wheeler and Dunne 1998; Williams 2004). In this environment, INGOs can achieve enormous results if they have political access, but if not, it may be hard for INGOs to find funding or leverage influence. For example, many NGO staffers point out that the hostility of the former secretary of state for international development, Clare Short, toward INGOs made working with government difficult (Sunderland 2004, 6–7).[43] At the same time, British INGOs have generally benefited from New Labour's emphasis on "joined-up" governance with civil society.[44]

There are many established structures for consultation between government officials and charitable organizations. For example, the Foreign and

---

42. BOND, *The How and Why of Advocacy, Guidance Notes No. 2* (March 2005), 4.

43. See also George Monbiot, "Don't Cry for Clare," *Guardian,* May 13, 2003.

44. The first Labour *White Paper on International Development* (1997) emphasized that DFID was not going to solve world poverty alone but must work in partnership with civil society, governments, and other donors.

Commonwealth Office (FCO) has four thematic panels that each meet twice a year. Each February, the FCO hosts a forum for NGOs to meet with the British delegation to the UN Commission on Human Rights.[45] The Department for International Development (DFID) is also required to host consultations with civil society organizations on a variety of issues. These opportunities for consultation focus on substantive policy discussions and seem generally appreciated and valued by British INGOs, in contrast to the French consultative structures discussed below. Still, DFID emphasizes that it seeks consultations with many types of civil society organizations, not just NGOs, and DFID officials generally see British INGOs as less critical to global development than their American counterparts (Wallace 2003, 565).

Beyond formal political structures, informal policy patterns affect the relationship that British INGOs have with state authorities. The greater receptiveness to cooperation with civil society that has existed since 1997 is still far from the decades-long American pattern of frequent and substantial cooperation with private organizations. Historically, the relationship between INGOs and the British government was centered around two limited issue areas: development research and short-term emergency assistance programs.[46] Collaboration between the state and NGOs has increased somewhat over the past two decades, evidenced by the increasing amount of aid that has been channeled through NGOs. Still, British INGOs are reluctant to seek more government funding if it will compromise their independence (OECD DAC 2006a, 34). The general state of relations between DFID and NGOs is thus one of limited cooperation; while they often work together on a functional basis, they also often hold very different policy views (Sunderland 2004, 9). The extensive postcolonial foreign policy apparatus in Britain, combined with the British INGO sector's concern with maintaining independence, makes it highly unlikely that even greater cooperation in the future will lead to convergence on the American model of government-INGO relations.

---

45. Foreign and Commonwealth Office, "Joined-up Government," *Annual Report on Human Rights 2003* (London: FCO, 2003), 61–86.

46. David Geer in Mary Braid, "Nongovernmental Organizations in France and Britain," report of a Franco-British Council seminar held in Leeds Castle, Brent, March 12 and 13, 2003 (on file with author).

Material Resources

The landscape of resource availability for international charities in Britain is quite different from that of the United States. The British government does not allocate enormous sums to INGO funding, though it is a relatively friendly donor. Private donations are the largest source of funding for INGOs, and while many Britons give to international causes, they tend to give spontaneously and in small amounts. Many British INGOs also avail themselves of funding opportunities at the European Union, though this source does not account for a substantial share of British INGO income. With five times as many INGOs per capita as in the United States, British INGOs must stay in the public eye in order to attract private donations.

The United Kingdom spends twice as much on official development assistance as the United States when measured as a share of gross national income, and in absolute terms it is one of the largest donors worldwide.[47] This international aid is distributed mainly through DFID, an agency created in 1997 from the previous Office of Development Assistance and made independent from the FCO. In 2004–5, DFID administered three-quarters of British official development assistance.[48] Other agencies that provide international aid include the FCO, the Export Credits Guarantee Department (mainly involved in debt relief) and the Commonwealth Development Corporation.

Since the mid-1980s, the British government has channeled an increasing amount of international assistance through NGOs—both INGOs and local NGOs in recipient countries.[49] According to DFID, support for voluntary organizations doubled between 1997 and 2004–5, when DFID channeled about 9% of its budget through civil society organizations.[50] In

---

47. In 2005, the United States and the UK spent 0.22% and 0.47% of GNI on foreign aid, respectively. OECD DAC, "Aid at a Glance," www.oecd.org.

48. DFID, *Statistics on International Development 2006* (East Kilbride: DFID Statistical Reporting Group, Oct 2006), table 3.1.

49. "In the ten years to 1993/94, the United Kingdom increased its official funding of NGOs by almost 400% to £68.7m, raising the share of total aid channeled to NGOs from 1.4% to 3.6%." Overseas Development Institute, *NGOs and Official Donors, ODI Briefing Paper* (April 1995). 3.1% of British overseas development aid was channeled through NGOs in 1998 (€102 million) (Paquot 2001).

50. National Audit Office, *Department for International Development: Working with Non-governmental and Other Civil Society Organizations to Promote Development* (London: NAO, July 2006), 1.

total, the OECD estimates that 5% of British official development assistance goes through INGOs. (OECD DAC 2010, 52). Unlike many other donors, however, DFID has several innovative funding schemes that support INGOs' research and overhead. For example, DFID's Partnership Programme Agreements provide large grants over three to five years to relief organizations and international volunteer-sending agencies, and about twenty such agreements are currently in place. Other civil society funding schemes provide smaller organizations the chance to access official funds, but DFID funding remains concentrated in the hands of just a few NGOs, particularly the "big five" relief organizations (Wallace 2003).[51] Thus, DFID programs reflect a limited but productive partnership between INGOs and the UK government. While Britain may not provide a large share of INGO income, the funding schemes allow INGOs flexibility and encourage research and advocacy. DFID also conducts research on its own to complement INGO and academic research: in 2001, it spent almost 5% of its budget on research and policy analysis, the third-highest level of any OECD donor government (Sunderland 2004, 10).

Private giving is the primary source of income for British INGOs. Britain ranks second worldwide in individual giving as a share of gross domestic product, though giving has declined slightly in recent decades (Wright 2001, 403). But unlike in the United States, international assistance is one of the top charitable causes to which the British public donates.[52] Private donors in Britain tend to give in spontaneous ways and small amounts. The Charities Aid Foundation reports that spontaneous methods of giving accounted for 66% of all donations in 2007.[53] Many of these cash donations are made to "chuggers," or charity muggers, who gather donations on the streets.[54] There are several national organizations that help raise and channel these private donations: proceeds from a national lottery (the

---

51. In 2004–5, ten organizations received 88% of all DFID funding (OECD/DAC 2006, 33).

52. The most popular charitable causes in Britain are health, social care, and international assistance; these three rotate spots as the number one cause. "Make Poverty Political," *Guardian,* February 15, 2006; Cathy Pharoah, "Fundraising: New Research on Giving to International Causes," *Networker* [BOND], May 2007.

53. Charities Aid Foundation, *UK Giving 2007,* 33. This figure was 68% in 2006. The report also shows that 48% of donors use cash methods of giving, but that these only account for 18% of the total amount of donations.

54. Liam Vaughn, "Chuggers: When Capitalism Works for Good," *New Statesman,* October 11, 2004, 18.

world's largest) go to general public projects and charities, while the Disasters Emergency Committee, which brings leading NGOs together with the British press and government agencies, helps launch appeals in cases of global humanitarian crises. These patterns of small and spontaneous contributions put great pressures on INGO fundraising departments, but private funds also provide NGOs with a great amount of program flexibility, as these individual donations are unrestricted.[55]

The British foundation sector is of moderate size, and far smaller than the American sector. The foundations prefer to give to UK-based activities—the Association of Charitable Foundations reports that "only a small proportion of UK trusts and foundations make grants outside the UK, and few give funds directly to organizations in other countries."[56] According to this report, international grants from British trusts and foundations totaled £98 million in 2001.

Many British NGOs also take advantage of their access to funding through the European Union. The European Commission's Humanitarian Aid and Civil Protection department (ECHO; formerly known as the European Community Humanitarian Aid Office) is one of the world's largest humanitarian aid donors and has long-standing partnerships, called Framework Partnership Agreements, with many leading British NGOs, including Action Aid, CAFOD, Christian Aid, PLAN International, Oxfam, and Save the Children. These agreements place high administrative demands on INGOs, but they are also regularly revised in consultation with NGOs, making for a more collaborative financing system. The EU's EuropeAid office manages EU external assistance and has extensive funding available for NGOs in the areas of development education in Europe, human rights and democracy promotion, and development work abroad. While specific information on EU aid to British INGOs is not available, overall, EU funding accounts for an average 13% of income of relief and development NGOs in Europe.[57]

---

55. The terms "restricted" and "unrestricted" are widely used by charities to differentiate funds given to specific projects versus funds "without strings attached." While organizations obviously solicit restricted funds, unrestricted funds allow INGOs more flexibility in choosing priorities and engaging in advocacy and sector-wide research.

56. *Guidance for Grant-seeking Organizations Outside the UK* (London: ACF, January 2007).

57. CONCORD, *The Truth behind the Figures: What the Official Figures Tell Us about European Aid and NGOs* (Brussels: CONCORD, May 2006).

Social networks

Geography, history, elite interactions, and staffing together create a tight social network for British charities. The small size of the UK and the concentration of charities in the London-Cambridge-Oxford triangle allow for regular interaction among INGOS and between INGOs and their counterparts in government and academia. Crossover of staff among INGOs and between NGOs and the government seems particularly high in Britain. According to David Lewis of the London School of Economics (2008), increasingly flexible government arrangements have increased personnel flows between the government and NGO sector.[58] In addition, Britain's colonial past has left it with research centers like the Institute for Development Studies and the London School of Hygiene and Tropical Medicine that provide information and support to both government and INGOs (Slim 2006, 5). Formally, interaction among NGOs often happens at BOND, an umbrella organization for relief and development NGOs that includes nearly half of all British development INGOs.[59] BOND acts a formal liaison with other European groups and pushes for continued consultation with and funding from the British government. Finally, the elite that make up the boards of directors at major NGOs come from a variety of other sectors, including the corporate world, academia, and government (Wallace et al. 1997, 83).

British NGOs are highly professionalized, much like their American counterparts, and the large organizations are run by professional staff based in and around London. There are two major differences from the American charitable sector, however. First, the emphasis on management and oversight came to British charities later than in the United States, and management is still understood as a less structured affair. A 1997 government-funded study of development NGOs found that most INGOs had tightened project management over the previous few years, but as recently

---

58. For a discussion of this phenomenon in the INGO sector, see "Crossing Boundaries," *The Networker* (April 2006); Cathy Shutt, *Changing the World by Changing Ourselves, Institute for Development Studies Practice Paper* (September 2009), 17.

59. The organization's name was originally an acronym that stood for British Overseas NGOs for Development. In line with its networking function, the name has since been changed to "BOND."

as 1989 few British NGOs understood the guidelines of the "logframe" approach so prevalent in the American setting (Wallace et al. 1997, 27). Another survey of British NGOs found that management training had increased but in a haphazard way that was supply-driven rather than demand-led (Amos-Wilson 1996). Thus, while younger INGO staffers often come from the corporate or public relations sector, many of those working at British INGOs are still not involved or not interested in the standardization of management practices.

Second, unlike at American charities, volunteers play an important role in the British INGO sector. National rates of volunteering are slightly higher in Britain than in the United States: 30% of the adult population compared to 22% in the United States. The differences are much starker within the subsector of international charities. Overseas assistance is one of the top five causes for which Britons volunteer (Charities Aid Foundation 1994). In addition, at least a hundred British INGOs welcome volunteers for fieldwork overseas (Sunderland 2004, 26). There are many reasons for this. Most obviously, volunteers provide a large and free workforce, but volunteers also help inform the identity of UK NGOs as partners and community activists.

The British Environment for INGOs

Britain is a supportive and fairly resource-rich environment for nonprofits, like the United States, although favorable tax treatment of charitable gifts is much newer to Britain and rates of charitable giving are lower. Although this may make private fundraising more difficult, British INGOs are fortunate to face a public deeply interested in international causes. This yields a large pool of small but numerous spontaneous private donations, and these unrestricted funds allow UK NGOs to engage in sector-wide research and multilevel advocacy and campaigning. Of course, organizations that can demonstrate their expertise and impact then may be more successful at attracting private donations to overseas causes (Desforges 2004). At the same time, the limited engagement of the British government with INGOs relative to the United States may also reward those groups that are capable of both insider lobbying and outsider campaigning. Finally, the small world of the British charitable community facilitates interagency cooperation and staff flows.

As in the United States, institutional and material features together reflect and reproduce a set of norms that define appropriate charitable action.
In contrast to American pragmatism focused on *outcomes,* the *process* of
charitable action is most important in Britain. Karen Wright of the London School of Economics refers to this as the difference between generosity
in the United States and altruism in Britain. As Wright describes it, the
British expect that giving "should be altruistic, even self-sacrificing," and
that the bulk of donations should go to "universal causes such as Oxfam
or Save the Children in which there is little direct or indirect benefit to the
giver" (2001, 412). The concern with process, that is, with true interest and
right motivation, may encourage British charities to be more embracing of
volunteers—who share a commitment to a particular cause—than their
American counterparts.

This concern also means that Britons do not prioritize efficiency in
the same way as their American peers. Scandals involving the misuse of
charitable funds are equally prevalent in both countries, but British donors (both private and government) do not subject charities to the same
scrutiny of spending on management and fundraising. For example, a
new British private watchdog group, Intelligent Giving, advises donors
not to "pay much attention to charities' overheads when deciding which
one to support. After all, no organization runs on thin air, and the few
that try are often disorganized and ineffective."[60] This more nuanced
understanding of "overhead" costs may be related to the stricter separation between the corporate and charitable sectors in Britain. Researchers
Fran Tonkiss and Andrew Passey refer to the divide as the difference
between "doing well" (the corporate emphasis on efficiency) and "doing
good" (the charitable emphasis on altruism). In a survey conducted in the
late 1990s, they found that half of respondents disagreed with the statement that "charities should be more like businesses" (Tonkiss and Passey
1999, 269). Donors in Britain, like donors elsewhere, are concerned that
their money be used well, but they lack the American preoccupation with
efficiency.

---

60. "Statistics We Like," www.intelligentgiving.com, accessed March 11, 2008. See also "Is He
Guiding Charities in the Right Direction?" *The Guardian,* February 20, 2008, 3.

France: Independent and Growing Charities

If the institutional environments for international charities in Britain and the United States appear surprisingly different, those differences may appear less stark in comparison to France, with its particular relationship between state and society. In France, the domination of the state in political thought and life runs parallel to a belief that private institutions fragment the "general will" represented by the state (Hall 1986; Archambault et al. 1999). French Revolutionary principles rejected the idea of any intermediary between citizen and state, and independent associations were outlawed until a 1901 law finally legalized them. Thus, the private charitable sector in France is much younger and smaller than in either Britain or the United States; in the words of one analyst, the French nonprofit sector has, "in a historical sense, really only recently begun to develop" (Archambault et al. 1999, 82). As of the early 1990s, one review suggested, French voluntary associations "on the whole lack the resources, expertise, and prestige necessary to maintain a consistent presence" in public discourse (Veugelers and Lamont 1991, 150), while another study found that France collected "almost no data either on formation of non-profit associations, financial gifts to charities, or voluntary work" (Charities Aid Foundation 1994, 14). Reliable historical data on specific charities and charitable giving are thus difficult to come by.

Yet the French charitable sector is growing. Since the 1960s there has been considerable growth in the number and size of associations, particularly following the Decentralization Acts in the 1980s that reduced the role of the state in the economy (Archambault 1996; Levy 1999). In 1995, nonprofit organizations accounted for 4.9% of all employment in France, less than in Britain (6.2%) and the United States (7.8%) (Archambault et al. 1999, 91). Concomitantly, a growing body of scholarly literature is tracing the dimensions of associational life in France. Still, the expanding sector is in no way a challenge to the authority of the French state. Although the French may be joining civic organizations in record numbers, these organizations operate in a political wilderness, unconnected to French policymakers (Appleton 2006). Unlike in the United States where the lines between the private and public sectors are increasingly blurred, the divisions between state and society remain firm in France (Bryant and Rubio 2006, 82).

Within this small but growing charitable sector, the subsector of international charities is particularly prominent. The most popular charitable causes include humanitarianism, environmentalism, and the *"sans"* movements—advocacy groups focused on the rights of those without housing, rights, or jobs (Dreano 2004), like the group Les Enfants de Don Quichotte that I encountered in Paris in early 2007. French INGOs are generally referred to as "international solidarity organizations," and they are much smaller in size than British or American INGOs. The largest French INGO, Médecins Sans Frontières, has an annual budget that is less than a third the size of Oxfam International's. The total size of the French INGO sector was estimated at €713 million for 2001, the equivalent of 15.4% of all French official development assistance (Fagnou 2004b). Even more than in Britain, the French NGO sector is dominated by a few large organizations. The income of the four largest INGOs accounts for a third of the total income of all French NGOs, and the top twenty NGOs account for more than three-quarters of the total (Fagnou 2004a). Alongside these big, privately funded NGOs, there are many small organizations, many of which have no paid staff and rely heavily on local and national authorities for funds.[61]

The modern NGO sector in France has gone through three waves of development. In the nineteenth and early twentieth centuries, early French humanitarians were involved in the alleviation of the consequences of European wars. The 1960s saw a second wave of internationalists concerned with Third World development, and in the 1970s a series of "emergency-only" organizations formed the third wave of INGOs (Hatton 2007). As perhaps a fourth wave, many newer organizations are small but vocal participants in the *altermondialiste* movement protesting the effects of globalization (Meunier 2000). The organizations that came out of these waves are often in public disagreement with one another over the principles of humanitarianism and international assistance.

Regulatory Environment

A dense network of French law governs charitable organizations, legally known as *associations*. The Law of 1 July 1901 defines an association as any

---

61. In contrast to the popular image of French INGOs as emergency doctors, there are actually many small INGOs that focus only on development (Cumming 2009).

group of two or more persons whose aim is a nonprofit one. To register, an association must formally lodge a declaration with the state and advertise its aims in the *Journal Officiel* (Archambault 1996, 58). Oversight for charities rests with several regulatory bodies. The Cour des comptes was authorized in 1991 to audit public charities, and its recent audits include some of the most high-profile charities in France.[62] In 1996, the Inspection générale des affaires sociales was given the authority to supervise the use of public donations to charities.[63] Finally, charities set up a private auditing mechanism in 1989, the Comité de la Charte, to reassure donors that their money was being well spent (Queinnec 2003, 512).

While tax benefits for charities have become more generous, the law surrounding tax exemption remains complicated. All French associations are exempt from commercial taxes, receive a reduced VAT rate on the purchase of certain goods, and can be exempt from taxes on earned income according to a complex formula (Council on Foundations 2006, 9). In order to be eligible for tax exemption for charitable donations, organizations need to either be general interest associations (those that advance philanthropic, education, humanitarian, and other causes) or to apply for designation as a public utility association (*association reconnue d'utilité publique*), a status that is difficult to achieve but affords important additional tax privileges. There are about two thousand public utility associations, out of a total of perhaps a million associations, and this special status allows these organizations to offer tax exemptions on larger donations, such as those made in private wills. Changes in the tax code in 2003 were meant to further encourage private donations, but the formula is still complicated. Individual donors can claim tax relief on 66% of the value of donations, up to 20% of an individual's income. One recent study of French tax returns found that the overall effect of these reforms has been quite small, resulting in little increase in private charitable giving (Fack and Landais 2010).

The French regulatory environment is the most permissive of those profiled here toward political activities of private associations. Essentially, nothing in the tax code says that associations may not engage in political activities (Newman 2001). General interest associations can engage in

---

62. Recent audits include organizations like the National League Against Cancer, the Abbé Pierre Foundation, and a sector-wide review after the 2004 Asian tsunami. "Contrôles des organismes faisant appel à générosité publique," www.ccomptes.fr (accessed March 13, 2008).

63. IGAS, *Close-up on IGAS* (March 2005), available at www.travail-solidarite.gouv.fr.

political activities to any extent, though a decision by the Council of State has clarified that public utility associations may not engage *primarily* in political action (Council on Foundations 2006, 8).

One final important aspect of French law relates to the legal protections afforded volunteers. There are two different types of volunteering in France, *bénévolat* and *volontariat*. The first type is more informal—anyone can give their time—while the second offers special legal status to those working with NGOs. According to the Law of 14 March 2000, those with *volontariat* status receive a monthly indemnity, health insurance, and two and a half vacation days per month. This legislation encourages active citizenship while ensuring social protections for those giving significant time to associations. The state offers additional support to international charities that send volunteers abroad. Individuals who volunteer for particular international development programs also receive a stipend upon return to help them "reintegrate" into French society. About two dozen French organizations are officially recognized by the Ministry of Foreign Affairs as those that receive support to send volunteers abroad. Around two thousand *volontariat* workers are sent abroad each year for an average two years overseas.[64] As another reflection of the voluntary nature of the associative sector, nonprofit managers are prohibited from receiving excessive salaries (Council on Foundations 2006, 6). In sum, French law encourages the charitable sector to remain voluntary.

Political Opportunities

The formal institutions of the French state and the limited informal opportunities for interaction with political authorities powerfully shape French charities. Particularly in foreign affairs, there is a broad acceptance of the primacy of the state in France. The president plays a central role in a foreign policy process that has lacked transparency (Lancaster 2007, 164). The authority and capacity of private organizations in foreign affairs have long been denied. In the postcolonial period, French NGOs had little direct contact with state agencies, and through the mid-1970s the primary

---

64. The European Volunteer Center, *Country Report on the Legal Status of Volunteers in France* (Brussels, 2005), 8.

point of contact for NGOs was a small, peripheral bureau in the development ministry (Cumming 2009, 74–75). In the past decade or so, the foreign affairs ministry and other government agencies have exhibited some limited willingness to cooperate with non-state actors. Part of this change in INGO-state relations occurred during sweeping reforms of the French foreign aid system in 1998, in which new consultative structures were established to facilitate dialogue with civil society representatives.

Officially, there are several points of contact for French NGOs at state agencies. Authority for international assistance lies with the Ministry of Foreign Affairs and the Ministry of Economic Affairs, Finance, and Industry. Outside these agencies, the Development Cooperation Commission was created in the early 1980s as an interdepartmental advisory committee made of both government and NGO representatives to address international issues. In the fields of humanitarianism and human rights, there are two consultative structures. The Haut Conseil de la coopération internationale, created in 1999, has forty civil society representatives that develop recommendations to the prime minister and government on international issues. The Commission nationale consultative des droits de l'homme was created in 1947 to protect France's special role in domestic and international human rights promotion; today it hosts discussions and helps organize training sessions for human rights protection abroad.

This official emphasis on cooperation has not resulted in much real change in the state-NGO relationship. According to an OECD review of French foreign aid, the new interest in dialogue "does not translate into use of NGOs as intermediaries in the management of official aid [which] NGOs put...down to official distrust of their capabilities and the durability of their activities" (OECD DAC 2000, I–25). The limitations of this new dialogue are seen in the extremely low levels of government support for INGOs (see below). Skeptic Samy Cohen (2006) argues that the new attention to NGOs by the state is a calculated move to strengthen French influence in the world, rather than a philosophical shift regarding the role of civil society. From the NGO perspective, these overtures have been deemed "insufficient to form the basis of a genuine rapprochement" (Cumming 2009, 88). The foreign affairs ministry explains this low level of state-NGO cooperation by pointing to the fact that France already has a considerable public bureaucracy for international cooperation, while other states may use INGOs to distribute aid instead of developing state capacity

(Paquot 2001). In other words, state officials feel they already have sufficient capacity to address international assistance and do not need the assistance of international NGOs.

The informal patterns of interaction between the state and private charities, including INGOs, are "essentially conflictual" (Biberson and Jean 1999). Many French INGOs are fiercely protective of their independence from politics, yet that independence has been basically forced upon them by a government unwilling to partner in international development and assistance. Despite the closed nature of the political system, French charities tend to make vocal demands that government officials recognize and act upon their obligations. Operating in the shadow of a powerful state, NGOs turn to that state for action: in France, "the average citizen still considers that it is up to the government to deal with any civic, social, or economic problem" (Archambault 1996, 17). Rony Brauman (1996, 80) has argued that NGOs have a responsibility to act as an "alarm bell" for states, alerting governments to their failures and demanding action. Where American INGOs and the U.S. government are partners, and British INGOs coexist and often collaborate with their government, French INGOs are vocal but subordinate critics of the state.

Material Resources

French charities in general and INGOs in particular have fewer sources of support than their counterparts in the United States and Britain, whether from the government, private donors, or private foundations. Many INGOs have turned to the European Union for help, but the relative lack of funding has kept the leading French INGOs smaller than British or American organizations.

The French foreign aid budget is comparable to that of the United Kingdom; according to the OECD, France spent US$10 billion on foreign aid in 2005, the equivalent of 0.47% of gross national income. Like many other Northern donor countries, France has pledged to increase its development assistance, and the French aid budget has grown noticeably. French foreign aid has traditionally relied upon bilateral mechanisms to help spread French culture and institutions, but France has dedicated increasing attention to debt relief, which accounts for much of the rise in its development aid (Schraeder et al. 1998). A 2003 policy document suggests that France, as an exemplary model of the universal values that constitute democracy, has an important role to play in nurturing governance systems abroad (Ministère des Affaires étrangères 2003, 10–11).

Unsurprisingly, given the state's hostility to NGOs, France ranks last among European governments in the amount of official development assistance channeled through private organizations, with about 1% of all foreign aid (Commission Coopération Développement 2005). French government funds accounted for 8.4% of the total income of all French INGOs in 2001 and even less in 2004 (Fagnou 2004b). Most of this support comes from an office within the Ministry of Foreign Affairs specially tasked with NGO cooperation. In funding NGO projects, the ministry will generally support no more than 50% of the total cost of any project.[65] The Agence Française de Développement, the French international development bank, also spends little through NGOs (about 7% of its total budget); interestingly, many local offices around France offer some support to INGOs (Ministère des Affaires étrangères 2004).

Given low levels of financial support from the French government, most of French NGOs that report getting "institutional" funds are actually receiving support from the European Union. From 1991 to 1999, EU support for French NGOs tripled, while French government funding for NGOs remained basically unchanged (Sanchez-Salgado 2001a). Of the two hundred organizations worldwide that currently have established partnership agreements with the EU's humanitarian office ECHO, about two dozen are French. Still, EU funding accounted for only 17% of the total income of the French INGO sector in 2003 (Commission Coopération Développement 2005). Thus, even though there is a strong push factor driving French NGOs abroad for resources, there has been no "Europeanization" of the sector's funding.

Private donations account for most of French NGOs' income. They received an average 60% of their resources from private sources between 1991 and 2003 (Commission Coopération Développement 2005, 10). Yet these private donations are hard-won. Compared with Americans and

---

65. "Cofinancement de projets et programmes," Ministère des Affaires étrangères, www.diplomatie.gouv.fr (accessed April 5, 2007). The ceiling was raised in 1996 in a scheme called the "la nouvelle contractualisation," but these new contracts account for only perhaps 20% of all government support for NGOs (Cumming 2009, 78; Commissariat Général du Plan 2002, 110).

Britons, only a small share of the French public gives to charity. A 1991 survey by the British Charities Aid Foundation found that a "strikingly low" proportion of the French population gave to charity, but interestingly, the average donation was quite high (Charities Aid Foundation 1994). The fact that privileged tax treatment for charitable donations is a recent phenomenon has kept many donors from giving (Archambault 1996, 70). In 2006, charitable giving was 0.14% of GDP in France, much lower than in Britain (0.84%) or the United States (1.67%) (Charities Aid Foundation 2006). Fortunately for internationally oriented charities, international assistance is a fairly popular cause. Humanitarian aid and Third World development together are perhaps the third most popular charitable cause in France behind social assistance and medical research.[66] Thus, while other French charities involved in social services and education receive heavy support from the French state, international charities effectively tap into the small pool of private donors (Archambault et al. 1999).

On top of a very small pool of government funds and a small but generous pool of donors, the French foundation sector is very weak. In the 1960s, the government helped support the creation of France's largest foundation, the Fondation de France, which today has a few small programs for "international solidarity."[67] In the 1980s, the law governing associations was changed to encourage the establishment of foundations, but grant-making foundations in France are still rare, and with less than 20 foundations per 100,000 inhabitants, the number of foundations per capita in France is one-twentieth the number in the United States.[68]

Thus, the French NGO sector has largely depended on relatively scarce private donors, with some smaller role for funds from European Union institutions. As in Britain, private donors are the primary source of income for INGOs, but the patterns of charitable giving are vastly different in each

---

66. Although the popularity of international assistance changes a bit depending on the survey, it is regularly in the top five charitable causes. Fondation de France, *Portrait de la générosité en France* (September 2006), 4–5.

67. Edith Archambault (2001, 121–2) explains this scarcity by pointing to a Jacobin tradition suspicious of private property held outside the state and a lack of social awareness of foundations.

68. "Enquête nationale auprès des fondations," *Contact* [monthly newsletter of Fondation de France] April 2005, 4.

country. In France, a small but committed donor pool, rather than a large pool of occasional donors as in Britain, keeps INGOs afloat.

Social Networks

The French split between a small group of large, wealthy, and somewhat professionalized NGOs, and a very large group of small, volunteer-run organizations roughly matches up with the divide between emergency-only organizations and development NGOs. Beyond the relief-development divide, other factors, like geography, the structure of INGO networks, and patterns of staff and volunteer recruitment shape the social interactions of these INGOs. Geographically, most French INGOs have a headquarters in Paris and a large national network of local volunteer offices (Commissariat Général du Plan 2002, 159). Organizational leaders are thus geographically concentrated and have multiple opportunities for interaction.

One of the most fascinating features of the French INGO landscape is the complex configuration of networks. The biggest umbrella organization, Coordination SUD (The French National Platform of International Solidarity NGOs), was created in 1994 as a meta-umbrella organization to manage the relationship between INGOs and the state. Coordination SUD is made up of direct member organizations as well as six independent INGO collectives, each of which has dozens of other member organizations. Though Coordination SUD has recently taken a leadership position, the French INGO landscape still remains an alphabet soup of simultaneously interlocking, overlapping, and competing organizations. For example, the Center for Development Research and Information (CRID) has fifty-four members, works from the same building as Coordination SUD, and focuses on education and campaigning in France on development issues. Another umbrella organization, the Forum of International Solidarity Organizations on Migrations Issues (FORIM), is also located in the same building but works only on migration. Yet another collective, Réseau IPAM (the "Initiatives for Another World" Network), an anticolonial, antiliberalization group, brings together six NGOs, while one member of IPAM, CEDETIM (the Center for International Solidarity Studies and Initiatives), is actually its own umbrella organization working with human rights groups and umbrella groups for migrant workers.

These inter-NGO partnerships are celebrated, contested, and very often are formed on the basis of shared principles rather than as attempts to improve program coordination.[69] Alongside this complex web of organizations, individual French citizens frequently jump from one association to another. Jean-Pierre Worms (2002, 159) refers to this phenomenon as "zapping," which he argues is an expression of "a desire for personal coherence, for step-by-step control of one's social investments." This creates a wide but fragmented set of social networks for activists.

In the broader context of French civil society, French INGOs are part of a larger Left-oriented group of social activists (Dreano 2004). As one activist explained, "the major NGOs within the French framework were formed as dissidents. . . . associations [here] are often quite political in their configurations."[70] For example, the leading French human rights organization, the Ligue des Droits de l'Homme, has had close ties to leading figures from the political Left since its creation (Irvine 2007). These domestic political connections are reflected in the fact that international charities are not as exclusively international as their American counterparts. Every major French INGO has important programs in France itself (Commissariat Général du Plan 2002, 37).

These informal links between international charities and domestic political groups become a conduit by which activists share and spread a principled orientation to charitable work. As the activist mentioned above stated, "before we have a practice, we have a *concept*. Then we have a practice, an action."[71] Program activities are chosen based on their compatibility with the charity's principles. The contrast between this principled French approach and American pragmatism is consistent with Michèle Lamont's (1992, 354) account of different social boundary patterns in each country: the French "value cultural sophistication through refinement, familiarity with high culture, and intellectualism, whereas Americans stress self-actualization, expertise, and cosmopolitanism." The French principled orientation often creates lively and critical debates in the NGO sector. The

---

69. While downplaying some differences between American and French NGOs, Samy Cohen (2006) argues that if there is anything unique about French NGOs it is their insistence on independence and thus their unwillingness to form durable coalitions.

70. Personal interview, February 22, 2007.

71. Personal interview, February 22, 2007.

quintessential example of this is the heated debate among French INGOs over the merits of emergency relief versus long-term development.[72]

A final important facet of the social networks of French INGOs relates to patterns of professionalization and volunteer involvement. The growth of the broad charitable sector has been accompanied by some professionalization of charitable organizations. Still, pay levels at French charities are quite low, a function of the small size of these organizations, the part-time nature of much of the workforce, and the fact that many workers accept lower pay because they are motivated to work for organizations with which they share ideals (Cumming 2008, 382). In the French charitable sector as a whole, volunteers are a crucial labor force. Though professionalization is high in charities dedicated to social services, education, and health, many other important sectors are primarily run by volunteers (Archambault et al. 1999, 86).

Among international charities, the topic of professionalization remains a contentious issue. According to a report from the Economic and Social Council, the top fifty French INGOs had an average staff size of sixteen and an average volunteer workforce of ninety in 1994 (Désir 1994, 74). Many leading French NGOs, including the Ligue des Droits de l'Homme, pride themselves on being volunteer-driven, if not fully volunteer-run. The famous split in the "French doctors" movement in 1980 was in substantial part caused by MSF's increasing professionalization, leading the new Médecins du Monde to claim the title of the "real" humanitarian organization. Since then, many of the larger INGOs have become more professionalized, but a volunteer ethic remains. One review of organizational management in the sector found that, when questioned about capacity building, French NGOs "tended to use words referring to quality (*qualité*) rather than the notions of organizational effectiveness and performance which are often emphasized by Anglophone organizations." The report continued that "questions about internal organizational issues appeared to be slightly sensitive. Organizational change is in most cases perceived as the privileged responsibility of directors.... It was recognized that approaches such as human resource management were not part of French culture" (Sorgenfrei 2004, 17–18). Referring to NGOs as "professional" is

---

72. For an example, see the roundtable discussion and other articles in "Logique d'urgence et pérennité," *Revue humanitaire* 14 (Spring 2006): 5–29.

still taboo in some circles, and professional staff are outnumbered by volunteers in humanitarian organizations (Ryfman 2005, 28). In a study of the staff of the largest French humanitarian INGOs, Johanna Siméant and Patrick Dauvin (2002) found an almost exponential increase in the number of salaried workers at each organization over the past fifteen years, but found many who claimed that activism and witnessing (*militantisme* and *témoignage*) are as important as technical proficiency.

Volunteerism in France is important both as a labor source and as part of the identity of the associative sector. Yet these activists are not as numerous as in the United States or Britain, as the figures for overall volunteering given earlier show. Given the encouraging regulations and benefits, however, the international charitable subsector successfully recruits many volunteers for work overseas. Perhaps because of this volunteer workforce, French NGOs often employ a higher percentage of expatriates in the field than their Anglo-Saxon counterparts (Brauman 2006, 10). These volunteers often go on to work permanently for INGOs as salaried employees. Based on interviews with hundreds of INGO staffers, Johanna Siméant (2001) suggests that volunteering abroad is a sort of nonreligious pilgrimage that transforms the way these volunteers view the world and motivates their future career choices. Even more than in Britain, volunteerism is a critical component of what is appropriate charitable action in France.

The French Environment for INGOs

In the state-centric environment of France, charitable organizations are run by political activists involved in struggles against the state. Frequently engaged in debate and conflict within a web of umbrella organizations, international charities use their loud voices to attract the private donors upon which they rely heavily. In the absence of big government coffers, the opportunity costs in France of refusing to accept government funds seem low. While protest against the state is the dominant means of political expression, many French INGOs demand higher levels of state support and, given the opportunity, can collaborate effectively with the French government. INGOs in France are generally younger and smaller than their counterparts in Britain or the United States, but their presence in the international NGO community is substantial.

In this environment, appropriate charitable action is that which is consistent with an established set of principles. As Lamont (1992, 60) described it, moral boundaries in France exclude "people who lack personal integrity and who show little solidarity with other human beings." Principled consistency and general solidarity are appropriate when acting on behalf of others. Internationally oriented charitable organizations are thus evaluated primarily by the processes by which they pursue certain ends, rather than by their ability to efficiently reach those ends.

Arguably, professionalization at French INGOs signals an increased concern with effectiveness, but it has not meant the abandonment of a principled orientation. Despite bringing in more paid staff with expertise, "we still find a much bigger tendency in France for organized civil society to protest and bring together individual citizens to represent their interests directly" (Saurugger 2007, 398). In other words, solidarity acts by ordinary citizens are the driving vision of French charities; this is not the individualistic American vision where one citizen directly serves another. Instead, citizens in France work together to advance the interests of others by calling upon the power of state authorities.

The comparative study of nonprofits and civil society is a growing field. This chapter has offered a systematic comparison of the charitable sectors in the United States, Britain, and France, with a particular focus on internationally oriented charities. Table 2 summarizes these findings. In each country, international charities face very different "varieties of activism." These have been shaped over decades by a complex web of material resources, political institutions, and social practices that inform particular notions of appropriate charitable action.

The profiles above focus on contemporary varieties of activism in these three countries, but a focus on the continuities within each country may appear overly static. While this study focuses on how national environments shape charities, organizations actively work to manage and change their environments. At the same time, there have been some important changes over time within each national environment. In tax legislation, for example, Britain and France have both tried to encourage more charitable giving, and in the case of Britain the reforms were intentionally designed to encourage a more "American-style" pattern. Yet any new incentives, in tax law or elsewhere, are introduced into a particular set of preexisting institutions, and must be interpreted according to preexisting norms within the charitable sector. National environments may evolve, but these adjustments happen within a limited range. While each international charitable

TABLE 2. The international charitable sector in three countries

	United States	Britain	France
Regulatory Environment			
Encouragement of charitable donations	High: tax law creates large planned donations	Moderate/high: creates small spontaneous donations	Low: Small group of dedicated donors
Restrictions on political activities	High	Moderate	Low
Relations with Government			
Centralization of foreign policymaking	Low	High	High
Informal patterns of govt-NGO interaction	Close cooperation	Limited cooperation	Antagonism
Material resources			
Foreign aid channeled through NGOs (%)	30	5	1
Centralization of government funding	Low/moderate	High	Moderate/high
Charitable giving as % GDP (2006)	1.67	0.73	0.14
Public interest in international causes	Low	High	High
Foundation support for international causes	High: $3.1 billion (2000)	Low: £98 million (2001)	Virtually none
Social Networks			
Formal social networks	InterAction, Human Rights Network	BOND	Coordination SUD; many small groups
Population that volunteers (%)	22	30	14

sector in the United States, Britain, and France may change over the coming decades, it is unlikely that all three will converge upon a single model of civil society. Thus, although national origin will not account for all of the practices of any particular organization, it can render understandable the patterned practices of INGOs in meaningful areas like fundraising, advocacy, professionalization, government relations, and issue selection. It is to the cases of particular INGOs that we now turn.

2

Humanitarian INGOs

Humanitarians attempt to improve the lives of those affected by war or natural disaster. The "humanitarian imperative" has driven major relief efforts from Biafra to Bali to Bosnia, and the impulse is an inherently universalistic project to alleviate the suffering of individuals anywhere in the world. Humanitarian organizations face this daunting task with limited resources and a wide array of possible strategies. How, then, do they choose particular practices? There is really very little information available on this question. There are many organizational histories and practitioner journals, but these offer largely descriptive and often uncritical accounts of different organizations' practices. We have evidence of *what* INGOs do, but few attempts to explain *why*.

In this chapter, I offer an explanation for important INGO practices that focuses on the national origins of leading humanitarian INGOs. American, British, and French INGOs have divergent causal beliefs about how to alleviate suffering and different constitutive beliefs about what it means to be a humanitarian. Those beliefs were established in reference to resources, institutions, and norms in each INGO's home country. At each INGO, purposeful actors have employed domestic resources, interpreted available organizational models, and built on domestic institutions to create distinctive organizations.

In order to gain a comparative, organizational perspective on the humanitarian relief sector in three countries, I focus here on three of the world's largest INGOs: CARE (Cooperative for Assistance and Relief Everywhere), founded in the United States; Oxfam, founded in Great Britain; and Médecins Sans Frontières (MSF), founded in France. These are the leading secular INGOs in their respective home countries, and each organization also has host country offices in the other two. In order to ascertain whether each organization's practices are shared by INGOs of the same country, I provide six additional "mini-cases" for comparison: World Vision (United States), the International Rescue Committee (United States), Save the Children UK, Christian Aid (UK), Action contre la Faim (France) and the Comité catholique contre la faim et pour le développement (France). These INGOs are subject to general pressures from the international environment in each of the four central areas of organizational practice studied here—professionalization, fundraising, advocacy, and relations with governments—but the domestic environment defines the range of likely responses to these pressures.

Unlike most of the human rights INGOs profiled in the next chapter, humanitarian INGOs are particularly interesting because they have offices in many developed countries, and these host country offices are often places where home country practices are carried into the international confederation. That is not to imply there is always a perfect match between an INGO's home country and host country practices; the particular history and structure of each international confederation is a critical determinant of the strength of home country influence on host country practices. Still, the general priorities and outlook of the INGO are set by the home country and often institutionalized in chapters abroad.

To begin with, I describe the development of the international humanitarian sector. While humanitarianism has developed into a global enterprise over the past two decades, the international humanitarian sector remains a very weakly institutionalized field in comparison with the domestic environments from which INGOs originate. Brief histories of CARE, Oxfam, and MSF then show how each organization has responded to this international environment by creating global structures. A look at the practices of the three INGOs in the four areas studied here reveals that there are substantial differences among the three INGOs along national lines; and comparison with a half-dozen other American, British, and French INGOs demonstrates that there are established national patterns for INGOs in the three countries. I conclude by arguing that the global humanitarian sector has created some broad trends for INGOs but national environments shape the specific responses to these trends.

The Internationalization of Humanitarian Action

While charitable acts to address the effects of war are as old as war itself, most analysts date the origins of the modern practice of humanitarianism to the 1860s. That decade saw the creation of the first international treaty governing the conduct of war, the Geneva Convention of 1864, as well as the establishment in 1863 of the aid organization that would become the International Committee of the Red Cross (ICRC) (Hoffman and Weiss 2006, esp., chap. 2). In the twentieth century, the body of international law governing humanitarian action has expanded considerably. Most notably, the 1949 Geneva Convention and the 1977 Additional Protocols established protections for civilians in wartime, offered basic guidelines for protecting civilians in intrastate conflicts, and explicitly empowered the ICRC, a nongovernmental organization, to help in the provision of assistance. Other treaties that govern humanitarian conduct include the 1989 Convention on the Rights of the Child and the 1998 Rome Treaty establishing the International Criminal Court. In general, international humanitarian law has increasingly challenged the immunity of sovereign states from international scrutiny.

Alongside developments in international law, formal organizations have served humanitarians in action. In response to the devastation of two world wars, both public intergovernmental organizations like the United Nations and private groups like Oxfam were created in the mid-twentieth century. Since then, developed countries have either funded these organizations or run their own operations in emergency situations. The OECD Development Assistance Committee, a club of donor governments, has provided a forum for discussing best practices in the provision of aid. At the same time, technological developments in communications and transportation since the late 1960s have changed the way the public views global humanitarian crises and have enabled more citizens to travel to places in crisis, enabling considerable growth in private humanitarianism.

Finally, ever since the 1860s, humanitarians have been guided by a set of shared norms that are more or less familiar to all actors within the humanitarian sector: independence from all other actors, neutrality toward the parties involved in conflict, and impartiality with regard to the provision of assistance to civilians. These norms emerged out of the tradition of humanitarianism originally conceived by Henri Dunant, and were aimed at creating a depoliticized "humanitarian space" within which aid could be delivered. Humanitarians rejected the political questions that had created conflict in the first place and instead sought to protect civilians from unnecessary suffering.

The conventional wisdom today is that these three factors—international law, organization, and humanitarian norms—in combination with new types of conflict at the end of the Cold War have created a well-defined and institutionalized sector, frequently referred to as the "international humanitarian system" or the "global humanitarian community" (ALNAP 2010; Minear and Weiss 1995). According to Michael Barnett, "in the 1990s humanitarianism became a field, with regular interactions among the members, an increase in the information and knowledge that members had to consider, a greater reliance on specialized knowledge, and a collective awareness that they were involved in a common enterprise" (Barnett 2005, 729). A number of factors have changed in the past several decades. Humanitarian aid as a share of all foreign assistance has grown over time, from less than 3% in the 1970s and 1980s to over 10% in the past two decades (Randel and German 2003). As this funding has increased, so has the number of governmental and nongovernmental organizations active in humanitarian relief (McCleary and Barro 2008). In response to concerns that resources were being provided unevenly in emergency situations, NGOs developed a set of codes in the early 1990s to enhance their own effectiveness and ultimately protect their legitimacy. The ICRC developed a ten-point code of conduct for humanitarian agencies and later contributed to the Sphere Project, an attempt to establish concrete standards for the provision of water, sanitation, nutrition, shelter, and health in relief operations (Barnett 2005, 730).

This expansion and standardization of post–Cold War humanitarian action has been accompanied by new global humanitarian structures. In 1988, the UN General Assembly formally recognized the rights of civilians to international assistance and the role of NGOs in humanitarian emergencies. Several years later, the UN established a coordinating office for UN efforts and an interagency committee that included other intergovernmental organizations and leading NGOs. More recently, the emergence of a new international norm surrounding the "responsibility to protect" civilians has given a humanitarian rationale to the conduct of war.

In sum, those active in the humanitarian sector today are conscious of the global dimensions of their enterprise. How does that awareness impact the individual actions of humanitarians? As the following analysis of three major humanitarian INGOs shows, they have been driven to demonstrate that they are rooted in a global community rather than in a particular country by establishing international confederations, but their core practices remain distinctive.

Three Humanitarian INGOs: Origins and Structures

CARE, Oxfam, and MSF are three of the largest and most prominent humanitarian relief organizations in the world.[1] CARE was founded in 1945 by a collective of American civic associations who began to send "CARE packages" to postwar Europe. Since then, CARE has embraced a wide variety of relief and development activities, with particular strengths in agricultural and nutritional assistance, and it has offices today in over seventy countries. CARE "sees itself and is perceived by others as a pragmatic, non-ideological organization" (Henry 1999, 116). Oxfam was founded in 1942 as the Oxford Committee for Famine Relief and has long been a highly visible charity in Britain. Oxfam is both a grant-making organization that funds local partner organizations and an operational agency

---

1. The line between relief and development is blurred. These three organizations all began as ways to channel emergency assistance abroad, but today the exact balance of short-term relief and long-term development work varies at each organization. Some scholars deal with the relief-development spectrum by only focusing on one type of organization or the other, but the balance between relief and development at INGOs is an outcome to be explained, not assumed away.

running programs on its own. In contrast to CARE's pragmatic approach which aims for the efficient delivery of the most aid to the most people, Oxfam's understanding of poverty is based upon solidarity with the poor, a notion that replaced traditional ideas of charity within the organization during the 1970s (Black 1992, 197).[2] Médecins Sans Frontières, founded in 1971, is the youngest of the three INGOs and focuses almost solely on emergency medical relief. MSF was founded by a group of French doctors frustrated with policy of the International Committee of the Red Cross to avoid speaking publicly about the maltreatment of civilians in conflict zones (Brauman 2004; Redfield 2006).[3] Today, MSF sees itself as independent, risk-taking organization in an essentially antagonistic relationship with government authorities (Biberson and Jean 1999, 108). In 1999, the international MSF confederation was honored with the Nobel Peace Prize.

Although these organizations remain based in their home countries, they have not been immune to the impact of globalization. The economic processes of globalization have created new sources of poverty and conflict, while growing public participation in humanitarian relief and development has generated pressures to develop inclusive decision-making structures at the global level (Lindenberg and Bryant 2001, esp. chap. 1). Thus, starting as early as the 1970s, these organizations have attempted to create more global structures that reflect a more cosmopolitan identity, with mixed results.

CARE has struggled to expand its organizational base beyond North America. Since its founding, CARE USA had been the "relief agency of choice" for the U.S. government, but by the 1980s CARE faced a more competitive environment at home and abroad (Lindenberg 2001; Campbell 1990). Transforming itself into a global INGO, rather than an American NGO operating internationally, seemed like the answer. In 1984, CARE USA's executive director stated that CARE needed to become "an international organization that is seen as not being politically tied to one country but sharing the views of several," to raise money globally, and to

---

2. "Solidarity" is a frequently used but often misunderstood term. I use it as employed by Smith and Bandy (2005, 3): solidarity organizations negotiate differences based on notions of equality, liberty, peace, tolerance, and emancipation.

3. MSF continues to share many other ICRC principles.

get access to countries where Americans were unwelcome.[4] CARE Canada had been around since the late 1940s, but in the 1980s, CARE established offices in many other developed countries, including CARE France (1983) and CARE UK (1985), to assist with fundraising and programming. In addition, CARE set up an international secretariat (CARE International, or CI) in Brussels, later moving it to Geneva in 2005. These new offices then demanded more autonomy and a greater role in decision making.[5] A particularly important role was played by Peter Bell, CARE USA president from 1995 to 2006. Bell had a strong background in Latin American affairs and human rights and he pushed the organization to become more overtly principled and more global in its outlook. CARE International has since been restructured with a streamlined board of directors, a new mission statement, and a new strategic plan.

Nevertheless, CARE USA still dominates the CARE International confederation. CARE's programs on the ground are organized around what CARE calls the "lead member model": in each country in which CARE is active, the field office is supervised by a single Northern CARE office, eliminating duplication. Only three CARE sections—USA, Canada, and Australia—act as lead members, running actual relief and development programs, while other sections raise money and public awareness. CARE USA is lead member for 60% of all of CARE's country offices. In addition, CARE USA accounted for 75–80% of the international confederation's total income between 2003 and 2009.[6] CARE responded to a set of internal and external challenges by trying to transform a national NGO with global activities into a truly global organization, but CARE USA is the overriding power within the confederation's international structure.

The international Oxfam confederation has a complex history. The first international Oxfam section was established in Canada in 1966, but this and other sections (in Belgium, the United States, and elsewhere) were established independently from Oxfam Great Britain (GB) and were each responsible for their own financing and programming. This fragmentation

---

4. "CARE Increasing Efforts to Expand Its International Base," *New York Times,* August 12, 1984, 15.

5. Lindenberg 2001; see also Denis Caillaux, "CARE International," *iCARE News* [internal CARE newsletter] 49 (June 2005), www.icare.to/.

6. CARE International, *CARE Facts and Figures* (various years). Available online at http://www.care-international.org (accessed October 27, 2010).

among organizations all using the same name was problematic. In 1974, the different Oxfams met to consider forming an international association, but "competing views of the rich world/poor world divide, and of how to tackle it" (Black 1992, 175), kept the different national Oxfam organizations from formal collaboration for the next several decades. By 1995, however, there was a general recognition that the long-term effectiveness of Oxfam's efforts, particularly in advocacy, rested on collective action (Scott and Brown 2004, 3). An Oxfam International (OI) secretariat was established with its offices in Oxford, across town from the headquarters of Oxfam GB.

The international confederation has focused on branding and the coordination of political advocacy. Before the creation of OI, the advocacy work of Oxfams outside Great Britain was limited and uneven (Anderson 2000). Today, the various Oxfams work together as a "global campaigning force" and organize their work under the heading of five basic rights.[7] In dramatic contrast with CARE, however, programs in the field are still run separately by each national chapter. A glance at South Asia, for example, shows that in 2005, eight separate Oxfams were at work in both India and Pakistan. This configuration of globally managed campaigns and independent programs is likely to continue through the foreseeable future.[8] Although Oxfam GB does not dominate the OI confederation financially (as CARE USA does CARE International), sources at both Oxfam GB and other Oxfams point out that Oxfam GB drives the OI advocacy agenda.[9]

The establishment of Oxfam International coincided with internal restructuring at Oxfam GB. A 1998 internal strategic review at Oxfam GB found that the organization's approach to problem solving was strong but that poor staff development and weak monitoring systems created uneven performance across different programs.[10] One of the recommendations

---

7. *Towards Global Equity: Strategic Plan 2001–2004* (London: Oxfam International, 2001).

8. Barbara Stocking. "How We Work with Oxfam International" (communication to Oxfam GB staff, February 2003) (on file with author). In March 2010, Oxfam began to construct what it calls a "single management structure" in each field office to minimize duplication. Even under this new system, which will establish a "managing affiliate," multiple Oxfams will still be working in a single country.

9. Personal interview, Oxfam GB staffer, October 19, 2006; personal interview, Oxfam GB staffer, November 2, 2006; Offenheiser et al. 1999, 128.

10. *Oxfam Strategic Review: Setting Course for the Twenty-first Century* (Oxford: Oxfam GB, July 1998).

for reform was for Oxfam to respond more effectively to the needs of its Southern partners. Still, the internal review did not recommend the abandonment of the organization's British roots: "Given that Oxfam's very existence is dependent on its profile and reputation in Great Britain...it would chart a dangerous course were it to neglect its British networks on the issues which concern poverty and suffering and more generally regarding the British voluntary sector."[11] In sum, the reconstruction of separate Oxfam chapters into a global confederation with shared policy positions has if anything increased the centrality of Oxfam GB, which is committed to retaining its deep ties to the British relief and development community.

The internationalization process at MSF began early as former volunteers for MSF France set up chapters in their home countries. In the early 1980s, MSF sections were established in Belgium, Switzerland, Holland, and Spain. Today, these five sections run programs in the field, while another fourteen sections in other developed countries like Britain and the United States largely focus on fundraising and recruiting volunteers. As at CARE and Oxfam, an international secretariat, MSF International, was established to bring these different chapters together formally and to address problems of operational overlap.

Within the MSF International confederation, the decision-making process is contentious. There is no financially dominant section, and the international secretariat has virtually no independent power. The national sections have different understandings of core organizational principles, including the balance between emergency and development work, the importance of "witnessing" (*témoignage*) in the MSF's mission, and the appropriateness of accepting money from governments (Sondorp 2006; Redfield 2006). In fact, MSF France once sued MSF Belgium's use of the name in a fight over the "true" heritage of the MSF movement.[12] In 2006, MSF reexamined its organizational structures and strategies through a series of meetings known as the "La Mancha Process," which revealed the continued salience of these divisions. MSF France remains the outspoken

---

11. Ibid., 158.
12. See Rony Brauman, "Constructive Disagreements," *Messages* [MSF France newsletter] 136 (May 2005): 20.

defender of the uniqueness of MSF, repeatedly avowing its "emergency-only" role and its commitment to political independence.[13]

Attempts at greater coordination through the international secretariat have achieved little success. Jean-Hervé Bradol, former president of MSF France, has argued that "we have to take the risk of running things democratically: contradictory debates must be sanctioned by votes...we are at a difficult stage [but] we do not need more central bureaucracy."[14] Analyst David Rieff argues that strengthening the international secretariat to increase the coherence of MSF would be futile anyway. "In the event of disagreement on a fundamental point involving MSF's identity, MSF France would be the first section to break the rule."[15] Thus, while the international movement may not be "simply French,"[16] the French section is the internal locus of debates and the external reference point; MSF is often referred to as the "French doctors." French citizens make up the largest share of all volunteers for all MSF projects—27% in 2003 (Bortolotti 2004, 64). Fifteen years of internationalization have not changed the centrality of the French section to MSF, and, as discussed below, the financial clout of MSF France relative to other sections has actually grown.

To put this historical detail together, CARE, Oxfam, and MSF have all tried to transform their global visions into global structures, with mixed results. MSF has arguably been the most successful at transcending its French roots, but the international "movement" today is highly fragmented. The warming of relations among the different Oxfam chapters that occurred in the early 1990s has resulted in a more cohesive international movement at Oxfam than at MSF, but the emphasis on global campaigning has put the parent body, Oxfam GB, back at the center of Oxfam International. CARE has created a relatively cohesive global structure but not a global identity, as CARE USA is still the center of gravity in fundraising and programming.

---

13. Sondorp 2006, 49. See also Guillermo Bertoletti, "Operations: Same Name, Same Action?" *Messages* 136 (May 2005): 7.

14. "How Many Divisions Does MSF Have?" *Messages* 136 (May 2005): 3. See also MSF, "Synthesis of the Debates," La Mancha Conference, Luxembourg, March 8–10, 2006.

15. David Reiff, "MSF, an International Movement? It Remains to Be Seen," *Messages* 136 (May 2005): 21. Perhaps in response to this point, the general director of MSF Holland argues that MSF's self-absorption is isolating. *Messages* 136 (May 2005): 21.

16. I do not claim that the French national environment shapes the practices of all MSF sections but rather that MSF France is deeply tied to its home country and remains powerful in the MSF International confederation (Redfield 2006, 20 n.14).

Organizational Practice: Fundraising

Global humanitarianism is based on universalistic values, and humanitarian INGOs have faced pressures to create more cosmopolitan identities and structures, but national environments have a powerful impact on fundraising, professionalization, advocacy, and relations with governments.

CARE, Oxfam, and MSF are all very successful at fundraising, and it is their large size that gives them a global presence. Yet these three groups have very different fundraising strategies. CARE USA relies heavily on government funding, Oxfam GB gets the majority of its revenue from private individuals in Britain, and MSF France is almost entirely funded by private donations, half of which come from France and half from abroad. The fundraising strategies of CARE and Oxfam at home are clearly evident in their offices abroad, and somewhat less so at MSF's international offices.

CARE has historically relied heavily on support from the U.S. government and is regularly one of the top NGO recipients of such support. CARE USA's income in 2009 was over $700 million, an increase in real income of 50% since 1997. Figure 1 breaks down this income by source, based on CARE USA's annual financial reports. From 1997 to 2009, CARE USA received an average 51% of its income from the U.S. government and an average 17% from individual American donors. Reliance on U.S. government funding is long-standing practice at CARE USA: from 1986 to 1996, it received an average 56% of its income from the U.S. government, and as much as 82% in 1970.[17] While government support has declined as a share of total revenue (from 58% in 1997 to 39% in 2009), it has climbed slightly in absolute terms (from $208m in 1997 to $274m in 2009).

Because of its small private donor base, CARE is able to keep fundraising costs low. For example, in 2003, fundraising accounted for just 4% of all CARE USA expenses.[18] The recent diversification of income streams has been possible not because of massive expansion of private donations, but rather due to modest growth in private donations combined with more extensive support from other members of the CI confederation.

---

17. USAID, *VOLAG: Report of Voluntary Agencies* (various years); McCleary 2009, 26.
18. CARE USA, *Annual Report 2004*, 41. The figure was 4.34% in 2002.

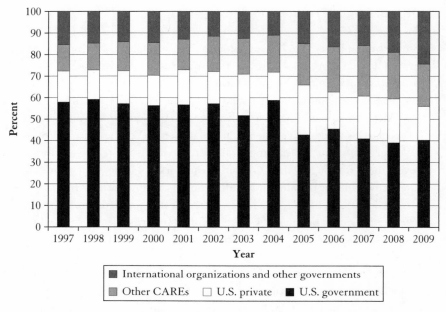

Figure 1. CARE USA sources of income as percent of total income

The international CARE sections share CARE USA's affinity for fund-ing from official agencies. From 2003 to 2009, CARE UK received an av-erage 47% of its income from the British government and another 24% from the European Union.[19] The same holds for CARE France: official donors accounted for about 57% of its income between 2003 and 2010.[20] CARE France has had a more difficult time than its British counterpart: it has a small staff, a name difficult to pronounce in French, and it works in a "not particularly friendly place for American organizations."[21] Thus, CARE France's "official" funding has come mainly from the EU and other international organizations rather than the French government. As one CARE France staffer explained,

> In the last few years, we have tried to be more integrated in the French
> NGO environment and with our donors. Before, a man at the French

---

19. *CARE International UK Report and Consolidated Accounts* (various years).

20. CARE France, *Rapports annuels* (various years). 2005 data missing.

21. The name is often confused with that of the Egyptian capital Cairo. Personal interview, CARE International staffer, February 27, 2007.

Ministère des Affaires étrangères told me that "as long as I am here, we will never fund you." Now we do get a little funding, but it depends on who you talk to—you may still get this image of being American...

The French government says it is quite happy to fund CARE France if it is a CARE France project, but not for U.S. projects. We really must change our image and show our independence and added value. I try to convince myself that CARE is a truly global organization. Our COs [country officers] are very independent, and our staffing is so international.... But it is also very true that we are very much an American organization, and if we could show that this is an international organization, it [would be] easier for us.[22]

CARE France's weak support from its host government distinguishes it from other CAREs but resembles the experiences of other French humanitarian NGOs. In order to expand its private donor base, CARE France has highlighted its emergency relief work, an issue to which the French public is very responsive.[23]

The Oxfams, by contrast, rely on private funds raised through different means. Like CARE, Oxfam GB has grown significantly over the past fifteen years, having doubled its real income between 1996 and 2009. Figure 2 compiles data from Oxfam GB's annual report and shows that most of the organization's revenue comes from private British donors. In addition to soliciting donors directly, Oxfam has an extensive national network of charity shops that create links to local communities and bring in steady if moderate revenue. Direct donations and income from charity shops accounted for 49.4% and 13.5% of total income, respectively, during this period. Attracting private donations is an expensive endeavor for Oxfam; in 2003, for example, 13% of Oxfam's budget was spent on fundraising alone.

Beyond its private base, two features of Oxfam GB fundraising are noteworthy. First, despite access to European funders, Oxfam GB is not a European NGO. It receives generous support from the European Union's humanitarian aid office, but British sources (including the government) accounted for an average 72% of Oxfam GB's income from 1996 to 2009. Second, Oxfam receives a lower quantity but arguably a higher quality of

---

22. Personal interview, CARE France, February 8, 2007.
23. Lévêque 2004. Examples can be seen in their annual reports; see particularly CARE France, *Comptes spéciaux? 2001, 2004.*

government funding than CARE. Support from the British aid agency DFID accounted for 10.6% of Oxfam GB's income from 1996 to 2009. This is considerably lower than the government funding for CARE USA, but Oxfam has benefited from a generous Partnership Program Agreement with DFID. Developed in consultation with the NGO, this funding scheme provides substantial support for improving both management and research in headquarters rather than strictly funding programs in the field.

Although members of the Oxfam confederation are operationally independent, the Oxfams in France and the United States share Oxfam GB's preference for private support. Founded in 1970, Oxfam America made an early decision not to accept U.S. government funds. As a result, Oxfam America is quite small among American humanitarian INGOs (about a tenth the size of CARE USA). Still, this pledge reflects Oxfam America's commitment to maintaining its independence (Offenheiser et al. 1999, 126), a priority that echoes the social movement concerns of its British

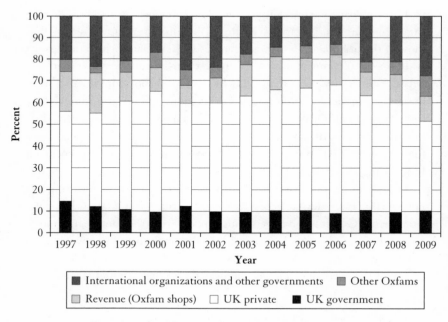

Figure 2. Oxfam GB sources of income as percent of total income

parent. Like Oxfam GB, Oxfam America relies heavily on individual private donations, which accounted for an average 67% of total income from 1999 to 2006, according to the group's annual reports. Oxfam France—the youngest member of Oxfam International, established when a fifteen-year old French NGO, Agir Ici, became an Oxfam affiliate, and later changed its name—had a budget of $2.1 million and a staff of sixteen in 2008. The section remains small, and it does not run programs in the field. In its fundraising, it takes no money from governments or corporations; in fact, according to its 2006 annual report, 40% of its funds come from the Oxfam International confederation. Direct donations and the sale of campaign materials account for the remainder of Oxfam France's income.

Finally, MSF exhibits the strongest preference for private sources in its fundraising. Although MSF France is the largest French relief INGO and has grown substantially over the past decade (more than doubling its income between 1994 and 2008), it is still small in global perspective. Figure 3 shows the breakdown of MSF France's income by source, based on data from its annual reports. A few features stand out in comparison to the other cases above. First, MSF receives virtually no support from its home government and surprisingly little from international organizations. From 2001 to 2008, MSF France derived an average 0.1% of income from local and national French authorities; the last time MSF France received even a token sum from the foreign affairs ministry was 2003. MSF France's largest "institutional" supporter is the European Union, but it accounted for only 4% of income during the same period.[24] Thus, the two largest sources of income for MSF France are private French donors and other MSF sections, whose fundraising efforts support MSF France programming. Since 1985, MSF has had legal status as an *association reconnue d'utilité publique,* allowing tax relief on larger donations and making it easier to raise private funds. Private French donors accounted for an average 36% of MSF France's income from 2001 to 2009, while another 38% came from partner sections in the United States, Australia, and Japan.[25] MSF USA accounts

---

24. The EU has numerable budget lines that support NGOs; the figure here includes funds from ECHO (the relief office). This figure for MSF France is comparable to those for all the MSF chapters combined, which derived an average 6.9% of income from the EU from 2000 to 2005. MSF International, *International Financial Report* (various years).

25. On the process of the creation of partner sections, see Siméant 2005.

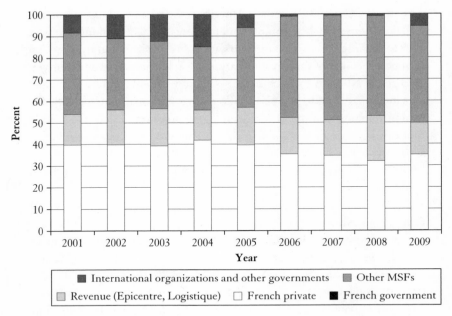

Figure 3. MSF France sources of income as percent of total income

for three-quarters of the total support from international sections, and nearly all of the partner section money is also privately raised. The fact that MSF derives a majority of its income from sections abroad allows it to claim low fundraising costs (only 5.7% of total expenses in 2008); fundraising expenses would appear much higher if international donations were excluded from the accounting.

It is more difficult to generalize about fundraising strategies within the international MSF confederation, since different sections are divided on whether to accept government funds (Siméant 2005). Generally, the international confederation as a whole has moved away from government funding, which accounted for 12% of all of MSF's international income in 2009 compared to around 20% a decade earlier.[26]

Unlike the operational sections that were set up by volunteers returned from the field, however, MSF USA and MSF UK were established in

---

26. MSF International, *Audited Facts and Figures 2009;* Marine Buissonnière, "MSF: A State of Affairs," presentation made at MSF La Mancha Conference, March 8, 2006.

a top-down fashion by other MSF sections looking for help with fund-raising, advocacy, public education, and volunteer recruitment. MSF USA, known to Americans as Doctors Without Borders, was set up in 1990 as the first partner section of MSF France. MSF USA is a cash cow for MSF International, providing about a third of MSF France's income and almost 15% of all of MSF International's total income in 2009.[27] The American section's bylaws require that at least 50% of its private funds go to MSF France and that the president of MSF France sit on its board of directors (Siméant 2005, 858). MSF's emergency profile appeals to private American donors, and MSF USA is able to reach the many wealthy individuals in the United States.[28] It also benefits from the generosity of American foundations, which provide about 12% of its income.[29] Like MSF France, MSF USA takes virtually no money from the government. The British section, MSF UK, was established in 1993 as a partner section of MSF Netherlands. It has also experienced rapid expansion, with its income more than tripling since 2000.[30] In contrast to the American and French sections, MSF UK receives substantial support from the British government, which is the largest government donor to any MSF chapter.[31] The British aid agency DFID is "relatively easier to work with" than other donors, according to one MSF UK staffer: "In my whole time here working with NGOs in the UK, I have never heard of someone being told, as a result of accepting DFID funds, what to do, either explicitly or behind closed doors. This was the whole impetus behind creating DFID—to take the politics out of foreign aid—and many of us thought at the time 'Wait—what do you mean? It's government aid.' But that's how it works."[32]

---

27. MSF International Movement, *MSF Financial Report 2009.*

28. Personal interview, MSF USA staffer, September 8, 2006; personal interview, MSF USA staffer, May 22, 2006.

29. This is the figure given in the 2005 and 2009 annual reports.

30. "Medecins Sans Frontieres UK," *Extract from the Central Register of Charities No. 1026588* (www.charity-commission.gov.uk, accessed June 4, 2007).

31. MSF UK received £12.1m in 2005 and £14.3 in 2004 from the UK's Department for International Development (DFID); MSF International Annual Report 2004. Among official donors, only the EU's ECHO gave more to the international MSF confederation.

32. Personal interview, MSF UK staffer [2], October 25, 2006. I conducted interviews with two MSF UK staffers on the same day, so I have designated them as MSF UK staffer [1] and MSF UK staffer [2].

MSF believes that DFID's apolitical funding schemes allow NGO partners to maintain their independence, a critical concern of the MSF movement. Funding from DFID is, however, limited by MSF's international pledge to keep government funds below 50% of total income.

Explaining Fundraising Strategies

As resource dependency scholars have long noted, donors may play a critical role in determining organizational priorities and strategies. What is less clear, however, is how organizations choose to rely on different donors. For major humanitarian INGOs like CARE, Oxfam, and MSF, resources and institutions in their domestic environments play an important role in shaping fundraising strategies. At CARE, cooperation with the U.S. government has long been a given for this "Wilsonian" NGO that sees a basic compatibility between its humanitarian aims and the state's foreign policy goals (Rieff 2003, 113; Stoddard 2006). Though some have argued that government funding compromises CARE's independence, three features of the American environment keep government support attractive. First, the American public is relatively uninterested in international affairs, making it difficult and costly to extract private donations. Second, pressures from watchdog groups to keep overhead low make private donations (which are costly to drum up) less attractive. CARE frequently touts its low overhead costs and efficiency, which have earned it high ratings from American watchdog groups like Charity Navigator and the Better Business Bureau.[33] Finally, there are simply enormous sums of government money available for INGOs.

Oxfam GB's fundraising is also tied to its home environment. Oxfam's public prominence in Britain is unequaled by American INGOs at home and reflects much higher public interest in international affairs. Private donors offer Oxfam a source of support without restrictions, but because Britons tend to give in small amounts and spontaneously, Oxfam has had to invest heavily in fundraising. The British government offers

---

33. Each annual report from 1997 to 2010 contains a chart showing management costs under 10%. This is long-standing practice; see "America's Best-Run Charities," *Fortune,* November 9, 1987, 145–49.

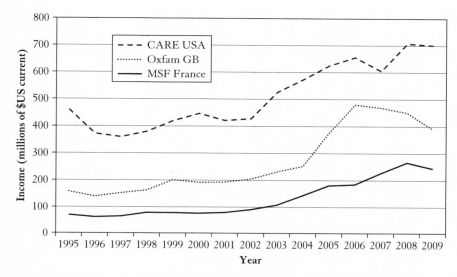

Figure 4. Total income at three humanitarian INGOs, 1995–2009 (millions of US$ current)

less funding to its INGOs, but DFID "block grants" have few strings attached and are attractive to large relief INGOs like Oxfam.

MSF France faces the most difficult environment for fundraising, given a weak French tradition of charitable giving and the French government's lack of support for NGOs. The opportunity costs for MSF of rejecting government funding are thus low, and MSF's principled stance against government funding in favor of independence also helps in attracting private donors. Because of this difficult environment, MSF has turned to the European Union and private donors abroad for support. While MSF may be relatively less reliant on home country donors, the initial need to go abroad for funds was informed by resource scarcity at the domestic level.

These fundraising strategies are important for at least three reasons. First, there is a relationship between income source and the selection of program activities. Private donors are most receptive to public appeals during emergencies like the Southeast Asian tsunami, while governments offer much more support for long-term development activities. There is a general correlation between private support and emergency programming at the three major INGOs. CARE has spent an average 27% of its budget on emergencies in the past decade, while Oxfam has spent between

40% and 50%.[34] And MSF, which is famous for its private donor base, is also famous for its emergency-only focus. Second, national origin may help account for the actual size of these organizations. The availability of resources for internationally oriented charities is high in the United States, moderate in the UK, and fairly low in France. As Figure 4 suggests, the size of each INGO's annual revenue varies according to resource availability at home. Finally, these financial ties are part of the isomorphic pressures surrounding INGOs. As Dimaggio and Powell (1983) argued, when organizations compete for both resources and legitimacy, they adopt a homogenous set of practices. The diverse outcomes at CARE, Oxfam, and MSF suggest that these organizations are not competing against each another but rather against their national counterparts.

Organizational Practice: Professionalization

The three organizations differ not only in their resource bases but also in their level of professionalization and rationalization. Although they have all paid increasing attention to the professionalization of the global humanitarian sector, the concept is interpreted in different ways at each organization. CARE is a fully professionalized organization with detailed and structured procedures for internal management that serve to advance efficiency goals. MSF prefers to refer to itself as a member-driven movement rather than an organization, and while it is the largest and most professional of the French INGOs, like its compatriot nonprofits, it prioritizes voluntarism over efficiency. Oxfam falls somewhere in between. Given that professionalization is a part of a broader move toward rationalization of internal practice, it is important to examine the balance of professionals and volunteers at each organization, hiring criteria and executive compensation, and the standardization of management.

CARE is the most professionalized of the three INGOs. Since the mid-1990s, it has produced multiple internal staff guidelines that establish

---

34. CARE average 1998–2006. CARE USA, *Annual Reports* (various years). Oxfam doesn't provide these figures consistently; using figures from 1998, 2000, and 2005–9, an average 43.5% of program spending went toward emergencies. Oxfam GB, *Annual Report and Accounts* (various years).

standards on a variety of issues, including principles for programming, partnership strategies, and ways to evaluate the impact of its work. The auditing procedures and information systems meant to assist with internal monitoring and evaluation are often taken directly from the corporate world.[35] For example, an organization-wide transformation at CARE USA in 1995 emphasized strategic planning for the years ahead, the importance of using common financial systems to trace financial flows, and the need for organizational learning (Henry 1999; Lindenberg and Bryant 2001, 43). Beyond CARE USA, system-wide reforms have sought the participation of many stakeholders across the different national offices, but of course not all CARE International members were equally enthusiastic about the systematization of CARE practices.[36] While the process sought input from multiple levels of the organization, the desire to create uniformity, update principles, and restructure management emanated primarily from CARE's American headquarters. Today, the standardization of procedures at CARE is enabled through the organization's online "learning library," where staff can access these many manuals.

The emphasis on efficient management is seen also in the CARE USA staff, known among NGO partners for their professionalism and technical expertise.[37] This is nothing new; a 1976 book on CARE refers to a long-standing "tradition of business efficiency" at the organization (Linden 1976, 9). Many CARE staffers come from the business rather than charitable sector. For example, the former head of human resources has argued that, in managing the organization's staff, "there is no fundamental difference whether the business is a corporation or a humanitarian organization like CARE."[38] CARE USA staff are compensated at levels competitive with the for-profit sector, and CARE executives receive some of the highest salaries among American INGOs. These salaries reflect the organization's

---

35. Several different for-profit models were used to generate the approaches to programming that CARE now uses (Lindenberg 2001, 254–56; Scott 1995).

36. Scott 1995; Peter Bell, email to author, February 8, 2010.

37. According to a 2006 survey of CARE partners in the field, 98% of partners believe CARE's staff are professional and skilled; another 89% consider technical expertise a strength of CARE. "Partner and Project Participant Views on CARE's Organizational Tensions and Challenges," *iCARE News* (February 2007). See Devone 1990, 64; Jude Rand, *CARE's Experiences with Adoption of a Rights Based Approach,* report, June 21, 2002 9.

38. "HR and the business of CARE." *HR Focus* 69 (January 1992): 24.

perceived need to compete with the business world.[39] In fact, CARE directly draws upon the corporate sector for leadership; in 2007, for example, fourteen out of twenty-three board members had corporate backgrounds, and only two had professional experience in the nonprofit world.[40] The line between the for-profit world and the nonprofit world is quite blurry for those involved in CARE.

Unlike at Oxfam and MSF, there are very few opportunities for volunteers at CARE, and the organization offers only a few chances for community participation in limited areas. These options include making a donation, joining a competitive fundraising network, sending a form letter to Congress, or setting up a "CARE Corps" website. Unlike MSF, CARE does not send volunteers into the field.[41] In management and professionalization, CARE imitates, competes with, and works with the corporate world, and generally shares the corporate sector's emphasis on efficient performance.

Other CARE sections are also professional and regularized. CARE UK draws heavily on the corporate sector for leadership.[42] Management is proud of its low overhead, comparing itself favorably to other British NGOs.[43] CARE France offers an intriguing perspective on the transfer of this practice. While most French INGOs rely heavily on volunteer workers, CARE France has only recently embraced volunteers. The low profile of volunteers combined with generous compensation for staff has created a curious situation where some CARE France staffers have objected to their own high salaries![44]

Oxfam GB is less structured than CARE USA in its management and more open to the participation of volunteers and community members.

---

39. According to former CARE president Peter Bell, "In setting executive salaries at CARE, we survey salaries more generally in the nonprofit and for-profit areas. Our salaries are competitive with our peer organizations, but are below those of for-profit corporations." "Outlook: The First Wave of Relief," *Washington Post* online forum, Monday January 3, 2005, 2 pm. www.washingtonpost.com (on file with author).

40. Seven of these directors had served on other nonprofit boards. The past two CARE presidents came directly from the Ford and Gates foundations.

41. A few volunteers work in CARE's regional fundraising offices or have internships in Atlanta. Personal interview, CARE staffer, June 12, 2007.

42. Personal interview, CARE UK, October 24, 2006. Of five senior executives in 2006, none came from within CARE, and all but one had substantial background in the corporate sector.

43. Personal interview, CARE UK, October 24, 2006.

44. Personal interview, CARE France staffer, February 8, 2007.

Strategic planning within Oxfam GB began a bit later than at CARE USA, but internal management procedures received much attention in the late 1990s. In 2001, Barbara Stocking, formerly of the National Health Service's modernization agency, became the chief executive of Oxfam GB. Stocking made explicit her goal of transforming the organization into one that was "modern, professional, and gets things done."[45] This required substantial standardization of decision-making procedures and human resources policy. Some staff questioned the link between being competent, which they valued, and establishing elaborate structures and rules, which they felt were stifling.[46]

Despite becoming more structured and professional, Oxfam's compensation practices suggest that it either cannot or will not compete with the corporate world. Oxfam staff salaries are competitive with major British nonprofits but still much lower than those of CARE USA. A comparison of the top salaries from 2001 to 2006 shows a large gap in executive compensation.[47] Overall staffing expenses at Oxfam GB are also lower than at the British chapter of CARE.[48] All of this supports the argument that Oxfam's point of reference is the community of British charities, not the global humanitarian sector.

In the mid-1990s, Oxfam was thought to be led in "an independent, unprofessional, slightly improvisational spirit."[49] That notion is somewhat misleading today, but important vestiges of that spirit remain. Oxfam maintains extensive and diverse links to the British public, and its long-standing status as a "British phenomenon" underpins its financial and political successes (Black 1992, 97). Dependent on numerous but small donations, Oxfam creates myriad opportunities for the public to give. To name just a few options, private supporters can set up a monthly account debit to Oxfam, get an Oxfam credit card, hold a bake sale or dance contest for Oxfam, recycle for Oxfam, attend an "Oxjam" concert, or help with

45. Barbara Stocking, *Annual Report 2001/02* (Oxford: Oxfam GB, 2002), 13.

46. Personal interview, former Oxfam staffer, November 2, 2006.

47. Based on an average of the top five highest-compensated staff, Oxfam GB's executive salaries were $78,000 to $124,000 lower than at CARE USA. This is an imperfect comparison; CARE gives exact salaries, but Oxfam shows salaries within £10,000 ranges.

48. *CARE International UK Annual Reports 2006; Oxfam GB Annual Reports 2005/06.*

49. Anthony Dworkin, "Doing Good for the Wrong Reasons," *New Statesman,* July 12, 1996, 12.

soliciting donations on the street. These efforts not only raise money but also increase public interest in and awareness of the organization.

Oxfam GB's desire to engage the community is also reflected in its approach to volunteers. Alongside salaried staff, several hundred volunteers work in Oxfam's offices,[50] and the organization's charity shops are staffed by a force of at least twenty thousand unpaid volunteers. Oxfam's strategic review recognized the instrumental value of this free labor but argued that volunteers offered two additional benefits: "volunteers will increase Oxfam's legitimacy and credibility [and] by working with volunteers Oxfam will play a role in developing a civil society in which values and beliefs are most likely to flourish."[51] Volunteers are thus central to the practical success and principled identity of Oxfam. Without volunteers, argued one staffer, "both in terms of financing and recruitment, the organization would collapse. Also, it would completely lose its social movement base. In order to campaign, it has to be seen as *voluntary*—and here voluntarism is about an act of *will* to change society."[52]

The commitment to voluntarism alongside professionalization is also found at Oxfam's chapters in the United States and France, both of which create many opportunities for ordinary members of the community to engage in the organization's work. At Oxfam America, volunteers play a key role in a country where most of the major INGOs have few volunteers. More than a hundred volunteers annually log around ten thousand hours.[53] Still, Oxfam America may feel the pressure to compete for skilled leaders in the American environment, and its salaries for top management are higher than at Oxfam GB.[54] Oxfam France, the recent arrival to the Oxfam International federation, has a small staff of sixteen, a handful of interns, and claims a network of thirty thousand people nationwide who regularly participate in the group's campaigns.[55]

50. In 2004–5, there were 211 volunteers in the offices with 3.91 average years of service. *Oxfam GB Human Resources Annual Report 2004–5* (Oxford: Oxfam, 2005), 21.

51. *Oxfam Strategic Review* 1998, 119.

52. Personal interview, former Oxfam staffer, February 27, 2007.

53. "Oxfam America: Interns and Volunteers," http://www.oxfamamerica.org/whoweare (accessed March 29, 2007).

54. An average difference of over $33,000 in 2002–6. Oxfam America, IRS Form 990 (various years); *Oxfam GB Annual Reports* (various years).

55. Oxfam France–Agir Ici, *Rapport annuel 2008.*

Médecins Sans Frontières may be the most professionalized French INGO but it is the least professionalized of the three INGOs profiled here. MSF still has a reputation as the risk-taking "cowboy" of humanitarian INGOs, though it has changed substantially since the early 1970s. As early as 1979, the issues of professionalization and regularization caused a split among the French doctors, some of whom went on to form Médecins du Monde. Subsequently, MSF began to focus on resolving a few management problems by paying small stipends to volunteer physicians in 1982 and expanding its fundraising capacity (Bortolotti 2004, 55). In the late 1980s, MSF began formalizing its management structures, centralizing a large proportion of decisions while regularizing and codifying many of its internal procedures (Queinnec 2003, 518–19).

Today, MSF has a small core of about two hundred paid staff, but the process of professionalization has not been entirely smooth. Siméant and Dauvin (2005, 109–15) found an almost exponential increase in the number of paid staff at MSF over the previous fifteen years, but they also found significant opposition to the transformation of humanitarian work into a "career." Today, many MSF leaders want to recall that they are first a "movement" and not a "bureaucracy," and many MSF workers like to highlight that the organization is flat rather than hierarchical (Bryant and Rubio 2006, 84–85; Biberson and Jean 1999; Leyton and Locke 1998). Anthropologist Peter Redfield (2005, 332) has noted the tension created by this aversion to professionalization: "A common apprehension of older MSF veterans is that the work might become 'just a job' for their successors, rather than a passionate, moral endeavor." Importantly, MSF's largely private donor base may keep it insulated from external pressures to create more formalized internal structures.[56] This discomfort with internal standardization is reflected in MSF's position on external codes of conduct in the humanitarian sector such as the Sphere Project. According to Abby Stoddard, Francophone agencies such as MSF "strongly oppose such initiatives on the grounds that they risk creating a set of rigid, lowest-common-denominator standards; inhibit innovation and independence;

---

56. MSF France's largest official donor is the European Union's humanitarian office (ECHO), which may be the least demanding in terms of oversight. Particularly in its early days, ECHO needed NGOs like MSF as much as MSF needed ECHO. Personal interview, NGO analyst, March 1, 2007.

are open to manipulation by donor governments; and solidify the dominance of the core group of major NGOs."[57]

Volunteers are essential to MSF's work and identity. MSF's international charter highlights the central role of volunteers and asks individuals to take responsibility for the risks involved in humanitarian action. Unpaid members (mostly medical professionals) make up the boards of directors of international sections, and these boards are accountable to the ordinary staffers and returning field workers that make up MSF associations.[58] Volunteers accounted for 37% of the workforce at all MSF headquarters in 2004, and they fill the 450 or so positions in MSF's offices in the field,[59] receiving health insurance and a monthly stipend as required by French law for international volunteers. Although the organization's salaried staff has grown, so has the number of volunteers in headquarters and field offices (Siméant and Dauvin 2002). Humanitarian work is still seen as a calling for MSF-ers rather than one of many career options, and for prospective leaders of MSF, business experience cannot substitute for humanitarian action in the field (Torrente 2005, 9). Professionalization and voluntarism co-exist at MSF, but the voluntary spirit is the touchstone of the organization.

The voluntarist orientation of MSF France is visible at MSF USA and MSF UK as well. MSF USA recruits a substantial number of volunteers for the field, though recruiting doctors for six-month assignments is difficult given the structure of an American health system which offers little opportunity for extended leaves.[60] The actual doctors of Doctors Without Borders USA are thus in short supply. MSF UK also exhibits a mix of professionals and volunteers. The UK office has a small professional staff, a sizable number of office volunteers, and significant recruitment for volunteers in the field.[61]

---

57. *Humanitarian NGOs: Challenges and Trends, HPG Briefing Paper* [British Overseas Development Institute] 12 (July 2003): 4.

58. Interview, MSF UK staff [1], October 25, 2006.

59. *MSF International Financial Activity Report 2004.* All field positions are volunteer except for *chefs de mission,* who are paid and housed separately (Siméant and Dauvin 2002, 301 n.1).

60. Interview, MSF USA staff, May 22, 2006. This is true for other medical relief NGOs in the United States. Personal interview, former Doctors of the World USA staff, September 5, 2006; personal interview, former Physicians for Human Rights staff, October 5, 2006.

61. In 2005, MSF UK had 39 paid staff, 250 volunteers in the field, and 72 weeks' worth of volunteer work at headquarters. *MSF UK Trustees Report and Financial Statement, 31st December 2005.*

As a basic illustration of the differences among the three organizations, consider compensation of their top five executives. Over a recent five-year period, the average salary of CARE executives was $211, 859, of Oxfam GB executives was $133,279, and of MSF executives was $62,215.[62] It should be clear that these organizations are not competing with each other to attract executives, but rather with charitable organizations in their domestic environments.

Explaining Levels of Professionalization

National origin helps account for these differences in professionalization, as material and normative pressures differ in the United States, Britain, and France. First, resource dependence at the national level has a heavy impact on professionalization. All three organizations have taken part in a global dialogue within the humanitarian sector over monitoring outputs through the adoption of approaches like "results-based management," but the issue may be more urgent for organizations that are more reliant on official donor agencies that themselves face enormous political pressure to demonstrate the efficacy of their foreign aid projects. In the United States, generous support from the government comes with substantial requirements for reporting and accountability, which has led American INGOs to develop highly structured management systems run by accounting professionals (Forman and Stoddard 2002). The British aid agency DFID and the European Union's humanitarian office ECHO also have reporting requirements, but USAID has been a leader in developing standards for monitoring and accountability at its NGO partners. Generally, the process for applying for government funding is much more technically demanding than for raising private revenue, which encourages the professionalization of fundraising staff. Although CARE has recently reduced its reliance on the U.S. government, five decades of close partnership helped establish rigorous internal systems of management. By contrast, Oxfam receives only 10% of its income from DFID and MSF gets a much smaller share

---

62. 2002–6 (inclusive). CARE IRS Form 990s (various years), Oxfam GB, *Annual Financial Reports* (various years); MSF, *Rapports annuels* (various years). All of these figures exclude benefits as health and social welfare programs differ substantially among the three countries.

from ECHO. These two agencies are relatively less demanding in their reporting requirements for NGOs, though ECHO's reporting requirements have grown significantly over time. DFID and ECHO also have partnership agreements with a select number of NGOs that enable the latter to enjoy fewer restrictions and to participate in the selection of projects in the field.[63]

There are also differences in how charitable organizations prioritize efficiency, which affect each organization's need for professional staff. In the United States, ratings systems—including Charity Navigator and the Better Business Bureau—reward nonprofits for limiting "wasteful" overhead. These measures of efficiency resonate with an American public averse to bureaucracy, and in response, organizations like CARE regularly report spending less that 10% of their budgets on management and fundraising. This pressure to maintain low overhead is unmatched in Britain or France. In Britain, the Charity Commission requires that large charities submit audited financial reports, but there is no equivalent assessment of "excessive" overhead spending; thus CARE UK staffers report being "shocked" at the administrative expenses of an organization like Oxfam.[64] In France, private donors demand transparency, but also expect that charities act in a fundamentally different way than businesses, making the language of resource maximization and efficiency somewhat incongruous.

The strength of the voluntarist norm also varies in the three countries. In the United States, volunteers have largely been crowded out by professional staffers who pursue efficiency goals. Though rates of volunteering are high in the United States, they are low in the field of international affairs. The weakness of the voluntarist norm in the international NGO community may also be attributable to the belief that charity work is not particularly sacred. This contrasts sharply with Britain, where professionalization has not displaced "ordinary" or "passionate" people who volunteer for international charities. Those volunteers underpin the political and fundraising successes of INGOs, even if they make internal management more challenging. Oxfam director Barbara Stocking made this discovery when she attempted to professionalize the staff of Oxfam shops. Rather

---

63. Versluys 2008; Adele Harmer, "The Road to Good Donorship," *Humanitarian Exchange* [Overseas Development Institute] 24 (July 2003), 33-36.
64. Personal interview, CARE UK staffer, October 24, 2006.

than leading to efficiency gains and revenue increases, the removal of volunteers sharply reduced profits, since volunteers had not only brought in their own donations but also anchored social networks that kept other community members involved in Oxfam.[65] In France, the professionalization of humanitarian work has caused real and enduring tension both within INGOs and in the relationship between INGOs and French public. In a country where the NGO sector is sharply divided between a very small set of large INGOs and a very large group of small, volunteer-based organizations, the word professionalization is still met with disapproval in many circles, which may explain MSF's preference for referring to itself as a movement.

Professionalization matters to humanitarians for several reasons. Practically, professionalization and standardization may affect an organization's success on the ground. There is a heated debate over this, manifested both within organizations and among global humanitarians considering the usefulness of global frameworks like the Sphere Project and the Humanitarian Accountability Partnership. Some argue that the expansion of technical expertise and uniformity is critical to service delivery and long-term effectiveness; critics respond that managerialism and professionalization rob humanitarianism of its moral power and attractiveness and will ultimately drive away the most passionate and capable people from humanitarian work (Torrente 2005; Roberts et al. 2005). It is possible that professionals are more successful at some activities, while volunteers are more effective at others. Arguably, CARE may be more successful at service delivery, while MSF may be better able to create political awareness and action.

Beyond the question of success, however, the location of an INGO on the professional-voluntarist spectrum speaks to its very identity. In the language of constructivists, the constitutive beliefs of INGOs—the answer to the question of "who we are"—are informed by the relative balance of professionals and volunteers in humanitarian work. CARE sees itself as a humanitarian organization able to bring considerable expertise to fight global poverty; Oxfam describes itself as a global movement of ordinary people (both professionals and citizens) combating poverty; and MSF sees

---

65. Personal interview, former Oxfam staffer, November 2, 2006.

itself as a voluntary community of medical professionals who bring the "do no harm" ethic of medicine to the traditional principles of humanitarian action. The growth of a global humanitarian sector has not been accompanied by the development of a single humanitarian identity.

Organizational Practice: Advocacy

If fundraising and professionalization are practices whose effects may be diffused throughout the range of an organization's activities, advocacy strategies have a more directly observable impact in both home and field offices. INGO advocacy may differ in many ways, but here I focus on the prioritization of advocacy as well as the type of advocacy strategies adopted. Beyond these two dimensions, the following analysis also considers the role of research at each organization, as research can be more or less policy-oriented. CARE does very little advocacy or research and prefers an insider approach; Oxfam heavily prioritizes advocacy and research and uses a wide range of strategies, including insider lobbying, outsider campaigning, and grassroots public education; and MSF puts a moderate amount of emphasis on advocacy and research and primarily uses an outsider approach to political action.

CARE regarded itself as a nonpolitical organization until the mid-1990s when Peter Bell became president. Bell was a proponent of greater advocacy, but in the face of internal resistance to more political work, he promised to make incremental changes and to root any advocacy in CARE's experiences in the field.[66] Since then, CARE has done more lobbying and campaigning, and in 2005 it established its first internal advocacy policy.[67] Still, advocacy remains a low priority. It is difficult to compare spending on advocacy across INGOs in different countries as the reporting requirements for charities are quite different. In 2008, CARE spent $141,882 on lobbying and $8.5 million on what it calls public information (this also serves fundraising goals and is thus more than advocacy). Even using the more generous figure, CARE still spent only 1.2% of its budget on public information, in contrast to Oxfam, which spent 6.5% of its 2008 budget on campaigning

66. Personal interview, Peter Bell, February 4, 2010.

67. Personal interview, CARE staffer, April 26, 2006; personal interview, CARE staffer, February 27, 2007.

and advocacy.[68] The big push at the top for more advocacy was not met with commensurate investment—for about five years, there was only one person running advocacy training at all of CARE's offices in the field.[69] An internal survey from 2005 reported that many CARE staffers "are, at best, skeptical of advocacy and do not see what it has to do with our work or what the various topics on the agenda have to do with each other."[70]

The advocacy that CARE does do is generally insider lobbying—face-to-face meetings with government officials and legislative campaigns (Stoddard 2006, 60). One well-placed CARE staffer, who described a "fairly open door" to the U.S. government, explained CARE's aversion to confrontational advocacy:

> Some organizations don't share our agenda, or they don't manage their relations with the Administration or Congress; they act in an uncomfortable manner, and we're not interested in joining with them.... Sometimes those organizations can say things and do things that we can't do—they push the envelope. This doesn't mean that we don't want to them to say or do those things, but they are pushing instead of keeping the door open or not being constructive. We don't work that way...we wouldn't be *accusatory*, we wouldn't be *rude*, we wouldn't be *pointing fingers*. For example, in Iraq, other CAREs wanted to use CARE International to "get to" the U.S. government, but CARE USA didn't want that to happen.[71]

CARE argues that confrontational advocacy would not only threaten its partnership with government but also endanger staff in the field.[72] CARE's conciliatory tone is evident in its recent "I Am Powerful" campaign, in which CARE makes a series of unobjectionable statements that highlight the role of women in combating poverty.

CARE staff claim the majority of its advocacy happens at the country level, as CARE tries to "speak to what we know."[73] Country-level advocacy

---

68. IRS Form 990 for period ending June 2008; CARE, *Annual Report 2008*. The Oxfam figures come from the annual report for the period ending April 2008.

69. Personal interview, former CARE staffer, February 5, 2010.

70. Barbara Larkin, "What's Advocacy Got to Do with It?" *iCARE News* 51 (September 2005).

71. Personal interview, CARE USA staffer, April 26, 2006, quoted in Stroup 2010.

72. Personal interview, CARE International staffer, February 27, 2007. Oxfam and MSF also have many field staff but engage in more confrontational advocacy.

73. Personal interview, CARE USA staffer, September 6, 2006.

has long been conservative. For example, a 1990 review of CARE's work in field offices argued that "as an international organization, it is not appropriate for CARE to become involved in internal politics" and suggested instead greater concern for the local context (Devone 1990, 64). Interestingly, there seems to be an unmet demand for advocacy by CARE. In 2007, 59% of CARE partners in the field reported that they would like the organization "to advocate with donors to change how projects are funded and measured."[74]

Without extensive campaigns, CARE's research and policy work focuses on the outputs of specific projects, rather than the sector-wide analysis characteristic of Oxfam. Consider two reports by CARE and Oxfam on Bangladesh. CARE's *Analyzing Power Structures in Rural Bangladesh* (2005) reported on a survey designed to help incorporate knowledge of community power relations into country office programming, while Oxfam's *Towards Ending Violence against Women* (2004) linked events in Bangladesh to global trends and made specific recommendations at both the local and global level. Both reports are detailed and well-documented, but CARE's audience is its own program staff, while Oxfam's report speaks to policymakers and the general public. As one CARE staff member explained, "The quality of advocacy is proportional to the policy analysis. The way CARE works is that the policy research is good on operational work in country, but much weaker at the global level. It's not part of the advocacy we do. But if you take Darfur, we have interesting concepts of the ways of advancing solutions to the conflict, which our field colleague invented."[75] Policy research at CARE is also made difficult by the fact that most of CARE's income is restricted funding, that is, grants and contracts marked for specific projects rather than unrestricted funding that can be used as the organization chooses. While CARE has worked to expand its private donor base, there has been contention over whether those funds should automatically go to advocacy or might be better spent on programs in the field.[76]

CARE USA's approach to advocacy and research is reflected at CARE UK and CARE France. A CARE UK staffer volunteered a comparison

---

74. "Partner and Project Participant Views," *iCARE News* (February 2007).
75. Personal interview, CARE UK staffer, February 27, 2007.
76. Personal interview, Peter Bell, February 4, 2010.

between CARE's advocacy style and that of Oxfam: "I don't understand [Oxfam's approach]—if they expect to work with the prime minister in a high profile capacity, it's a bit offensive to say 'Tony Blair's policy is totally wrong.'...I don't think that approach pays dividends. I might personally think that the policies are awful, and on Iraq, for example, I completely disagree with the entire affair, but I won't publicly say, 'Tony Blair is to blame.' I will say 'a readjustment is needed.'"[77]

However, one area in which CARE UK differs from other CARE offices is in its interest in research. CARE UK does not run programs in the field, but it conducts investigations into topics like HIV/AIDS and urban poverty to complement these programs. According to one person at CARE UK, CARE generally had a reputation as "being a bit thick, just getting the job done," but the interviewee said that CARE UK is considered "the thinking CARE" of the international confederation: "The UK is one of the richest NGO sectors in the world...and what flows from that is that there is a strong flow of people from academia in the UK that flow to British NGOs....We are part of that family, which means we bring that baggage, those expectations from our peers, to the CARE confederation...our presence here, our Britishness, if you will, is helpful in that way."[78] This approach to research may be a function of public expectations of NGOs within Britain, but also is related to CARE UK's financial support. Unlike the major American aid agencies, DFID provides block grants that support evaluation and learning initiatives at CARE UK—and research at CARE UK did not take off until this money arrived.[79]

The CARE approach to advocacy is particularly challenging in France, with its limited political opportunities and confrontational political culture. Using an insider approach, CARE France does occasionally consult with French officials on humanitarian issues, and it is a member of the NGO umbrella organization Coordination SUD (Lévêque 2004). But the staff of CARE France struggle to use a conciliatory tone in a country where vocal protest is the norm: "We follow the CARE International rules, but spontaneously we react the way that French NGOs react. This means

77. Personal interview, CARE UK staffer, October 24, 2006.

78. Personal interview, CARE UK staffer, November 1, 2006.

79. DFID, *CARE—Partnership Programme Agreement* (2005). The timing was described by a CARE UK staffer. Personal interview, November 1, 2006.

that... we'd be tempted to say things that are more reactive, do denuncia-
tion like MSF or others do.... We are tempted to do political advocacy, but
in the [CI] network it's mostly Anglo-Saxons—there is a culture of compromise, of getting input from everybody... CARE's object in advocacy ultimately is *not* to affect program implementation, and I think that is good.
In a more Latin or French culture, though, we would... speak out and *then*
face the consequences...."[80] While a limited, cooperative, and insider approach to advocacy may be the norm at CARE and in the American relief
and development community more generally, that approach is perceived as
peculiar by British and French CARE staffers.

Things are much different at Oxfam. Oxfam GB has been involved in
advocacy since its inception, and it has a reputation among other NGOs and
donor agencies as being particularly effective at influencing decision makers. Oxfam has had a formal Public Affairs Unit since the 1970s (now called
the Campaigns and Policy Unit) (Bryer and Magrath 1999, 173). Over the
past decade, Oxfam GB has invested between 6% and 8% of its total annual
budget in political action and education, according to its annual reports.
In contrast to CARE, Oxfam's advocacy is concentrated at the global and
structural level rather than the local or project level (Edwards 1993, 164).

Oxfam uses a wide range of advocacy strategies, including insider lobbying, outsider campaigning, and broad public education. Oxfam sees effective advocacy as a multipronged strategy that demonstrates the links
between conditions and causes while operating at all levels of the policy
process (Bryer and Magrath 1999, 171). According to one former Oxfam
staffer, a vague rule of thumb there has been to start with insider lobbying
but to then work with campaigners to bring public attention and pressure to
an issue if lobbying fails.[81] The same person described the potential of these
campaigns: "we have so many members.... Political parties... have maybe
three-quarters of a million members.... In the 'Make Poverty History' campaign, we had 10 to 12 million people—that's a huge constituency." Yet
throughout these campaigns, Oxfam maintains its access to government:

> If Oxfam is going to send out a press release, or a policy paper, that is criti-
> cal of the government, it is *always* shown to the government first. Not so the

---

80. Personal interview, CARE France, February 8, 2007.
81. Personal interview, former Oxfam GB staffer, October 19, 2006; Bryer and Magrath
1999, 172.

government can say "you can't publish it," but so they won't be surprised. So if Oxfam says that Blair's policy on such-and-such is bad, they won't be surprised. I think this comes first out of respect—respect for the interaction—but also it demonstrates that there really is a lot of contact between Oxfam and the government.

If Barbara Stocking wanted to, she could get Gordon Brown on the phone in half an hour, no matter where he was. This organization has got those close contacts, and those contacts are only generated by on ongoing dialogue, a reflection of the enormous interaction. And there are lots of private briefings in both directions—from us to them, and from them to us.[82]

Though the long-term relationship is protected, in the short term, critical campaigns help Oxfam demonstrate its independence and integrity (Bryer and Cairns 1998, 35).

Oxfam's advocacy work is built upon an extensive research capacity. Besides doing many evaluations of its projects out in the field, Oxfam GB also produces sector-wide research directed at governments, international institutions, and the general public. Oxfam excels at translating complex issues like trade protectionism into simple, striking messages for public consumption.[83] Provocatively titled reports—like *Mugged: Poverty in Your Coffee Cup* and *Offside! Labour Rights and Sportswear Production in Asia*—provide the evidence upon which lobbying efforts and campaigns rest. Oxfam also houses two development journals which act as forums for exchange among practitioners and academics. One former board member traces this penchant for research to Oxfam's intellectual Oxford roots, which drive the organization to explore and reveal the structural causes underlying poverty, and approach that has made it world's leader in campaigning NGOs (Slim 2006, 40–41). With unrestricted funding from both the public and DFID, Oxfam has the luxury of choosing to spend its money on things other than specific projects run by field offices.

Two additional points are worth mentioning. First, the style and content of Oxfam GB's work is carried into the global OI confederation.

---

82. Personal interview, former Oxfam staffer, November 2, 2006.
83. "Collaborating with an Advocacy NGO," *International Trade Forum* 2 (2006): 9.

According to a director at Oxfam America, a "bright idea" at Oxfam GB often ends up as an OI priority: "You have some people...working full time on a particular issue. They do a very initial draft of a very initial paper...and before you know it, it's a snowball—it gains momentum and by the time it gets to the table at Oxfam International, there's almost a precooked campaign with precooked messages" (Scott and Brown 2004, 19). By one estimate, perhaps 70% of the Policy Division staff at Oxfam GB work on global policy issues rather than domestic campaigns.[84] Second, Oxfam's advocacy work has gotten the unwanted attention of the Charity Commission. In particular, a 1990 censure of Oxfam's "political abuse of its charitable status" led to restructuring within Oxfam and the clarification by the Charity Commission of proper political activities (Burnell 1992, 311). This reveals an interesting contrast with the United States: while there is less oversight of charities' political actions in the United States, CARE is very wary of advocacy; meanwhile, with more intrusive oversight in Britain, Oxfam regularly engages in large and provocative campaigns.

The other Oxfams are heavily committed to multipronged advocacy. The American chapter used to be less involved in campaigning: between 1981 and 1996, Oxfam America's spending on advocacy dropped from 10.4% to 5.3% of total expenditures (Anderson 2000, 447). This declining emphasis on advocacy brought Oxfam America closer in line with its American counterparts. Since the creation of Oxfam International, however, Oxfam America's advocacy work has expanded, reflected in greater investment in the Washington advocacy office (Scott and Brown 2004, 1; Offenheiser et al. 1999, 128). Today, both Oxfam GB and Oxfam America have about a fifth of their staff working in campaigns and policy. With this high level of political activity, Oxfam America has been concerned about running afoul of American tax law. In 2004, the INGO created the Oxfam America Advocacy Fund to conduct its campaigns with support from non–tax-exempt donations. In addition, because of America's global power, campaigning in the United States is a priority for the entire Oxfam confederation, but there has been some tension with Oxfam GB over who controls the advocacy agenda.[85] When asked where the center of gravity

---

84. Personal interview, Oxfam staffer, November 2, 2006.
85. Scott and Brown 2004, 20; personal interview, former Oxfam staffer, February 27, 2007.

was for advocacy work within the Oxfam International confederation, one Oxfam America staffer said:

> It's somewhere just off the European coast. In the Atlantic. Which is very different from where it was five years ago. Five years ago it was in Oxford with everybody else wishing it was somewhere else. And what's happened is the other European Oxfams,... have pulled it southward, slightly, and we are pulling it westwards. It's still very much European centered, I would say, but for the reasons I have mentioned.... If you look at where the major money is coming from for campaign and advocacy... my instinct is that it's overwhelmingly now coming from the [United] States...
>
> A lot of that money's going to go to other Oxfams. We will lead—we will manage the grant but we will go to other Oxfams, including OGB [Oxfam Great Britain] etc. But even the fact that we're sort of facilitating the grant... it moves it slightly—to just off the coast of Ireland as I like to say.[86]

While other chapters like Oxfam America may have levers they can use to move Oxfam's global advocacy agenda, however, Oxfam GB retains the lion's share of control.

Oxfam France is really a campaigning-only organization. Its initial incarnation, the French NGO Agir Ici, had a strong record of advocacy, having conducted over seventy separate campaigns over fifteen years. Of the three or four annual campaigns of Oxfam France today, three overlap with Oxfam's global agenda, but Oxfam France maintains at least one campaign that is not driven by the international confederation.[87] The willingness of Oxfam to partner with a campaigning-only organization signals the centrality of advocacy in the entire Oxfam confederation.

Like Oxfam, MSF speaks of a commitment to advocacy, but unlike CARE and Oxfam, MSF generally favors outsider protest strategies. In a country where political engagement among NGOs is high, MSF is perhaps the most outspoken of the French INGOs, with an established policy of clearly denouncing human rights violations and state failures.[88] In recent years, there has been an increasing emphasis at MSF on *témoignage*—actively using the media to speak out on the horrors of conflict and critique

---

86. Personal interview, September 3, 2010.
87. Personal interview, Oxfam France, February 7, 2007.
88. Personal interview, Groupe URD, March 7, 2007.

state and international policies. At the global level, MSF's most visible and successful advocacy has happened through its now decade-long "Access to Essential Medicines" campaign.

Former MSF president Rony Brauman has argued that the job of NGOs is to act as an "alarm bell" for states and international institutions, "pulling them towards crisis areas and getting them to react" (Brauman 2004, 408; see also Brauman 1996). *Témoignage* differs somewhat from advocacy. For MSF, witnessing cannot be separated from humanitarian action in the field, where it sees the abuse of particular populations or violations of international humanitarian law by belligerents. This makes accounting for advocacy expenditures difficult. Spending by MSF's French headquarters on what MSF calls "raising public awareness" accounted for an average 1.64% of total expenditures from 2001 to 2008.[89]

MSF's confrontational activism is rooted in its social movement history. MSF has been criticized for having inconsistent policy positions, but what matters most for it "is its continued projection of a sense of authenticity, rather than its adoption of a particular position on a specific issue" (Redfield 2006, 10). For MSF, there is nothing inherently valuable about maintaining good relations with political authorities. Former MSF International secretary Rafa Vilasanjuan unfavorably contrasts the "Anglo-Saxon" approach of silent diplomacy with the "Latin vision," which brings "a problem into the public and assert[s] itself despite tensions with authorities.... The 'no comment' policy is not a solution at MSF!"[90]

As at Oxfam, MSF's recent campaigns have combined detailed research with multilevel advocacy, but unlike Oxfam, MSF research is generally critical (rather than solution-oriented) and directed at MSF programs. As one subject explained, "the role of research is particularly important for MSF.... They have a very critical self-presentation—they like to say they are always the first to criticize themselves. But they don't pretend to contribute to the academic sector."[91] Although careful and detailed research is an integral part of MSF's technical work in the field and underpins individual and collective *témoignage,* MSF's research profile is narrower in

---

89. Author's calculations from MSF France, *Rapports annuels* (various years).
90. "Speaking Out: Think Politics." *Messages* 136 (May 2005): 10.
91. Personal interview, NGO analyst, March 1 2007.

scope than at Oxfam.[92] Country-level research is generally limited to documenting health-related problems and to epidemiological studies. MSF also has a few satellite organizations like Fondation MSF and Epicentre, which create opportunities for research with other NGOs and international organizations on technical issues.

The "Access to Essential Medicines" campaign is one in which MSF has, since the late 1990s, combined careful research in the field with clear and consistent policy positions, but MSF's tone has remained provocative. The campaign began with a focus on access to HIV/AIDS medications and has since expanded in scope, all along requiring detailed knowledge of the global rules governing intellectual property and patent law (Sell 2002). MSF emerged as an early leader in the global campaign, and the timing of its 1999 Nobel Peace Prize helped elevate the campaign's status. Still, throughout its participation in this global coalition, MSF has provocatively made claims for state authorities to take responsibility. The best example of this comes from the Nobel Prize acceptance speech of the president of MSF International:

> As civil society we exist relative to the state, to its institutions and its power....Ours is not to displace the responsibility of the state....If civil society identifies a problem, it is not theirs to provide a solution, but it is theirs to expect that states will translate this into concrete and just solutions. Only the state has the legitimacy and power to do this. Today, a growing injustice confronts us. More than 90% of all death and suffering from infectious diseases occurs in the developing world....Life saving essential medicines are either too expensive [or] are not available because they are not seen as financially viable, or...there is virtually no new research and development for priority tropical diseases. This market failure is our next challenge. The challenge however, is not ours alone. It is also for governments, International Government Institutions, the Pharmaceutical Industry and other NGOs to confront this injustice. What we as a civil society movement demand is change, not charity. (Orbinski 1999)

Another example of MSF's confrontational tone comes from an editorial written by MSF's campaign directors: "To put it simply: greed in the

---

92. An MSF Holland director suggested that the medical ethic propels MSF to focus on the individual patient and his or her present condition, rather than looking for extramedical (and perhaps deeper) causes of the patient's situation. Sondorp 2006, 54.

West curtails the availability of life-saving drugs for all" (Veeken and Pecoul 1999).

This approach to advocacy gets translated into slightly different practices at MSF USA and MSF UK. Like MSF France, MSF USA is uncompromising in its defense of its duty to speak out, and it does not focus on making specific policy recommendations: "We're not prescriptive, and we don't claim to have the skill to figure out the context in a political solution. I don't think humanitarian actors ought to be doing that. We try and rely on what we see and present that in the most compelling way possible—but that is not necessarily telling people what needs to happen. I think that oversteps the role of the humanitarian organization."[93] This stance may serve the American section well as it tries to raise private donations in a country where political action by charities is seen as suspect. Meanwhile, MSF UK stands out within the MSF confederation for its contribution to research. When asked about MSF UK's strengths, one staffer replied that MSF UK's "operational research and...links with academia here [have] to do with being located in the hub of London, in terms of the work that is being done here in technical issues and medical ethics."[94] MSF's British section has adopted the British INGO community's practice of focusing on ethical and technical research, though again, this research does not lead to policy recommendations in the style of Oxfam.

Altogether, the three organizations have vastly different approaches to advocacy, a dimension of INGO practice that has received increasing attention over the past decade. These differences can be linked to the home environment of each INGO, while variation across each INGO's confederation reflects the intersection of home and host environments.

Explaining Advocacy Strategies

Political action by INGOs is shaped by the political opportunities, legal regulations, and political culture in each INGO's home environment. In the United States, several factors help account for CARE's low prioritization of and conciliatory insider approach to advocacy. Most basically, American tax law prohibits nonprofits from engaging in a substantive amount

---

93. Phone interview, May 22, 2006.
94. Personal interview, MSF UK staffer [1], October 25, 2006.

of political activity. Beyond the legal dimension, American nonprofits also believe that accepting government funds legally restricts their political activities more than it actually does. Thus, one CARE staffer took great pains to point out that the organization's small Washington advocacy office was funded only by private donations.[95] This creates a self-reinforcing dynamic: low private donations make advocacy unlikely since INGOs lack the necessary unrestricted funds, and low advocacy keeps them from attracting the interest and support of private donors. Finally, available American models of interest group politics in the past three decades suggest that advocacy is a professional activity undertaken by specialized staff rather than a participatory process involving ordinary citizens (Skocpol 2002, 134).

In Britain, by contrast, Oxfam's heavy investment in a multilevel, multipronged approach to advocacy is part of a larger orientation of openness toward the British community. Because public visibility is necessary to maintain a private donor base, grassroots campaigns and controversial policy statements serve fundraising goals as well as perhaps solving relief and development problems. In a dynamic that reverses the process at CARE, unrestricted private funds allow Oxfam to invest heavily in research and advocacy. Geography and political opportunities also matter. The concentration of officials and elites in southern England, a government that is centralized and open to input from INGOs, and the dense networks among officials, academics, and INGO leaders create many opportunities for lobbying and campaigning. An Oxfam America staffer described the differences in political opportunities: "There's no doubt that Oxfam GB doesn't just influence, it almost frames and shapes certain debates. They literally have direct lines. Plus it's somewhat simpler there. If you happen to have three former Oxfam-ers sitting in 10 Downing Street as we had for a period, okay. Game over, at some level. Over here, you create a great relationship with Senator Luger or John Kerry, or Hilary Clinton's Chief of Staff or whoever it is, you're just starting a very complicated conversation."[96] Furthermore, the policy-directed research that underpins Oxfam's advocacy work is widely supported in Britain by academic institutions like the Institute for Development Studies, well-placed think tanks

---

95. Personal interview, CARE USA, April 26, 2006.

96. Personal interview, September 3, 2010.

like the Overseas Development Institute, and DFID's funding schemes.[97] Oxfam benefits from these postcolonial institutions that continue a long-standing tradition of research on Third World development. Finally, whether it's called paternalism, do-gooderism, or simple ambition, voluntary organizations in Britain embody the normative understanding that they can and should try to solve major problems abroad. This norm is robust at Oxfam, even in the face of sanctioning by the Charity Commission. For British INGOs, effective advocacy is central to their legitimacy and capacity as charities (Hudson 2002).

Finally, French institutions and culture help account for MSF's commitment to witnessing but relative disinterest in specific policy change. The relatively young non-state sector in France is rooted in a set of social movements with a history of protest against the state (Siméant and Dauvin 2002). Witnessing and volunteerism, as well as MSF's "fieldwork'" in France, fulfill a need for engagement but leave the work of problem-solving to the state, which is understood as the legitimate, capable, and ultimately responsible power. This logic was evident in the Nobel Prize acceptance speech of former MSF International president James Orbinski, in which he described MSF's *témoignage* as an "ethic of refusal"—an act of indignation against political powers. Protest is an act of legitimation for NGOs in France, in contrast to the Anglo-Saxon "culture of compromise" that the French doctors deride. Finally, the closed nature of the French policy process means that policy-directed advocacy is fairly futile. In a country where the state is the one to define and address political problems, unsolicited input from civil society is much less welcome than in either the United States or UK. This approach to advocacy helps account for MSF's research strategy—while professional doctors undertake careful and detailed epidemiological studies necessary to continue fieldwork and support fundraising, MSF lacks the sector-wide research capacity that would support policy-oriented advocacy.

The issue of how INGOs select advocacy strategies is a critical one for scholars of international relations. Studies of transnational advocacy and campaigning reveal surprisingly little about who joins campaigns, how frequently collaboration on advocacy occurs, and which tactics are most

---

97. Personal interview, November 2, 2006; Sunderland 2004.

successful. The above cases suggest at least several implications about patterns of INGO advocacy. First, though Keck and Sikkink's (1998) discussion of transnational advocacy networks suggests a world of loud organizations that prioritize campaigning, many INGOs, perhaps most of the large American ones, participate in a transnational associative sphere but generally stay away from major campaigns. In addition, the diversity of advocacy approaches suggests that durable transnational coalitions may be rather infrequent phenomena, as organizations are likely to have difficulty collaborating on stylistic or substantive matters. Finally, advocacy campaigns are likely to succeed when the style of the INGO matches the expectations of the target. We know that context, political ties, and tactics matter for effective advocacy; INGOs use different political strategies because they come from different political systems.

INGO Practice: Government Relations

Political independence and neutrality are general foundational principles of global humanitarianism, but it is quite clear that humanitarians differ substantially among themselves in the way that they engage political authorities (Weiss 1999). Abby Stoddard differentiates broadly between "Wilsonian" NGOs that see a basic compatibility in the goals of humanitarians and states and "Dunantist" NGOs that are more protective of their independence from governments (Stoddard 2006). These categories elucidate important differences between American and European organizations, but there is substantial variation among European INGOs as well in the ways they relate to government authorities, and the dividing lines are often national ones.

CARE has consistently chosen to cooperate with the American government as the way to most efficiently address global poverty. Working with the myriad Cabinet-level agencies involved in the provision of development assistance and the formulation of policy, CARE has a strong network of contacts within the American government.[98] CARE is also often willing to work with the American military, as in Somalia and (until recently) in

---

98. Personal interview, CARE USA staffer, April 26, 2006.

Iraq (Stoddard 2006, 95–106). This close relationship has been strained recently by the U.S. government's increasing politicization of humanitarian relief, but CARE nevertheless works to retain and protect its relationship with the U.S. government.

In general, it is difficult to assess the success of INGOs like CARE in changing specific government policies. CARE is well respected within USAID for its consistent service delivery.[99] For example, as one of the largest providers of food aid, CARE has been active in the formulation and reform of policy in that area.[100] In other realms, where it is often excluded from discussions of the budget or organizational reforms (as are other American NGOs), CARE's partnership with the U.S. government is most certainly unequal.[101] What is different about CARE as an INGO may not be its weakness vis-à-vis the government but how it chooses to respond to this issue. In repeated instances, rather than go it alone or criticize policy, CARE opts to work with the government.

The positive orientation toward governments and political authorities is shared at CARE UK and CARE France, but with wildly different results. CARE UK has taken advantage of the British government's willingness to share information and provide financing. It participates in DFID policy discussions and, as noted above, it receives generous DFID support. CARE France shares the orientation of the other CAREs toward working with the state, but the relationship with the French state remains distant. The organization has enjoyed greater political access in the past decade, including several opportunities to brief French policymakers (Lévêque 2004). Still, CARE France brings an openness toward government to a political system largely closed to civil society actors.

Oxfam simultaneously criticizes and cooperates with the British government. Extensive formal and informal channels of communication enable both strategies. Most notably, Oxfam is part of the informal five-member British Overseas Aid Group, which meets regularly with the prime minister. Oxfam also participates in recurring consultations at DFID, which

---

99. Personal interview, CARE USA staffer, May 31, 2006.

100. Barrett and Maxwell, 2005; "In a War, Even Food Aid Can Kill," *New York Times,* December 5, 1999; "Federal Budget Cuts Mean Less Food For Peace," *Philanthropy News Digest,* April 18, 2005.

101. "New Developments in US Foreign Assistance," *iCARE News* 57 (March 2006).

claims its relationship with Oxfam is "one of the strongest we have with a civil society organization."[102] This close association is not dependent on the party in power, though the bond has been particularly strong under Labour. Former Overseas Development Minister Christopher Patten (1986–89), for example, reported that Oxfam's director had essentially unlimited access to him during his tenure (Burnell 1992, 325). Still, the government seems to appreciate Oxfam's desire to maintain financial and political independence. For example, in its evaluations of Oxfam, DFID acknowledges that the two sometimes differ on substantive positions, yet this does not affect chances for future collaboration.[103] This relationship is strengthened by personal ties, though the exchange of personnel is difficult to measure systematically.[104] On the other hand, Oxfam does maintain some distance from the government and often bluntly criticizes officials.

These practices travel in different ways throughout the Oxfam confederation. Oxfam France, as a campaigns-only organization, has always been very independent of the French state and political authorities in general. The American branch of Oxfam is perhaps even more independent than its British counterpart, but the nature of Oxfam America's interaction with U.S. government officials has changed substantially since creation of global campaigning through Oxfam International. Before the mid-1990s, Oxfam America was largely removed from interaction with the U.S. government, as it basically functioned as a grant-making operation with left-wing sympathies. Even though leaders were aware that forswearing government funding had limited the size of the organization, "both board and staff remain committed to the principle that Oxfam America should remain independent of U.S. foreign policy interests and are unlikely to alter this position in the short to medium term" (Offenheiser et al. 1999, 126). The introduction of global campaigning has not changed Oxfam America's financial relationship with

102. DFID, *Oxfam Partnership Programme Agreement 2004/05* (February 2006), 4; *Oxfam GB Partnership Programme Agreement (PPA) 2005/06 Annual Report—DFID Response* (February 2007), 1.

103. For example, DFID notes Oxfam's decision to not apply for DFID funds for Iraq but states this did not affect Oxfam's subsequent involvement in NGO meetings on Iraq. Mike Battock, *Oxfam PPA Annual Review 2004*, 5.

104. Personal interview, former Oxfam staff, November 2, 2006; Katharine Quarmby, "Why Oxfam Is Failing Africa," *New Statesman*, May 30, 2005; Barbara Stocking, "Oxfam Bites Back," New Statesman, June 6, 2005.

the state, but it has dramatically expanded its policy work and introduced more confrontational tactics. In keeping with its American peers, Oxfam America's policy director described its baseline advocacy strategy as an "insider" and "bipartisan" approach, but the newly created Oxfam International confederation pushed Oxfam America to be more provocative, through tactics like open opposition to the U.S. war in Afghanistan (Scott and Brown 2004). Thus, while Oxfam America may at heart be very independent from the U.S. government, the office tries to moderate its provocativeness in an environment where such an approach would cut off its political access.

Independence from government authorities is almost the raison d'être of MSF France. From its earliest days, MSF has maintained an antagonistic position toward political authorities, and it has avoided making value statements about particular ideologies or even about democracy as a political system (Bell and Carens 2004; Torrente 2004). For MSF, states have clear responsibilities toward their citizens, and working with states would implicitly absolve those states of their duties. Professor Samy Cohen argues that MSF is by far the most outspoken of French NGOs on this subject, but admits that outside France "there are practically no NGOs like MSF that refuse to surrender an ounce of their independence and live like a 'counter-culture'" (2006, 100, 130). MSF France has been particularly critical of "state humanitarianism," when states claim to advance humanitarian goals and aim to work alongside INGOs (Rouillé d'Orfeuil 2006, 147–48; Torrente 2004). For MSF, humanitarianism is about the impartial distribution of aid based on need alone, while states' foreign policies are inherently partial and political. Especially when the state is a party to the conflict, MSF argues, state humanitarianism blurs the line between the private and public sectors and puts humanitarian workers at risk.

In terms of its access to officials and policymakers, MSF is a household name in France, and its visibility and that of other humanitarian INGOs has created some limited space for state-NGO consultation (Doucin 2002). Unlike other leading French NGOs, however, MSF has no representative at the government liaison group, the Haut Conseil de la coopération internationale. According to some sources, as the largest INGO in France, MSF could have direct access to government officials, but that access is not advertised publicly by the organization, given its insistence on independence.[105]

---

105. This contrasts starkly with CARE or Oxfam. Personal interview, French NGO analyst, March 2, 2007.

The question of political independence is one where several MSF international sections depart markedly from the French section, one of the effects of a highly decentralized international structure. Thus, while MSF France has almost entirely eliminated government offices as sources of support, it has been less successful in pushing the entire MSF confederation in this direction.[106] MSF UK, for one, works closely with the British government, though this is made easier by the facts that the British government is arguably one of the most tolerant of criticism from its NGO partners.

MSF USA, however, is an exception to this pattern. It follows the lead of MSF France in fiercely protecting its independence and its duty to speak out. Asked if MSF USA was more or less cooperative with its home country government than MSF France, one staffer said,

> I wouldn't characterize us as more cooperative. Actually, it would probably be the other way around. In terms of sharing information…participating in events that they sponsor in preparing NGOs for conflict situations, we're really sensitive about the things that are developed by the U.S. government. I can't say that I really know enough about MSF France's engagement with the French government, but MSF is not engaged with the U.S. government. We are engaged to the point that we want our positions to be known, we want to call responsible parties to take responsibility. Perhaps we are even less cooperative, because the U.S. government is active in so many contexts where we work.[107]

The aversion to working with government officials seems equally strong at both MSF France and MSF USA.

Explaining Government Relations

At CARE, Oxfam, and MSF, there are fundamentally different understandings of the appropriate relationship between NGOs and the state that then shape the way that these INGOs engage with their home country governments and political authorities in general. This dimension of INGO practice is related to the fundraising and advocacy strategies discussed

---

106. "Synthesis of the Debates," La Mancha conference 2006, 14; Lindenberg and Bryant 2001, 38.

107. Personal interview, MSF USA, May 22, 2006.

above, but arguably comes prior to each. In order for an INGO to decide where to get its funds, or how to push for political change, the INGO must first have an understanding of what constitutes appropriate engagement with political authorities. CARE favors engagement and collaboration, Oxfam is engaged but independent, and MSF prefers disengagement and independence. A look at each INGO's national origin helps explain these orientations.

In the United States, CARE's willingness to work with government authorities in a cooperative manner is shaped by American political opportunities, social networks, and political culture. The American government sees NGOs as a partner in international relief and development, perhaps even, as Colin Powell declared, as a "force multiplier." This openness toward INGOs exists in a fragmented political system that makes large-scale change unlikely, thereby encouraging INGOs to work with governments on the micro level of service delivery and policy implementation. At the individual level, social networks may link the nonprofit and government sectors in ways that encourage a more conciliatory or cooperative approach. More broadly, American political culture may inform the baseline orientation of American INGOs in their approach to political authorities. I suggested in the previous chapter that pragmatism was an important norm in the U.S. charitable community—the ability to "get the job done" is inherently valuable. This may drive American organizations to work more closely with governments at home and abroad. The American government offers great resources and leverage for INGOs; host governments like Britain and France provide these advantages as well. An additional way in which we could explore an INGO's relations to political authorities would be to look at the practices of field offices. While that is outside the realm of the present study, anecdotal evidence suggests that many CARE field offices also work closely with local authorities.

National political opportunities, social networks, and political culture also affect how Oxfam relates to political authorities. The structure of political opportunities in Britain is one that tolerates more independence than in the United States but also does not encourage more collaboration. In Britain, Oxfam works with policymakers who understand the benefits of occasional collaboration while accepting that the interests of government and civil society may often diverge. The government-NGO relationship in Britain is thus one of weak partnership. British officials do not punish INGOs for confrontational advocacy, but they also don't reward them with large sums of money. Within these opportunities, however, social networks are important. Although the formal political structure could equally create a disconnect between civil society and government, the "Establishment radicals" of Oxfam are firmly linked with the political elite. To give just a single example, the former director of campaigns and policy at Oxfam, Justin Forsyth, went on to work for two British prime ministers as adviser on development issues before becoming the head of Save the Children UK in the fall of 2010. Geographical proximity between INGOs and government enables these close networks and increases the chances of successful collaboration. The orientation toward greater independence is framed as an expression of global humanitarian principles but its precise content is informed by domestic understandings of the appropriate role of charities in society—the understanding of charities as vehicles for principled work ("doing good") rather than as ways to efficiently achieve a goal ("doing well").

Finally, MSF is the most antagonistic toward its government. The INGO faces a French government that is fundamentally skeptical of the value and power of civil society. With little willingness to grant access to decision-making channels and few funding schemes that might facilitate cooperation, the doors and purses of French officials are closed. In its rhetoric, the French government has recently indicated some willingness to collaborate with NGOs, but this has led to little substantive change. When cooperation does happen, it is quite clear that it will be on unequal terms. On an individual level, those who work for French charities appear to travel in circles distant from government officials. This is obviously incredibly difficult to measure, and of course Bernard Kouchner stands out as an exception, but many of the major French INGOs were established as dissident associations coming out of the social movements of the 1960s. Ultimately, political culture matters. The principled orientation of French charities is clearly manifest in MSF's relationship to government authorities. Having decided that independence from political authorities is important, MSF often appears to take this thinking to the extreme.

Why does an INGO's orientation toward political authorities matter? The strategic choices that INGOs make about cooperating with governments affect the success of advocacy strategies and the effectiveness of aid delivery. In advocacy work, existing organizational practices may be appropriate in one setting but ineffective in another; recall the CARE UK worker confused about the confrontational nature of British INGOs' advocacy work. For humanitarian INGOs to be successful, they need to devise advocacy strategies based on a more sophisticated understanding of government-NGO relations in different countries. In the field, habits of NGO-government cooperation affect the delivery of services. This is starkly illustrated in the controversial U.S. invasion of Iraq in 2003 and the American government's position that NGOs were either "with or against" the war effort—a subject discussed in chapter 4.

From the Individual INGO to National Patterns

The implicit assumption underlying this book is that the effects of national origin will be felt at many other INGOs beyond the three that have been studied so far. The "mini-cases" from the United States, Britain, and France to which I now turn will demonstrate that there are real national patterns in fundraising, professionalization, advocacy, and government relations, even though the effects of national origin may not be entirely uniform across all INGOs.

Other American INGOs

First, let us compare CARE to two other American humanitarian INGOs—World Vision International (WVI) and the International Rescue Committee (IRC). The three groups have unique histories, leaders, and skills, but all were established in the United States and retain a substantial presence there. Recall that even in the face of changes in the international environment, CARE's central practices remained fairly constant and tied to its national origin. CARE is professional and efficient, wary of advocacy, and reliant on the American government as a financier and partner in the field. World Vision and the IRC, respectively founded in 1950 and 1933, share these practices to a greater or lesser extent.

World Vision is unique in at least two ways. First, it is a Christian relief organization that, unlike CARE and other secular agencies, receives enormous private support from churches and religiously minded donors. Thus, support from the U.S. government accounted for only 28%

of World Vision US income from 2002 to 2008, despite the fact that it is one of the largest recipients of such support in absolute terms.[108] Of course, high rates of religious giving among Americans make possible this vast private support base (see Stoddard 2006, 19). Second, World Vision is arguably the most advanced INGO worldwide in making its board and governance truly transnational. The organization began the process of internationalization as early as 1978 in an attempt "to break from its U.S.-centric past" (Whaites 1999, 415). Its offices in the developing world possess much more autonomy than field offices of other INGOs (Lindenberg and Bryant 2001). Still, about 44% of WVI's global income comes from the United States, while another 25% comes from the Canadian and Australian sections.[109] Compared to other INGOs, we should expect a more limited transfer of American organizational practices to other World Vision offices.

Despite these important differences in funding and global structure, World Vision shares other practices with CARE. Like CARE, World Vision is a fully professionalized organization that uses business models to pursue efficiency goals. Even two decades ago, Jonathan Benthall (1993, 167) wrote that the organization was nearest to the ideal of a humanitarian agency modeled on "the integrated, market-oriented, multi-national corporation." World Vision's management has long subscribed to the idea of "run your non-profit organization like a business" (Johnson 1993, 22; see also Lindenberg and Bryant 2001, 46). The corporate profile of World Vision leadership reinforces this orientation. For example, Richard Stearns, who moved from the tableware company Lenox to become president of World Vision US in 1998, has argued that "it is essential to apply rigorous business standards to an NGO or any nonprofit with the objective of driving down costs, cutting wasteful spending and eliminating unnecessary or duplicative systems."[110] World Vision regularly emphasizes its low overhead, and advertises its certification by Charity Navigator and the Better Business Bureau.

---

108. World Vision International, *Annual Reports* (various years).

109. World Vision International, *World Vision International and Consolidated Affiliates Consolidated Financial Statements September 30, 2009 and 2008.*

110. Richard Stearns, "Greater Scrutiny of NGOs Demands Leaders' Focus on HQ Effectiveness," *Monday Developments* [InterAction USA magazine] (April 2007): 29.

World Vision also shares CARE's approach to advocacy. Like other humanitarian organizations, World Vision became more political in the 1990s, addressing explicitly "issues of power, governance, and justice" that shaped humanitarian relief (Barnett 2009, 648). Yet while it may have followed a global trend of being more politically aware, its strategies follow a distinctly American profile. Spending on what World Vision calls "public awareness and education" accounted for an average 0.9% of all expenditures from 2004 to 2009.[111] Not only is advocacy a low priority, but World Vision also employs insider lobbying tactics and a cooperative tone when it engages in policy work. In 1997, the director of policy explained that World Vision maintained "a tenor of constructive criticism... while it has major criticisms of donor policies it has in the past chosen not to engage in that which some NGOs term 'campaigning'" (Commins 1997, 152). Ten years later, the same approach was evident in World Vision's 2006 annual review, which argued: "Policy influence is not a dramatic field of work. Rather, it is a quiet, determined persistence that operates in meetings, parliaments and committees."[112] This statement offers an even more conservative vision of advocacy than that of CARE USA.

The second U.S. "mini-case," the International Rescue Committee, is the world's largest secular refugee organization. Established in the United States in 1933 and with an office in London since 1997, the IRC's nine hundred employees and its budget of almost $300 million are put to work abroad and at home on refugee protection and resettlement.[113] The IRC shares many practices with CARE and World Vision. First, like CARE, the IRC has a close financial relationship with the U.S. government, which is the single largest donor to the organization. Between 2005 and 2008, the IRC received an average 30% of its income from the U.S. government and another 29% from international organizations and other governments.[114] Much of its private funding comes not from individual donors but from foundations and corporations, including the Gates Foundation, the Mellon Foundation, General Electric, and Johnson & Johnson.

111. World Vision, *Annual Reports* (various years).
112. *World Vision International Annual Review 2006*, 19.
113. International Rescue Committee, *Annual Report 2009*.
114. International Rescue Committee, *IRS Form 990* (various years).

Like CARE and World Vision, the IRC emphasizes its efficiency and professionalism. Reliance upon a few large donors helps keep fundraising costs down and demonstrates efficiency: like the other two American INGOs, the IRC always reports overhead below 10% of total expenses, and advertises its certification by the Better Business Bureau and *Forbes* magazine. The main policy and programming work is done by professionals in New York and Washington. Volunteers do have a larger place at the IRC than at CARE, as they play an important role in running the organization's regional resettlement offices within the United States. Still, according to David Rieff (2002), the IRC, like other American relief groups, has a business-oriented culture, sustained in part by leaders like former IRC president Reynold Levy who come from the corporate world.[115]

Advocacy at the IRC follows the American pattern. Like other humanitarian INGOs, the IRC became increasingly aware in the 1990s of how political forces shaped humanitarian assistance and it has responded by using a human rights framework to respond to humanitarian crises.[116] The IRC claims to be more involved in advocacy than CARE or World Vision, and its leadership and board are politically well connected. The IRC's prioritization of advocacy is difficult to measure, as it does not report on advocacy or public education in its annual reports. According to tax forms, lobbying expenditures are low—an average 0.1% of total spending between 2003 and 2005.[117] The specific examples of its advocacy work that the organization offers include testifying before Congress, organizing high-level conferences, and working on resolutions at the UN Security Council—typical insider lobbying strategies far from the protest politics of MSF or the global campaigns of Oxfam.[118] Finally, though the IRC may have become more protective of its independence from the U.S. government recently, it has long been criticized as overly supportive of American foreign policy interests.

---

115. Levy was a former AT&T executive (Rieff 2002, 228). The current president, George Rupp, comes from academia but had lengthy management experience as the former president of both Columbia and Rice Universities.

116. Gerald Martone, "The Compartmentalization of Humanitarian Action," *Humanitarian Exchange Magazine* 21 (July 2002): 36–38.

117. International Rescue Committee, *IRS Form 990* (various years).

118. IRC, *Annual Report 2008* (New York), 24–25. The Washington office meets with the executive branch and Congress "to raise issues of concern and advocate for change in U.S. government policies" while working with other NGOs. "Campaigns" consist of sending form emails to Congressmen. www.theirc.org (accessed March 7, 2010).

These short profiles do not do justice to either World Vision or the IRC, but they do offer some insight into the power of national origin in shaping the practices of humanitarian INGOs. CARE's practices are not idiosyncratic but part of a broader pattern for American humanitarian organizations. Clearly, there are other dimensions of an INGO's history and identity beyond national origin that may have powerful effects, particularly religion as in the case of World Vision. Still, while World Vision's Christian identity may have helped create different resource streams and a different commitment to internationalization, World Vision US is, like CARE, a professionalized organization with a limited and cooperative approach to advocacy. The IRC is an easier case for the argument that national origin matters, given the limited internationalization of the group's structure, and the similarities between CARE and the IRC are striking.

Other British INGOs

If the American humanitarian INGOs share important practices among themselves, is the same true of British relief groups? Yes, based on a comparison between Oxfam and two other British INGOs, Save the Children UK (SC-UK) and Christian Aid. These three organizations differ in age, religious affiliation, and in the nature of their overseas networks, but all share common a British heritage. As a result, all three rely heavily on private citizens for both financial support and volunteer efforts. All three also have excellent access to British policymakers but maintain their political independence. Finally, Oxfam, Save the Children UK, and Christian Aid place great emphasis on campaigning and advocacy and are willing to use blunt language in confronting their official counterparts.

Save the Children UK is the second largest relief INGO in Britain and is several decades older than Oxfam (having been established in 1919). Like Oxfam, Save the Children has many international sections that have operated independently for most of the twentieth century, with the largest offices in Britain and the United States.[119] In 1996, the International Save

---

119. In 2006, Save the Children US and UK together accounted for 65.1% of the income of the international alliance. *Opening Doors: International Save the Children Alliance Annual Report 2006* (London: SC Secretariat, 2006), 25.

the Children Alliance agreed to cooperate on common goals and strategies, while still operating as autonomous organizations, yet "prejudices and national values implicit in old structures and behavioral patterns" still remain (Gnaerig and MacCormack 1999, 145). Today, the international alliance is in the midst of another restructuring process, this time trying to create a more robust global structure that will coordinate programs in the field.[120]

Save the Children UK and Oxfam GB have similar fundraising strategies and spending patterns. SC-UK receives the largest share of its income from private donors in Britain, whose direct donations and spending at the organization's charity shops accounted for 57% of its income from 2005 to 2008.[121] Save the Children UK has one of the highly sought-after partnership agreements with DFID, but support from the British government accounted for only an average 10% of SC-UK's income from 2005 to 2008, while support from international organizations accounted for another 23%. Like Oxfam GB, SC-UK is a member of the Disasters Emergency Committee, the collective fundraising group that raises and distributes private donations.

The organization is professionalized but also embraces volunteers. The founder of the organization, Eglantyne Jebb, insisted that the new charity "must have some clear conception of its job, and seek to compass them with the same care, the same intelligence as is to be found in the best enterprises."[122] Since the mid-1990s, SC-UK has been working to develop more rigorous standards for monitoring and evaluation across all levels of the organization (Lindenberg and Bryant 2001, 227, 231). Still, like Oxfam, the organization uses volunteers extensively—in 2006, over ten thousand of them worked in its campaigns, charity shops, and fundraising offices.

Save the Children UK benefits from the same social networks and friendly home government as Oxfam, and like Oxfam it maintains its

---

120. Personal interview, Charlie MacCormack, October 29, 2010.

121. Save the Children UK, *Annual Reports and Accounts* (various years). I have adjusted the reported figures to be consistent with those for the other INGOs under examination here; thus private income includes both donations and retail sales and excludes private donations gathered by other Save the Children offices. The 2009 data are not included because the organization changed its fiscal year calendar, making comparisons difficult.

122. "Save the Children's History," http://www.savethechildren.net/alliance/about_us/1928_jebbdies.html (accessed December 7, 2010).

political independence and is deeply committed to advocacy. It is a member of the British Overseas Aid Group, the elite group of NGOs that meets with the prime minister, and Princess Anne has served as its president since 1970. The organization invests a great deal in advocacy, though its approach is perhaps slightly less confrontational than that of Oxfam. Like Oxfam, which spends 6%–8% of its budget on campaigning and education, SC-UK spent an average 5.5% of its budget on "information, campaigning, and awareness" from 2005 to 2008. Benthall (1993, 68) describes a wide range of campaigning activity by SC-UK, but suggests that its campaign culture is "more pragmatic, less politically engaged" than that of Oxfam. Within the International Save the Children alliance, SC-UK invests much more in advocacy than the American branch (Lindenberg and Bryant 2001, 189).

Another major British humanitarian INGO is Christian Aid, a Protestant group that was established in 1945 and maintains close ties with the churches. A primarily grant-making agency, Christian Aid does not have the operational capacity of Oxfam, and it is much smaller than either Oxfam or Save the Children. Like Oxfam, Christian Aid spends a large portion of its programming budget on emergencies (50% in 2006) and also receives only a minor share of income (17%) from governmental authorities.[123] Like Oxfam and Save the Children, Christian Aid is a member of the Disasters Emergency Committee and the British Overseas Aid Group, and it also uses volunteers extensively. Not only does it have about 450 volunteers in its offices in Britain, but Christian Aid has received an intra-industry accreditation that recognizes effective training and support for volunteers by nonprofits.[124]

Advocacy is central to Christian Aid's work. It spent more than twice as much as Oxfam as a percentage of total spending on education and campaigning in 2006. In the early 1990s, then-director Michael Taylor considered general campaigning for fundamental political change to be at least as important as anything else that Christian Aid did (Benthall 1993, 70). As

---

123. *The Face of Courage: Christian Aid's Annual Review 2005/06.* The report does not distinguish among the sources of government grants (UK versus others). The remaining income came from a variety of public appeals, including Christian Aid Week (16%), emergency appeals (28.7%), and donations (34.7%).

124. "Christian Aid Awarded Investing in Volunteers Standard," *Christian Today,* May 29, 2009.

one staffer said, "I know some of the smaller organizations might laugh to hear this, but Christian Aid sees itself as quite radical, pushing government to take an explicit pro-poor position. We also feel that our role vis-à-vis the government is to give a voice to poor countries here in the UK....Christian Aid *is* capable of taking a hard line against the government, perhaps because it is a Church-based organization."[125] This emphasis on "giving voice" drives Christian Aid to employ both insider lobbying and broad-based public advocacy in its advocacy work. These tactics are effective in Britain, but perhaps not elsewhere. One case study of a Christian Aid campaign found this multipronged strategy most effective when targeted at the British government and public (Nelson 2000, 483). In other words, Christian Aid has adopted an advocacy strategy that is effectively tailored to a certain set of political opportunities, and that strategy encounters difficulty in other settings.

Despite the development of a global humanitarian sector, the strategies of British humanitarian INGOs have remained fairly stable. The mix of professionalism and voluntarism, the reliance on small and frequent private donations, and the embrace of both cooperation and confrontation with political authorities distinguish the practices of Oxfam, Save the Children UK, and Christian Aid from their American counterparts. The very public profiles of these humanitarian INGOs build upon features of the British environment: the popularity of international causes, a tradition of volunteerism, many postcolonial research institutions, and a close network of links to policymakers and other activists. As with the American INGOs, however, much of the approach of Oxfam and its peers could be described as pragmatic, in contrast to the very principled approach to humanitarian work found not only at MSF but also at the other French INGOs to which we now turn.

Other French INGOs

As with the American and British humanitarian groups, there is a national pattern among French humanitarian INGOs. Recall that MSF France brings a principled, risk-accepting, and confrontational ethos to its

---

125. Personal interview, October 24, 2006.

humanitarian work. MSF is singular in many ways, but perhaps more importantly, the French INGO sector as a whole is smaller, with a few large organizations and many smaller INGOs. Thus, the French INGO sector may be somewhat less institutionalized than its American or British counterparts, and the idiosyncrasies of a single organization may stand out more starkly. Still, a brief comparison of MSF to two other French INGOs, Action contre la Faim (ACF) and the Comité catholique contre la faim et pour le développement (CCFD), reveals some important shared practices. Like MSF, these organizations protect their independence, adopt protest strategies, and employ professionals who prefer to think of themselves as part of a social movement.

Action contre la Faim, or "Action Against Hunger," was formed in 1979 and today is the fourth largest INGO in France. It has been involved in both relief and development over its history, but since the 1990s its emergency programming has increased.[126] ACF opened offices abroad in the 1990s in the United States, Spain, and Britain, first as fundraising arms and later as operational centers.[127] ACF differs from MSF in terms of fundraising strategies, receiving substantial support from governments and international institutions. Over the past decade, international organizations have provided 50–60% of ACF France's income.[128] In addition, the French government has provided anywhere from 3% to 9% of income, and one government ministry has provided ACF with a blanket subsidy every year since 1999.[129] Still, despite making different choices about where to go for funds, ACF and MSF both receive limited monies from their home government. ACF France has recently expanded its private donor base, and was awarded status as a public utility association in 1994. This has enabled further private fundraising, despite a scandal in 2002 that arose from allegations by former ACF president Sylvie Brunel that ACF staff led "freewheeling lifestyles" (Cumming 2009, 163).

Still, ACF and MSF share strategies in terms of professionalization and management. Philippe Ryfman (2006, 23) describes ACF France as

---

126. Table Ronde, "Logique d'urgence et perennité," *Revue humanitaire* 14 (Spring 2004): 11.

127. Siméant 2005, esp. 859, 865. Action Against Hunger USA was initially a fundraising office called Friends of ACF and did not begin its own programs until 1992. ACF Spain and ACF UK were established in 1995. ACF opened an office in Montreal in 2005.

128. Action Contre La Faim, *Rapport Financier 2006;* Commission Coopération Développement 2003, 2005.

129. Commission Coopération Développement 2003, 2005; Cumming 2009, 57.

part of the youngest generation of French relief and development INGOs, one that embraces professionalism. ACF has created professional, stream-lined management structures, but this has not meant closing the door to volunteers, which would involve "the risk of becoming corporate—you cut your links with students, with the local community."[130] One staffer described the difficult balance of running an organization and meeting public expectations:

> We *are* professionalized. I hope you would hear the same thing at MDM [Médecins du Monde] or MSF. In France, it is very difficult to make people understand this! People have…an image of humanitarian actors. There is some kind of mythology…that we go into the field with a bag of rice slung over our shoulders and put it down in the villages and la! that's it!…We need to recruit professionals for finance, for marketing, for communi-cations, etc., because in the field, we work in countries where we *cannot* improvise.…Sometimes people get angry because we have lots of sala-ried workers, but then they want us to publish all these reports and be so transparent—they want it both ways![131]

Struggling to balance professional responsibilities with social expecta-tions in France, ACF does not offer salaries competitive with its Brit-ish or American counterparts.[132] It does employ a significant number of volunteers—about 20 at headquarters and 293 in the field in 2006, com-pared with 139 salaried staff in headquarters.[133]

As at MSF, advocacy is an important task for ACF staffers, who think that "this is our job—to speak out about it [crises]…this is why we were created."[134] Though ACF has at times described itself as an apolitical orga-nization, it argues that only broad political engagement allows humanitar-ians to assert needs-based values and ensure that governments create space for humanitarians.[135] ACF is also careful to defend its independence from

130. Personal interview, Action Against Hunger UK, November 6, 2006.

131. Personal interview, ACF France staffer, March 2, 2007.

132. "L'interview: Benoit Mirabel." Communication Sans Frontières, February 2006 [avail-able online, accessed July 18, 2007, www.communicationsansfrontieres.net]. See also Cumming 2009, 102–3.

133. Action contre la Faim, *Rapport activité 2006*, 16, 43.

134. Interview, ACF France staffer, March 2, 2007.

135. James Phelan (now communications officer for ACF-USA), "Advocacy as Humanitar-ian Politics" (M.A. thesis, Humboldt State University, December 2006): 18–19, 178.

the French government. It does receive a small amount of money from the French government, but it is wary of cooperating with French authorities in the field.

A seemingly different approach to relief and development can be found at CCFD, a confederation of twenty-eight church groups formed in 1961 as part of an earlier generation of French NGOs that focused on development activities as a means of expressing international solidarity (Sorgenfrei 2004). The two main CCFD priorities are development projects in the global South and public education at home in France. One of the ten largest INGOs in France, CCFD has a budget of around €35 million, with over 90% of its resources coming from private donations (much like MSF). The CCFD is a grant-making organization and thus does not send volunteers abroad on missions but rather sends funds to partners in the South. In 1993, the CCFD was named a "grande cause nationale" by the prime minister, but despite the media exposure offered by this opportunity, the organization is less prominent than its emergency-oriented counterparts.

Although older and more development-oriented than MSF and ACF, CCFD shares the openness of these groups to volunteers and emphasizes confrontational advocacy. Fifteen thousand nationwide volunteers occupy a prominent place in the organization's work in France and work alongside a paid staff of 170.[136] In addition, public education and activism are organizational priorities, and CCFD has been a part of prominent initiatives such as the Jubilee 2000 debt relief campaign. Alone and through several umbrella organizations, CCFD works frequently to target and engage political leaders.[137] Still, its approach to advocacy involves making claims upon the French state to take action, an orientation that resembles that of MSF.[138]

While MSF may be unusual among both global INGOs and French nongovernmental organizations in general, it still shares many features with other French INGOs. MSF, ACF, and CCFD are all large by French

136. "Qui sommes-nous?" www.ccfd.asso.fr (accessed July 23, 2007).

137. Embassy of France to the United States, "Nongovernmental Cooperation," *Newsletter* 15 (May 2007).

138. For examples, see Sèbastian Fourmy and Jean Merckaert, "Fiasco pour la Banque Mondiale," *Le Monde,* June 27, 2007; Antoine Dulin and Jean Merckaert, "Biens mal acquis: À qui profite le crime?" *CCFD—Terre Solidaire* (June 2009): 13.

standards but much smaller than their Anglo-Saxon counterparts, as financial resources are scarce in France for INGOs. In this environment, the turn of MSF and ACF toward international organizations, particularly the EU, can be explained by this lack of domestic support. Though ACF and MSF may be the most professionalized humanitarian INGOs in France, the professionalization process has been met by resistance from both the French public and by INGO staffers themselves who value the voluntarist spirit of these international relief workers. In their advocacy work and government relations, these French INGOs rarely work with the French government and embrace protest strategies. Finally, working in solidarity with victims internationally and domestically is a priority for these principled French humanitarians.

The core practices of CARE, Oxfam, and MSF, three of the most transnationally active INGOs, have remained fairly stable in the face of globalization. In fundraising, professionalization, advocacy, and government relations, different INGO practices can be traced to institutions, resources, and norms in each INGO's home environment. These differences are summarized in table 3.

Of course, in tracing similarities among both countries and organizations, the above cases may underplay dynamism both within particular organizations and within the INGO sector. While the development of a global humanitarian sector has not resulted in radical change at any of these INGOs, there have been some important developments both within countries and at particular INGOs. For example, the French government has turned its attention to the issue of government-NGO cooperation in the past five years, and while the reality of government funding may not fully match the rhetoric of engagement with civil society, the political climate in France may become more favorable for INGOs. Within a particular organization, CARE president Peter Bell worked hard to boost the campaigning and advocacy work of CARE, and while it remains limited in comparative perspective, it is a noteworthy shift in the organization's trajectory.

Still, several decades of data on each INGO reveal that change comes slowly to these organizations, and is ultimately unlikely to lead to large-scale convergence upon a single global model of relief and development work. The global humanitarian sector has introduced some important

TABLE 3. Comparing three humanitarian INGOs

	CARE USA	OXFAM GB	MSF France
Size	$701m budget (2009) 470 staff in headquarters (2006)	$390m budget (2009) 1,735 staff in headquarters (2006)	$244 million budget (2009) 252 staff in headquarters (2006)
Internationalization	CARE USA = 77% of CI spending (2009) 3 operational sections Lead member model	Oxfam GB = 26% of OI spending (2005) 13 operational sections No program coordination	MSF France = 22% of MSF-I spending (2005) 5 operational sections No program coordination
Program Type	27% emergencies Multisector	44% emergencies Multisector	Almost all emergencies Medical/health sector
Fundraising: *Sources of Support*	U.S. govt 51% Other govt/intl org 15% U.S. private 17% Other CAREs 17% (1997–2009 average)	UK govt 11% Other govt/intl org 21% UK private 63% Other Oxfams 5% (1996–2009 average)	French govt 0.1% Other govt/intl org 6.5% Fr private 36% Other MSFs 38% Other revenue 16% (2001–9 average)
Professionalization	Average salary of top five executives $230,000 Led by largely corporate board No volunteers at headquarters No volunteers in field	Average salary of top five executives $127,000 Led by academic/government trustees 10% of headquarters staff is volunteer No volunteers in field but many at Oxfam shops	Average salary of top five executives $62,000 Led by membership council 37% of headquarters staff is volunteer 450 volunteers in field
Advocacy	1% budget (2008) Insider lobbying	7% budget (2008) Lobbying, campaigns, public education	2% budget (2008) Campaigns, witnessing
Research	Project based Focus on output	Sector-wide Focus on outcomes, impact	Project/country based Focus on output, outcomes
Relations with Government	Engaged Collaborative	Engaged Independent	Disengaged Independent

concerns, including the need to develop a more international organizational structure and an awareness of how political factors shape the delivery of assistance. Yet CARE, Oxfam, and MSF derive resources and legitimacy from their home countries, and they will continue to pay careful attention to powerful and specific incentives and constraints in their domestic environments rather than respond to vague trends and pressures at the global level.

Continued divergence in organizational practice may be a key impediment to realizing the kind of interagency coordination that humanitarians aspire to but rarely achieve (Minear 2002). For many analysts, the disjointed delivery of aid stands in the way of achieving the ultimate goal of alleviating suffering: Hoffman and Weiss (2006, 136) write that "the notion that somehow the dynamism and decentralization of the humanitarian family outweigh the disadvantages of centralization and integration has been open to question for some time." Do humanitarians fail to collaborate because they fail to understand the implications for the provision of relief? Efforts like the Sphere Project demonstrate that NGOs believe that better coordination should lead to more effective aid delivery.

Still, because humanitarian INGOs actually do very different things and see themselves in very different ways, robust collaboration may be elusive for reasons other than interagency competition (Cooley and Ron 2002). For example, there is a heated debate over the increasing rejection of humanitarianism's apolitical roots—roots protected by MSF—in favor of humanitarian intervention and postconflict nation-building—policy positions often touted by Oxfam (Rieff 2002). These political differences may make humanitarian agencies less willing to collaborate with each other. Meanwhile, there is substantial controversy surrounding the professionalization and standardization of what were previously understood as voluntary undertakings and over the embrace of corporate practices and partners in a values-driven sector. The nationally derived varieties of activism may help explain why the global humanitarian "community" does not act very communally.

This chapter has offered a very detailed examination of four organizational practices of humanitarian INGOs. While these dimensions may seem rather technical, these are not merely "standard operating procedures." They reflect fundamental choices about what it means to be a humanitarian and to engage in global relief and development. These day-to-day practices directly affect the big questions that humanitarian INGOs face: Where should we intervene? What types of programs should we run? Should we participate in a transnational campaign, and if so, what strategies should we adopt? The answers to these questions determine whether campaigns succeed and whether relief operations work. Some scholars have already acknowledged that a meaningful divide exists between INGOs from the developed North and the less-developed South, but the cases here show that there is not just a North/South divide, but a North/North divide as well. And these national differences also manifest themselves in a different sector—that of human rights.

3

HUMAN RIGHTS INGOs

The concept of human rights is an explicitly universalist one, and human rights activists seek to transcend cultural and political boundaries to protect the rights of all humanity. In practice, of course, each human rights INGO can only address a bounded set of issues given limited time and resources. How can we explain the process by which human rights INGOs select arsenals of strategies and structures? One critique emanating from the global South is that the leading human rights INGOs only address those human rights claims related to classic Western liberal values. Here I explore how the national origin of human rights INGO acts as a more specific source of constraint and opportunity. Unlike the majority of humanitarian relief organizations, several leading human rights INGOs initially began as transnational organizations. Still, at the world's largest human rights INGOs, national origin continues to exert meaningful pressure on INGO strategies and structures.

Here, too, I focus on three major and six minor case studies as a way to gain a comparative, organizational perspective on human rights activism.

The major organizations are the American group Human Rights Watch (HRW); Amnesty International (AI), founded in Britain; and the Fédération Internationale des ligues des Droits de l'Homme (FIDH), headquartered in Paris. It is important to note that the international human rights sector is different in at least four ways from that of humanitarian relief. First, the sector is dominated globally by Amnesty International, whose combined international income is almost eight times larger than that of the next largest INGO, Human Rights Watch. This fact alone would make comparisons among organizations difficult, but the analysis is further complicated by Amnesty's many idiosyncratic features, including its wide membership base, powerful international secretariat, and adherence to a fairly limited set of issues. A second feature of the human rights community is that human rights INGOs are fewer in number and smaller in size than in the humanitarian sector. This makes generalizations about any particular country's human rights sector more challenging. Third, many human rights NGOs worldwide have been created and sustained by contributions from American grant-making foundations (Carmichael 2001, 248; Korey 2007; Osviovitch 1998). Unlike in the humanitarian sector, where organizations depend on resources from their home countries, most of the nine INGOs profiled below received substantial funding from a few American foundations, including Ford, MacArthur, and the Open Society Institute; this subjects the INGOs to a different set of pressures than those that emanate from the individual and official donors in their home countries. Finally, because of the nature of their work, human rights INGOs are in general much more involved in advocacy and political action than their humanitarian counterparts. This complicates comparison across the two sectors and makes some strategic choices more sensitive for human rights groups. For example, there is a division among human rights INGOs over whether it is appropriate to accept government funds. One group of INGOs, including most American groups and Amnesty, sees government funding as a threat to independence and impartiality. In Western Europe, by contrast, human rights INGOs believe that impartial policy work can occur with the financial support of governments. The fact that human rights organizations spend most of their time pushing for policy change creates a different dynamic than in the relief sector.

Despite these differences, we can see some common effects of national origin across both sectors. Like its American humanitarian counterpart

CARE, Human Rights Watch has a professional organizational structure that serves the values of efficiency, and it largely abstains from grassroots campaigning and focuses its advocacy work on insider lobbying. We can also observe similarities between Amnesty International and its British peer Oxfam. The organizations emphasize both voluntarism and efficiency: while Amnesty and Oxfam each employ sizable cadres of capable professionals, they also create ample space for volunteers, engaging grassroots activists and community members. With these broad bases of support, Oxfam and Amnesty are better positioned than their American counterparts to employ insider and outsider advocacy strategies.[1] Finally, the French INGOs FIDH and MSF prioritize voluntarism and solidarity over efficiency, expressed in their decentralized organizational structures and in the fact that both organizations realize these principles through substantive work at home in France as well as abroad.

National origin shapes the strategies and structures of human rights INGOs, though perhaps in a less pronounced fashion than in the humanitarian sector. The more limited role of national origin is not a result of the progressive evolution of a global human rights community, as some might claim, but rather due to a few unique features of this relatively small sector. In fact, there is reason to believe that nationality may become more, not less, important in the future. For example, at Amnesty, the different national chapters like Amnesty UK and Amnesty USA have been given more leeway to work on issues in their own countries and pressure their home governments for policy change. This decentralization should actually create greater diversity among Amnesty's many national sections.

In this chapter, I first explore the history of the international human rights community in order to understand those pressures that human rights INGOs might face at the global level. Next, I briefly describe the history and structure of HRW, Amnesty, and FIDH. The heart of the discussion is an analysis of four practices of human rights INGOs—fundraising,

---

1. The phrase "better positioned" is crucial here, as AI makes very careful choices about its engagement in policy work. Concerns about impartiality have historically dominated the organization, but the national chapters of AI have been given greater leeway in choosing campaigns and lobbying their home governments. As explained below, this has created substantive differences among Amnesty's chapters in Britain, the United States, and France.

professionalization, and advocacy and research as with humanitarian relief INGOs, and issue selection. The "mini-cases" are Human Rights First and Global Rights from the United States, Interights and Article 19 from Britain, and two French groups, Reporters sans frontières and ATD [Aide à toute détresse] Quart-Monde.

Human Rights as an International Concern

While the concept of human rights has ancient roots, the advent of human rights as a global concern is decidedly a twentieth-century phenomenon. The idea of human rights is based on the assumption that "all human beings are born free and equal" and that everyone is entitled to enjoy certain rights and freedoms.[2] Yet for much of the history of the modern state system, any state's treatment of individuals was understood as a domestic matter to be addressed by each sovereign state. Human rights stands as a challenge to state sovereignty, and the growing global human rights community has worked for half a century to ensure basic and equal standards of rights protection for individuals around the globe.

As in the issue area of humanitarianism, a set of international laws, formal organizations, and universal norms has helped shaped the modern global human rights community. The development of international human rights law happened in three waves. The first important international legal texts were signed in the wake of World War II and reflected the progressive hopes of the postwar West. The 1945 charter of the United Nations lists the promotion and encouragement of respect for human rights as one of its four main purposes, and Article 68 required the establishment of a UN Commission on Human Rights. Three years later, the UN General Assembly adopted the Universal Declaration of Human Rights, and although the declaration was not binding on member states, it offered an important enumeration of those rights that should be considered universal, including rights to private property, protections against slavery and torture, and rights to education and social security. These developments at the UN and elsewhere laid the international institutional

---

2. Universal Declaration of Human Rights (1948), Articles 1 and 2.

foundation for human rights protection, but it was the human rights treaties of the 1970s, particularly the two International Covenants that entered
into force in 1976, that expressed a new interest in human rights and in
enforcing them as global standards of state behavior. Other more narrow
treaties addressed torture, racial discrimination, women's rights, and children's rights, and each has a mechanism for monitoring compliance. The
last wave in the development of international human rights law came at
the turn of the century. In 2002, a decades-long effort to establish an international criminal court came to fruition with the ratification of the Rome
Statute, and the Human Rights Commission was replaced by a new, pur-
portedly stronger UN Human Rights Council in 2006.

The growth of international human rights law reflected the efforts of a
growing number of private human rights organizations, and later of state
agencies, dedicated to human rights protection. According to William
Korey (1998, 2), "it was the NGOs who would take on the challenge of
transforming the [Universal] Declaration from a standard into a reality."
In 1953, there were three dozen human rights INGOs; this number had
more than doubled by the 1980s and then doubled again over the course
of the next decade (Keck and Sikkink 1998, 11). Amnesty International,
founded in the early 1960s, was a leader; the late 1970s saw another wave
of human rights INGOs established, including the Watch Committees
(later Human Rights Watch), the Lawyers Committee for Human Rights,
and the International Human Rights Law Group. Samuel Moyn (2010) argues
that these organizations were embodiments of a small group of activists whose human rights ideology became increasingly prominent in the 1970s
as other Cold War "-isms" lost credibility. As the cause of human rights
gained global attention, states also created formal structures for monitoring and promoting these rights. France was an early mover in establishing
a national human rights commission in 1947, but national human rights
institutions remained largely confined to Western Europe until the 1980s,
when they began to spread around the globe (Mertus 2009). States also established structures to incorporate human rights concerns into foreign policymaking; an early and important example was the creation of a human
rights bureau at the U.S. State Department under Jimmy Carter (Moyn
2010; Donnelly 2007, esp. chap. 1). All together, both private human rights
groups and expanding state structures provided the organizational scaf-
folding upon which global human rights norms were built.

While the content of universal human rights is supposedly clear, some rights enjoy greater global consensus than others. Going back several centuries, Jack Donnelly (1999, 82) argues that the concept of human rights has gradually expanded the recognized subjects of human rights; "gender, race, property and religion have been formally eliminated as legitimate grounds for denying the enjoyment of natural or human rights." More recently, analysts have somewhat uncomfortably divided human rights into "first generation" (civil and political) rights and "second generation" (economic, social, and cultural [ESC]) rights. This division reflected in part the Western origins of the human rights concept—civil and political rights arose from Enlightenment ideals of natural liberty, while ESC rights involved positive obligations placed on the state, a more contentious issue in the West. This focus on first-generation rights has become a source of discontent for human rights activists in the developing world, who argue that powerful human rights groups are "(at best) adopting an inadequate approach to human rights advocacy and (at worst)...blocking the full potential of the human rights framework to promote the rights of peoples hardest hit by economic globalization" (Nelson and Dorsey 2008, 52). As the discussion below reveals, this critique has prompted some attention to ESC rights, but within the organizations and elites that populate the global human rights community, the emphasis on protecting individuals *from* the state (rather than imposing positive obligations *on* the state) remains strong.

As Donnelly (1999, 84) points out, "the particular list of rights that we take as authoritative today reflects a contingent response to historically specific conditions." It is the confluence of the above-described developments in international law, formal organization, and global norms that has today created a particular global human rights community. The human rights sector is smaller and younger than the humanitarian sector, and its origins are more clearly traced to the international realm. According to James Ron and his colleagues (2005, 559), "it is at the level of global rhetoric, standards, and symbolism...that human rights have registered their clearest achievements." While humanitarians may vary in the way they interpret the principle of neutrality, for example, human rights activists generally agree on the meaning of their fundamental principles and speak in very similar terms about their work. In addition, following in the footsteps of the humanitarian community, the past decade has seen growing professionalization and standardization among those working for human rights in the field (O'Flaherty and Ulrich 2010). Still, perhaps because of its small size, the global human rights community is less structured than the humanitarian one. There is no global human rights NGO code of conduct, and other structures for collaboration are weak; coalitions arise in ad hoc fashion around particular issues.

The human rights community may be more internationalized and smaller that its humanitarian counterpart, but for that very reason a deep understanding of the leading human rights INGOs is necessary. As I will show, human rights organizations may use similar rhetoric, but they look quite different in terms of actual practices. These differences reflect the different home environments in which each INGO was created and in which it continues to be based. To begin with, a brief comparative history of the leading human rights INGOs outlines the ways in which they have responded to the global human rights environment described above.

The Origins and Structure of Three Human Rights INGOs

Human Rights Watch, Amnesty, and FIDH are the largest human rights INGOs in the United States, Britain, and France, and the first two are indisputably leaders within the global human rights community. Each of them has a history that emerges from the general background of the human rights sector within their countries.

Human rights have a complex history in the United States. The fundamental distrust of government present in American society has created an active and autonomous civil society with a tremendous concern for the protection of civil liberties (Lipset 1996). Despite the leadership of the United States in drafting key documents like the 1945 Universal Declaration of Human Rights, however, human rights issues have been understood as solely foreign policy concerns, and they garnered little attention until the 1970s. Michael Ignatieff (2005, 9) characterizes this view as "legal isolationism"—Americans tend to believe that international law may be enriched by the American legal tradition, but that it should not be employed in a domestic setting. Throughout the twentieth century, American human rights INGOs have played a central role in integrating human rights concerns into American foreign policy, and in the last several years, a few of these organizations have begun programs in the United States as well.[3] Despite this formal separation, the leaders of human rights INGOs have strong roots in domestic rights organizations—figures like Roger Baldwin and Aryeh Neier were leaders in the American domestic civil liberties community before they founded, respectively, the International League of Human Rights (1942) and Human Rights Watch (1978) (Neier 2003). Domestic and international rights organizations have also historically shared funders (including the Ford Foundation), strategies (such as litigation), and goals (such as the prioritization of civil liberties over the positive obligations of government) (Tolley 1990–91). Like other American charities, human rights INGOs benefit from a wealth of resources and a supportive legal environment. Today, there are over two hundred organizations in the United States primarily concerned with international human rights–related issues.[4] The largest of these is Human Rights Watch.

The organization was established in 1978 as Helsinki Watch, an American sister organization to citizens' groups in the Soviet bloc concerned with human rights violations by their governments. Other regional "Watch" committees soon followed, and in 1988 the regional organizations united as a single organization, Human Rights Watch. HRW was not the first international human rights organization in the United States, but it grew steadily in size and scope to become the largest American human rights INGO today. Throughout its history, the main focus of the organization's advocacy has been the U.S. government, which HRW sees as a "surrogate villain" supporting human rights violators worldwide (Neier 2003, xxvi).

Structurally, the leadership at HRW has played a central role in determining the practices and priorities of the organization. HRW has a much smaller staff than the larger humanitarian organizations, and thus has historically had less need for formalized structures for management and accountability. In its thirty-plus-year history, the organization has had just two executive directors. The first, Aryeh Neier, was one of the founders

---

3. For an example, see the U.S. Human Rights Network (www.ushrnetwork.org). Alan Jenkins and Larry Cox, "Bringing Human Rights Home," *The Nation,* June 27, 2005, 27.

4. The IRS categorization of international nonprofits is haphazard; refugee and human rights organizations are counted in the same category, while "democracy and civil society" organizations are separate. The number above combines those two categories from 2003.

of the organization. In 1993, the torch was passed to then deputy director Kenneth Roth, a thirty-something lawyer who had been with the organization since 1987. After Neier's departure, a core management group was created to standardize internal policies, reducing somewhat the power of the executive director (Korey 1998, 345–48). Still, "if Ken Roth decides to do something, it gets done," making HRW quite capable of quickly changing tactics or adopting new issues.[5]

Like other INGOs, Human Rights Watch has attempted to reform its structures to reflect a more global identity. The process of internationalization at Human Rights Watch can be traced to a stormy period in the early 1990s when the organization retooled internal management practices and reexamined its scope (Laber 2002, 375). An external review of the organization from November 1993 said that HRW needed to resolve the "key question" of whether it would remain a primarily American institution or pursue the internationalization of its strategies (quoted in Korey 1998, 350). While the organization does now have offices in eight countries worldwide, it remains deeply rooted in the United States. According to staff figures from July 2005, 149 out of 195 staffers (76%) were based in the United States.[6] HRW is also dependent on American funders, mainly wealthy individuals and foundations; funds raised by international offices remain trivial.[7] In recognition of the fundamentally American identity of Human Rights Watch, the billionaire philanthropist George Soros announced in September 2010 a challenge grant of $100 million for the organization. According to Soros, "I cut my teeth in philanthropy with Human Rights Watch, so I know them very well.... It's an American organization. And that has become a drawback, because America has lost the moral high ground for promoting human rights. So I want the organization to become truly international with maybe the American members in a minority."[8] Obviously, this grant to an organization whose budget is around $40 million has enormous transformative potential. For now, though, Human

5. Personal interview, AI-USA staffer, April 19, 2006.
6. "Human Rights Watch: Staff," www.hrw.org, accessed July 29, 2005 (on file with author).
7. HRW London accounted for about of total HRW revenue in 2004 and 2005. *Extract from the Central Register of Charities, Charity No. 1100101* (www.charity-commission.gov.uk, accessed January 21, 2008).
8. "Soros Donates $100 Million to Human Rights Watch," *Morning Edition* (National Public Radio), September 7, 2010.

Rights Watch remains an organization whose concerns are international but whose identity is not.

Moving across the Atlantic, international human rights organizations are prevalent in Britain, including the world's largest, Amnesty International, and perhaps the oldest, Anti-Slavery International, founded in 1839 (Madsen 2004). Many British human rights INGOs focus on narrow issue areas, including slavery, tribal peoples, freedom of expression, torture, and the death penalty.[9] The constellation of human rights INGOs in Britain in some ways reflects Britain's political position between the United States and Europe. Like their European counterparts, British human rights groups may be more accepting of the reach of international law than American ones, rely more on government funds, and create more opportunities for grassroots activism. But like the American groups, many British human rights INGOs are staffed with professional specialists, and focus more on civil and political than on ESC rights. As in the United States, the issue of human rights was traditionally understood as a foreign policy issue, but starting in the early 1990s, the issue gained a popular foothold in British domestic politics. Making generalizations about the British human rights community is difficult, however, because of the dominant presence of Amnesty International.

Amnesty International was founded in 1961 by a British lawyer, Peter Benenson, concerned with individuals imprisoned because of their political beliefs whom he termed "prisoners of conscience." Amnesty's origins have been traced to a British concern over apartheid, activism in the British Left on political imprisonment, and "a strong tradition [in Britain] of trying to rescue people."[10] Benenson later reflected that he could not imagine Amnesty being created in the United States, "because at that time America was...one of the major combatants [in the Cold War], and this was essentially a neutralist initiative" (Rabben 2002, 195–96). Over time, Amnesty slowly expanded its mandate beyond prisoners of conscience to include torture, disappearances, and extrajudicial executions. In the past few years, AI's mandate has been broadened and is now referred to as the mission, but the process of deciding what is and isn't an "Amnesty issue" remains

---

9. The organizations include Survival International, Article 19, Reprieve, and Redress.

10. These are the views, respectively, of Sean MacBride, Tom Buchanan, and David Astor (Buchanan 2002, 579; Rabben 2002, 196).

contentious.[11] AI has always been particularly concerned with maintaining impartiality, a concern that has manifested itself in a policy that prevented its members from working on human rights issues in their home countries. As this rule has been relaxed, national sections, particularly Amnesty USA, have become increasingly powerful.

Amnesty's founders consciously tried to construct an organization that transcended national boundaries. The process of internationalization at Amnesty began almost immediately, as representatives from France, Belgium, and Switzerland were included in early meetings (Hopgood 2006, 68–69). A chapter was set up in the United States in 1965 and in France in 1971; today, Amnesty has national sections in over eighty countries. Thus, like the humanitarian organizations but unlike most other human rights groups, Amnesty has many offices worldwide. But unlike any other INGO profiled in this study, Amnesty has a central office that is actually invested with considerable decision-making power. Ostensibly, AI has a democratic structure driven by its worldwide membership. In practice, most daily decisions are made at the International Secretariat (IS) in London, which houses AI's research department and coordinates international campaigning. The national sections of Amnesty provide funding for the IS while conducting campaigns and recruiting members (Winston 2001, 32). This centralization is reflected in Amnesty's international expenditures: of an estimated global budget of almost $200 million, the IS controls $56.8 million.[12]

The national sections do, however, have financial clout and the power to change the agenda through their membership. It can be difficult to get staffers to share detailed information on the national sections; in at least half a dozen interviews, I was pointedly told that Amnesty members think of themselves as part of a global movement first, and only then as members of a national human rights community. Still, AI sections operate in different domestic environments, and as with humanitarian organizations, this is where the global rubber meets the national road. As the discussions below of specific organizational practices reveal, while Amnesty places enormous value on uniformity across national sections there are also meaningful divides.

---

11. Personal interview, AI-USA staffer, May 19, 2006.

12. The IS budget accounts for approximately 25% of AI's total income. *Combined Financial Accounts, Amnesty International Limited and Amnesty International Charity Limited* (2005–6).

The French human rights sector looks quite different from those in the United States and UK. As perhaps the "fatherland of human rights," France has long had a vibrant domestic and international human rights sector. Many organizations were formed in the early twentieth century and then disbanded during World War II, but human rights activism was revitalized in France by the Algerian crisis, the protests of 1968, and the ratification of the European Convention of Human Rights (Madsen 2004). Unlike in Britain and the United States, many groups that work in the field do so while also furthering many other causes, including fair trade, antiracism, and antiglobalization (Fagnou 2004b). As with other French charities, French human rights INGOs have access to limited resources and face a hostile state generally disinterested in working with civil society. French human rights groups cobble together support from a variety of sources and espouse a voluntarist ethic, working in solidarity with victims of human rights violations.

The Fédération Internationale des ligues des Droits de l'Homme was created in 1922 by the French domestic human rights group, the Ligue des Droits de l'Homme (LDH). The international federation was largely inactive during and after World War II, but found a new life during the 1970s and began sending observer missions abroad in cooperation with the LDH and other French human rights NGOs. Today, the federation includes 141 member organizations worldwide. It operates on a small but growing budget, $6.3 million in 2008.[13]

FIDH has always been a loose confederation that brought together national human rights organizations that exist independently of it. Thus, the FIDH International Secretariat is in some ways a reverse image of the IS at Amnesty: "There is a bottom-up relationship here in the daily functioning of the organization.... In Amnesty, when Amnesty and the International Secretariat decide something, it is very top down—very efficient, I guess. There have a different capacity for mobilization, which is very strong.... But I think it is very top-down there! So [the FIDH structure] is both a strength and a weakness. A strength because we are well-placed to grasp local realities and address them properly, but it is a weakness because sometimes our local NGOs won't want to work."[14] The

---

13. FIDH, *Comptes d'exploitation* (2000–8) (on file with author).
14. Personal interview, FIDH staffer, February 20, 2007.

structure serves practical concerns for local activists, but decision making is firmly in the hands of the national member groups. Since the late 1980s, when the international secretariat gained a capacity independent from the LDH, the focus of the secretariat has been to serve the national chapters generally rather than to focus on the interests of the French section.[15] The FIDH secretariat has little independent power, and local members can block FIDH from participating in transnational campaigns with other NGOs.[16]

As FIDH has become more independent from the LDH, it has tried to increase its international profile. A turning point was its 2001 International Congress in Casablanca, where Senegalese lawyer Sidiki Kaba was elected as the first non-French president and more seats on the board of directors went to international rather than French activists. In 2001, FIDH welcomed its first American affiliate, the Center for Constitutional Rights, and in 2006 it opened an office in New York.[17] Despite having being set up as an international organization, however, FIDH has been largely driven by the French LDH and a concern with the Francophone world.

Human Rights Watch, Amnesty, and FIDH have very different histories and structures, but all have been important participants in the creation of a global understanding of human rights norms. If their values are ostensibly cosmopolitan, shouldn't their practices be similarly uniform? In fact, the story is much more complex. Global forces, including values and funding, intersect with the institutions of each INGO's home country, creating a distinct constellation of practices at each INGO.

Fundraising

As with the humanitarian groups, the relative availability of resources in the domestic environment has an important effect on the size of human rights INGOs and their sources of funding. Thus, the American origins of Human Rights Watch help account for the organization's enormous

---

15. Yves Hardy, *La Chronique d'Amnesty* (February 2000): 24. In 1990, the FIDH international secretariat had only two staff members (Landman and Abraham 2004).

16. Personal interview, FIDH staffer, February 20, 2007.

17. "Notre bureau FIDH à New York a déjà 1 an!" *La Lettre de la FIDH* 84 (December 2006): 15. FIDH had a volunteer representative to the UN until 1999 (Martens 2006, 25).

size—expenditures totaled $44 million in 2009, up from $12 million in 1997. The organization benefits from the generous giving habits and concentration of wealth in the United States. The fundraising efforts of HRW are narrowly targeted at several prominent foundations and a small group of wealthy individuals. As noted above, grant-making foundations were critical sources of initial support and continue to make significant contributions to general management as well as to the INGO's endowment. From 1998 to 2002, HRW received an average 37% of its income from foundations and corporations.[18] Three foundations—Ford, Carnegie, and Macarthur—have been generous and regular supporters.[19] The other pillar of HRW fundraising is reliance on wealthy individuals. From 1998 to 2002, the INGO received an average 54% of its income from individual donors.[20] In each annual report, HRW lists its large donors by name and levels of giving. While exact information on the size of each donation is not available, it is clear that a few large donors, rather than many small ones, fund the organization's work. In 2001, for example, two dozen individuals contributed $100,000 or more each, accounting for at least $2.4 million out of a total $11.8 million raised from individual donors. HRW has long had a strict policy of not seeking funds from any government, a position it also shares with Amnesty and other American human rights groups but not with most of its European counterparts.

Amnesty's fundraising centers around the fact that it is a membership organization. Being an Amnesty member means much more than just writing a check, but Amnesty members and other supporters are the prime source of support. Thus, like HRW, Amnesty relies on private individuals, but it receives many small donations rather than a handful of large ones. In 2005, three-quarters of the combined income of all Amnesty sections came from the over two million members and supporters of the

18. "Financials," *HRW Annual Reports* (various years). HRW's fiscal year ran from April to March during this period, so these years are adjusted (thus the 2002 figure is for HRW's fiscal year 2003).

19. HRW received $8.5 million from these three groups from 1990 to 1996 (Osviovitch 1998, 357). In mid-1999, Ford in particular approved a large grant that included $5 million toward the endowment and $1 million for operating reserves (Carmichael 2001, 254).

20. HRW, "Financials," *Annual Reports* (various years).

organization.[21] Another 14% came from sales, fundraising events, and individual bequests, and the remaining 11% came from foundations, corporations, and a few grants from government agencies (including DFID)
for human rights education. Amnesty, like HRW, largely avoids financing from governments; the education grants received by AI-UK may be
a reflection of both the close government-INGO relationship in Britain
and the fact that this type of program is fairly apolitical. Compared to
HRW, though, Amnesty has been much more wary of accepting funds
from foundations (Welch 2001).

Amnesty's strategy of relying on small donations worked well in a country where the public tends to give often to charitable causes but in small
amounts. Carried abroad, this fundraising strategy has worked well for
other sections but for none so well as for AI-USA, based in a country where
many people give to charities but tend to give in larger amounts than in
Britain (Wright 2001). Much of AI-USA's financial support has come not
from the membership but from less-involved donors, an issue that created
some debate within the international Amnesty confederation (Hopgood
2006, 108–11). If we take a careful look at the income of Amnesty's sections
in the United States, Britain, and France, the size of each section reflects
the availability of resources in that country. AI-USA is the largest section,
AI-UK comes next, and AI-France comes in fourth after the Netherlands;
the respective income of these sections in 2009 was $44 million, $36 million,
and $21 million. Together, these four sections accounted for 51% of the
combined income of all Amnesty offices around the world in 2008.[22]

Compared to Amnesty and Human Rights Watch, FIDH is quite small
but its budget has grown steadily. The limited availability of funds for
charities in France has driven the organization to seek funds from a wide
array of actors. Unlike AI and HRW, FIDH does accept funding from
governments, and the expansion of the organization over the past decade
is in large part due to the receipt of greater government and foundation
grants. FIDH receives substantial funding from the French Ministry of

---

21. Amnesty International Secretariat, *INGO Accountability Charter Annual Compliance Report 2007* (July): 10.

22. Amnesty International, *INGO Accountability Charter Global Compliance Report 2009*
(March 2010).

Foreign Affairs.[23] Meanwhile, FIDH's reliance on private donors has been declining. Less than 20% of FIDH's revenue came from private sources between 2001 and 2006.[24] The organization has set up a number of mechanisms to increase its private donor base and diversify its income, but these have had limited success.[25] FIDH does not report specific grant amounts, but its regular donors include the EU and other government agencies like the Netherlands Ministry of Foreign Affairs. FIDH also gets support from foundations like Ford, Fondation de France, and the Dutch organization Novib, and corporations such as Air France and the retailers Carrefour and FNAC.

Explaining Fundraising Strategies

Fundraising strategies are affected by supply and demand factors. The availability of funding sources limits the range of choices organizations can make, but whether organizations choose to pursue particular supporters is affected by how they understand the "strings attached." Human rights work may be somewhat less flashy than emergency relief work, making private fundraising more challenging for all human rights INGOs. At the same time, these rights groups offer more limited information on their finances than their humanitarian peers, so the figures offered here are less precise than in the previous chapter.

National origin accounts for the differences in size among human rights INGOs based on the availability of funds. In the United States, human rights INGOs enjoy a vast amount of resources as well as a strong tradition of charitable giving. In particular, the concentration of wealth in the United States has allowed American human rights INGOs, including both HRW and AI-USA, to successfully target a small group of wealthy individual

---

23. Neither FIDH nor the Ministère des Affaires étrangeres report specific grant amounts. The partnership between the two began around 2001, and the ministry supports FIDH's Observatory for the Protection of Human Rights Defenders. *Institutional Cooperation in Figures, 2000–2002: France's Action around the World* (Paris: MAE, 2002), 12–13.

24. An average of 18.9%, compared to an average 35.8% from 1996 to 2000. FIDH, *Comptes* (various years); "Profile: FIDH," www.observatoire-humanitaire.org, last updated September 12, 2010.

25. FIDH has been an *association reconnue d'utilité publique* since September 2003. Individuals and businesses accounted for an average of only €15,560 from 2003 to 2005. FIDH also has an "ethical" fund set up with assistance from the post office. *Rapport Général du Commissionaire aux Comptes: FIDH, Associations RUP* (31 December 2005): 16.

donors. In France, NGOs rustle up a range of supporters, none of whom give in large amounts. In Britain, the story is a bit more complex. As the "mini-cases" will show, Amnesty International's fundraising strategies are actually quite different from those of many other British human rights groups. In Britain, foundation support for international charities is weak and fundraising from private donors (who give in small amounts and spontaneously) is costly for small organizations, so many of the smaller human rights groups turn to American foundations and the British government for support. Amnesty is much larger and a membership organization, which makes a different pool of funds available. Today, Amnesty can absorb the costs of private fundraising given its large size, but it relied on small private donations from members even in its early days. Of course, given that funding from American foundations was not prevalent in the 1960s when Amnesty was formed, its reliance on small private donations makes sense. I am not arguing that "being British" somehow made Amnesty become a membership organization or determined that Amnesty should not seek big donors—obviously the ethos of this staunchly apolitical organization played a role in those choices. But attention to national origin does help account for the effectiveness of those choices in raising resources both at different national chapters and for the international organization as a whole. Amnesty's reliance on its private members may have been costly at first but attracted many supporters in the United States and Britain, the two countries that have the highest rates of private charitable giving worldwide.

National origin also helps us understand why, out of all the potential donors, INGOs choose some over others. Like other American charities, human rights INGOs in the United States are concerned that the acceptance of funds from governments, particularly from their home government, will compromise their ability to engage in political activities. Amnesty shares the aversion to government funding, but Amnesty's justification is that it is *apolitical*—a different argument from the position of Human Rights Watch that it needs to be free to critique the United States government. The "all or nothing" approach to government funding is less prominent in either Britain or France, where INGOs reject the idea that accepting government funds compromises their independence, though both British and French INGOs report being careful about funding for sensitive projects. British INGOs benefit from government grants with few restrictions and enjoy opportunities to collaborate with policymakers. In France, some human rights INGOs benefit from small grants from the central government and localities, but French organizations also rely on European governments and the European Union. Ultimately, the more transnational nature of human rights funding—either from the American foundation sector or from international organizations, particularly the EU (Sanchez-Salgado 2001b)—may be a primary factor in explaining the greater convergence in organizational practices, particularly in the professionalization of the human rights sector.

Professionalization

The second important INGO practice to consider is who works for the group and how the work environment is structured. Is the organization fully professionalized with rigorous internal management structures, and what space exists in the organization for volunteers? Human Rights Watch is a highly professionalized and efficient organization, like many other American nonprofits. Notably, the organization was started not by grassroots activists but with a professional staff hired with a $400,000 grant from the Ford Foundation (Laber 2002, 99). Professionalism and efficiency have been encouraged by the funders and board of directors at Human Rights Watch. As a principal donor, the Ford Foundation participated in the 1993 restructuring process and recommended the management study that led to administrative reforms (Korey 1998, 348; Brown 2001, 82)— a typical example of an American foundation pushing for the establishment of more rigorous internal procedures. In terms of management, the board of Human Rights Watch looks quite different from those of Amnesty and FIDH, which are largely staffed by activists and academics. According to former advocacy director Widney Brown (2001, 77–78), HRW's board "has evolved into a more traditional model in which members *bring particular expertise in institution building* to the organization, not the least of which is fundraising" (emphasis added). This has left virtually no space for volunteers and ordinary community members, particularly since the mid-1990s.[26] HRW has little interest in building "large constituencies in

---

26. One former staff member and former intern recalled that "the last time that amateurs were welcomed into the organization" was in 1994. Personal interview, February 14, 2006. See also Korey 1998, 349–50.

the West," according to director Kenneth Roth (2007, 177), who explains that "even a relatively large organization such as Human Rights Watch has finite resources, so devoting more of them to constituency building would mean having fewer resources available for research and advocacy. It is far from clear that the tradeoff would be worthwhile." This stands in stark contrast to the British and French INGOs, where "constituency building" and "advocacy" are thought of as two sides of the same political process coin. Human Rights Watch is clearly not in the business of constructing a popular human rights movement. The outsider amateurs who do participate in HRW's work are drawn from a narrow group of wealthy elites, mainly from California and New York. As described in its annual reports, the organization has an advisory council made up of several hundred "opinion leaders."

This professional orientation carries into the INGO's practices abroad. Consider the description of a 2006 event in London: "Human Rights Watch... was on a recruitment drive among the best and brightest London can offer. Lawyers, writers, financiers, actors, diplomats, and designers were there to hear how they could help.... These days activism can be more subtle than sit-ins, placards and letter-writing, and London's bright young things are as valuable for their CVs and contacts books as for their raw commitment. HRW wants their skills, whether they are designers who can lay out a pamphlet or business executives who can lobby their companies."[27] This narrow focus in HRW's recruitment contrasts sharply with Amnesty's attempts to be "a movement of the masses, for the masses."[28] For HRW, human rights work is a technically demanding task reserved for salaried specialists.

Amnesty International is run by both professionals and volunteers. At the center, the International Secretariat has a large professional staff of over 450 in 2007 and more than 100 volunteers.[29] Even this most transnationalized INGO has a largely Western staff (76% of IS staff come from Western countries, and the majority of the IS staff are British nationals (51.6%).[30] The many volunteers at the IS take on substantive tasks, including research

---

27. "Observations: Human Rights Chic," *New Statesman,* September 11, 2006, 19.

28. Irene Khan, "AI at a Crossroads," *The Wire* [AI newsletter], September 2001.

29. 2007 figures from *Amnesty International Annual Compliance Report 2007* (INGO Accountability Charter); Volunteer figures from "Amnesty International Today" (no date), www.amnesty.org.uk (on file with author).

30. Averages, 1993–2002. Figures from Hopgood 2006, 163.

and campaigning. As described by Stephen Hopgood (2006, 16), the staff
at Amnesty have historically "kept (and passed on) a commitment to the
ethos that was not professional but vocational ('not a job, but a life choice')."
These "keepers of the flame," as Hopgood (2006, 12) refers to them, have
been challenged by a recent reform movement within Amnesty that aims to
professionalize the organization and standardize internal procedures. This
tension between activism and professionalism is not new to Amnesty, and
reflects Amnesty's only partially realized desire to be a social movement
before being an organization.[31] Interestingly, the view of human rights as a
calling is found both among members and among many paid staff. Compared to HRW, the ethos of voluntarism is strong at this organization that
claims to be a movement of "ordinary" people working for human rights.

The national sections of Amnesty share this mix of professionalism and
voluntarism. AI-UK has over 100 volunteers working alongside its 130 staff
members. One staffer from AI-UK explained it this way:

> We absolutely, definitely could not function without volunteers. Not just
> in terms of our workload, which is part of it, but also because they bring
> such a rich culture to our work...there is a culture within the organiza-
> tion to allow people from different areas and walks of life, who may have
> no professional qualifications but have the commitment, to participate. This
> brings diversity and richness to Amnesty.
>
> The thing is, the staff is very white, very middle-class—probably upper
> middle class. But lots of our volunteers come from all over the world and
> from all over Britain.... Volunteers work in almost every department ex-
> cept the directorate. And they do everything from press clippings to having
> high-level internships in the government affairs office.[32]

The openness of AI-UK to ordinary people is visible in its newly built
Human Rights Action Centre, which not only houses AI-UK staff but also
provides a forum for Amnesty members and the general public to learn
more about human rights.[33]

---

31. Personal interview, former AI staffer, November 3, 2006.
32. Personal interview, November 9, 2006.
33. "Campaigning for Impact," *Amnesty* [UK newsletter], May/June 2005, 18. AI-UK has
grown significantly from 3,500 members (1988) to 143,100 (1998), to 270,000 today. "AGM Decisions," *Amnesty* [UK], May/June 1998, 27.

The issue of professionalism has created more turmoil at the American chapter. AI-USA stands out among other American human rights groups because of its large grassroots network of members and supporters. Its leaders believe that grassroots activists, rather than professionals and lobbyists, are who will effect the greatest change in human rights protection.[34] While the organization has a large professional staff, the volunteer ethic remains strong. This has created some internal conflict. Consider the internal crisis triggered by the allegations of AI-USA member and volunteer country specialist Barbara Bocek. Bocek claimed in 2002 that she had been threatened and attacked by Guatemalan thugs while back in the United States.[35] Doubts about the facts of the incident, as well as a larger divide between staff and volunteers, led to a major confrontation at a board meeting. Several members of the board resigned, "citing the need for a professional, reliable staff."[36] In response, the membership passed several resolutions at AI-USA's annual meetings that chided the board for its reaction and praised Bocek.[37] The tensions between professionals and volunteers at AI-USA are substantial, but the American chapter of Amnesty maintains the larger Amnesty interest in involving "ordinary people" in human rights work.

Like at AI-UK and AI-USA, volunteers contribute meaningfully to the work of Amnesty France, but Amnesty France is especially concerned with maintaining *l'identité associative* and avoiding bureaucratization.[38] Reflecting mixed emotions, one AI France staff member described the tension: "In Amnesty volunteers are the most difficult thing to handle! Everyone has to make a point on everything, and it can be difficult to make decisions.... But I am most impressed with the democratic process within Amnesty, both at the national and international levels. They [volunteers] own the organization.... But thus it is hard for staff people—they feel like they are working hard, doing their job, and they have to wait for the approval

34. Jane Savitt Tennen, "Broadening Support for Human Rights," *Philanthropy Journal,* April 26, 2006 (http://www.philanthropyjournal.org/archive/112418).

35. Ian Parker, "Victims and Volunteers," *New Yorker,* January 26, 2004, Academic One-File; "Policy Doubts about Attack Cast Cloud on Rights Group," *New York Times,* May 6, 2002.

36. Personal interview, former AI-USA staffer, February 14, 2006.

37. "A Human Rights Defender, AIUSA Volunteer," Resolution 9 (2003); "Decision Regarding Accountability, Healing, and Restoration of Trust," AGM Resolution G-12 (2004).

38. For examples, Eric Poinsot, "Professionalisme et vigueur militante," and "Turbulences identitaires," both in *La Chronique* [AI-France newsletter], February 2007.

of someone who is only here once a week."[39] At Amnesty France, as at other French NGOs, the balance between professionalism and vibrant activism is a sensitive subject.

Likewise, FIDH is less rationalized than HRW and Amnesty. It has seen a substantial expansion of its professional staff, from only two in 1990 to almost forty in 2010.[40] Still, the ethic remains voluntarist. Like Amnesty and Human Rights Watch, the office has a handful of short-term interns, but research missions abroad are carried out by volunteers.[41] FIDH's growth led its international board to create a set of internal management principles in March 2001, but decision making is still fairly ad hoc. According to an external review of FIDH, recent reforms have created better internal feedback and monitoring, but systematic evaluation processes still do not exist (Landman and Abraham 2004). Salaried staff members, working in a somewhat structured environment, coexist with a focus on local service and activism. The staff-activist tension that is so strong at Amnesty is absent at FIDH. The limited power of the FIDH secretariat is an expression of solidarity with and prioritization of local chapters' needs, many of which are themselves run by volunteers.

Explaining Levels of Professionalization

Human rights INGOs vary significantly in the level of professionalization. The three organizations profiled here could be arranged on a spectrum, with the fully professionalized Human Rights Watch on one end and FIDH somewhere near the other. None of the organizations are fully volunteer run, which is not surprising given that they were chosen for their international size and prominence, which may have been enabled by some measure of professionalization.

As with fundraising, there are logics of both supply and demand that influence the professionalization of an INGO. On the supply side, resource availability affects whether an organization *can* hire a professional staff

---

39. Personal interview, Amnesty France volunteer, March 1, 2007.

40. FIDH, *Comptes* (various years); Landman and Abraham 2004. Both staff and budget have tripled since 1998.

41. "Entretien avec Patrick Baudoin," *La Chronique d'Amnesty* (March 2001): 25. Also, as at other French NGOs, *bénévoles* receive a *ticket restaurant* (to cover the cost of meals) and are reimbursed for transportation costs.

as well the size of that staff (Martens 2006). On the demand side, each INGO's understanding of appropriate charitable work affects whether the INGO *will* hire professionals and systematize internal management procedures. National origin thus affects the ability of INGOs to become professionalized and their interest in doing so. In the United States, generous support from foundations and wealthy individuals allows these organizations to hire a highly professionalized staff. Equally as important, however, foundations actually encourage organizations to adopt structured systems of management staffed by experts. Perhaps as a result, international human rights work is understood in the United States as a technical task reserved for lawyers, country specialists, and public relations staff. These demand-side pressures can be seen at the non-American INGOs discussed below that also receive significant support from American foundations. In this instance, the globalization of grant-making by American foundations has produced convergence among some INGOs in the area of professionalization.

In Europe, however, human rights INGOs are much more committed to two norms—solidarity and voluntarism. The supply of human rights professionals is thus smaller, as human rights work is understood as a calling rather than a job. Amnesty's adoption of individual prisoners of conscience has long created solidarity between activist and victim; professional staff members are asked to join in the determination and sacrifice of the Amnesty "movement."[42] FIDH's commitment to solidarity is present not only in its public statements but also in its loose federative structure where decisions are driven by local activists. To different degrees, both Amnesty and FIDH welcome and rely on volunteers, to both help do daily work and maintain the spirit of voluntary action that underlies the British and French understandings of charity.[43] Of course, the volunteers at FIDH also receive cost-of-living allowances and social welfare protection under French law.

---

42. See Hopgood 2006 for a provocative account of the creation of moral authority at Amnesty.

43. Comparing Amnesty to French INGOs, one scholar makes the following comment about Amnesty's strategies: "all are precise and systematic, improvisation and amateurishness no longer fit. Local autonomy and creativity are not lacking, but they are subject to the strategic direction of the movement and to the approval of its authorities" (Poinsot 2004, 405).

Professionalization of the human rights sector matters for at least two reasons. First, it may have an immediate impact on the success of international advocacy. In her study of human rights representatives at the United Nations, Kerstin Martens (2006) argues that the UN offices of Amnesty and Human Rights Watch recruit staff based on their legal training and sector-specific expertise. Without this capacity, it may be difficult for human rights INGOs to provide information, shame governments, use leverage, or hold rights violators accountable (see Keck and Sikkink 1998; Risse et al. 1999). At the same time, professionalization may undermine the long-term achievement of human rights improvements. Some human rights activists, particularly those from the global South, argue that the creation of a broad human rights culture is necessary for the large-scale improvement in human rights conditions (Dudai 2007). The French human rights group ATD Quart-Monde profiled below argues that only by learning directly from the impoverished and the disenfranchised can outsiders find appropriate solutions and strategies. In other words, distant professionals may offer the wrong solutions or fail to achieve deeper cultural change. This is a difficult question for the human rights community, but whether a human rights INGO is professionalized or volunteer-based affects its relationships with the victims of human rights violations.

Advocacy and Research

Advocacy, and the careful research that underlies that advocacy, is the primary tool of human rights organizations striving for the political and social change necessary for human rights protection. Thus, unlike at humanitarian organizations which are heavily involved in service delivery, there is little variation among human rights organizations in terms of the prioritization of advocacy. But we can observe substantial variation among these INGOs in the types of advocacy strategies they prefer, using the simple but oft-used distinction between insider and outsider strategies. As with the humanitarians, American human rights INGOs most heavily favor insider lobbying, the French prefer outsider protest strategies, and the British use both.

The majority of Human Rights Watch's work in both advocacy and research centers on the strategy of "shaming." This involves both providing information and getting it to key actors as well as calling upon more powerful actors (Keck and Sikkink 1998). Importantly, consistent with legal restrictions in the United States on lobbying by nonprofits, this advocacy work is not concentrated on pushing for specific legislative changes.[44] Instead, HRW excels at producing meticulously researched reports that trace human rights violations while documenting the role of the U.S. government and international actors in those violations. It then uses that information to pressure government actors, as described by director Ken Roth (2007, 172): "The essence of [our] methodology ... is not the ability to mobilize people in the streets, to engage in litigation, to press for broad national plans, or to provide technical assistance. Rather, the core of the methodology is the ability to investigate, expose, and shame. Groups like Human Rights Watch are at our most effective when we can hold governmental (or, in some cases, nongovernmental) conduct up to a disapproving public." HRW maintains a large communications department that disseminates information on abuses to national and international policymakers.[45] To the chagrin of many at Amnesty, Human Rights Watch has long been seen as very media-savvy, and the timing of these reports is meant to coincide with key external events.[46]

The target of this shaming approach is most frequently the U.S. government. While HRW today does more work at intergovernmental organizations than in the past, American policy remains the focus of HRW advocacy work. Aryeh Neier (2003, 169) argues that the "international eminence" of HRW is "unquestionably" due in part to its status as "an organization based in the United States that exercised influence over US policy" (see also Rieff 1999, 38). Neier and others argue that HRW today is more internationalized, but the United States remains the focus of the organization; as one former staffer described the organization's approach to American policymakers, "they know how the system works."[47]

---

44. Between 1997 and 2005, HRW reported spending an average $94,992, or 0.45% of its total budget, on direct lobbying. IRS Form 990s (various years).

45. Welch 2001; Korey 1998. The communications and advocacy offices are roughly equivalent in size. "Staff and Committees," www.hrw.org (accessed August 2, 2005; on file with author).

46. Historically, Amnesty's reports received little attention in the United States, as they were not always timely and lacked the political analysis that policy makers seek (Winston 2001, 37).

47. Personal interview, former HRW staffer, February 14, 2006.

At Amnesty, advocacy and research are roughly divided between the national sections and the International Secretariat. The secretariat is the research hub of the international movement, assembling and releasing the reports that provide the evidentiary basis for the national sections' campaigns. Research and publication account for about half of the total secretariat budget.[48] Set up to be an impartial base, the International Secretariat is not directly involved in most political questions, and national sections often take the lead in pushing for new campaigns.[49]

Fact-finding is central to Amnesty's work, just as at HRW. Yet at Amnesty, as at Oxfam, research is in some ways a valuable end in itself. One staffer at AI-USA explained how this related to the organization's roots and affected AI's work:

> I wouldn't want to overstate it, but I would say yes, this is a British organization. The organization has traditionally been very centralized—all communication is to London, and if I want to find out what's going on in [Country X] I don't call AI-[Country X], I call London and ask about AI-[Country X]. Because of this centralization, therefore, the characteristics and style of the whole organization are influenced by London and that culture has permeated the organization. It's subtle, but it's there.
>
> The way in which this manifests itself for us here in the United States is that the research and recommendations tend to be kind of more academic, whereas we'd like to see timely, quick-hitting reports—even if they're only 10 pages, we see that as more important than waiting six months for a report on torture in Mexico. We in the U.S. tend to think in terms of timeliness and impact, but they think in a way that is unhurried, more thorough, and these are cultural differences.... To me, it sometimes feels like a group of people in universities in London developing long, detailed documents.[50]

---

48. Exact figures are available for three years: 2002 (53%), 2005 (52.79%), and 2006 (51.72%). *Facts and Figures: The World of Amnesty International, January to December 2002,* www.amnesty. org, May 28, 2003; AI Limited and AI Charity Limited, *Combined Statements for the Year Ending March 31, 2007.*

49. See for example the adoption of extrajudicial executions by Amnesty (Clark 2001, 101–13).

50. Personal interview, AI-USA staffer, May 19, 2006. This sentiment was echoed by a former IS staffer: "Would Amnesty be different if the International Secretariat was in the United States? Probably—they would be more obsessive over the media and hitting the headlines." Personal interview, November 9, 2006.

The Americans see the practical value of research, while for the British Amnesty, research itself is a valuable process that reveals truths.[51] This aversion to policy-oriented research may also arise from a strong conviction within many at Amnesty that the organization inhabits an apolitical sphere.[52] Today, Amnesty has moved closer to the "research for advocacy" model, beginning in the early 1990s under the direction of Secretary General Pierre Sane, who prioritized campaigning. Still, for many at the IS, research and documentation is an end in itself, in contrast to the targeted, policy-oriented research of Human Rights Watch.

AI-UK has long used the multilevel, multimethod approach of many of its British counterparts in its campaigns and advocacy work. While AI-UK meets with Foreign Office officials (often accompanied by researchers from the IS), it also uses multiple techniques to mobilize the greater public.[53] A 1994 study of AI-UK advocacy found that, like Oxfam, the section would first approach British government offices (some of whom received AI-UK quite warmly), but if it felt those overtures were unproductive, it would turn to "'rather provocative campaigns' and parliamentary lobbying of an outsider group nature" (Christiansen and Dowding 1994, 23). More recently, one source in Amnesty UK said that he "really didn't understand" the distinction between insider and outsider strategies, as the issue was really how to choose the proper channels to accomplish campaign objectives: "I think that the UK government is a rather easy one in that it is willing to meet with us and talk with us. But we do as much meeting with civil servants, who really decide policy, as we do with the political representatives above them.... In any one week we might be meeting with the foreign secretary to talk about government intervention on a particular issue, and then the next day we might condemn the government policy on the radio. And that condemnation really doesn't affect our access."[54] This is almost the exact sentiment expressed by campaigners at Oxfam GB.

---

51. Amnesty insists on discovering those truths itself (Hopgood 2009, 245).

52. Hopgood 2006, 231; Clark 2001, 12–15. Given this stand, it has stung both the AI secretariat and AI-UK that it has not been fully granted charitable status in the UK. Discussions of British charity law reform suggest that this may change. Personal interview, November 7, 2006.

53. Personal interview, November 3, 2006. The 2004 Amnesty UK national meeting (which involved an anti–domestic violence march through Manchester) is an example of Amnesty's protest politics. "AI Campaigners on the March," *Amnesty* [UK] (May/June 2004):17.

54. Personal interview, November 7, 2006.

In the United States, AI-USA has struggled to find a way to use its large membership base in a politically effective way to differentiate itself from Human Rights Watch. AI-USA stands out among other American human rights groups because of its large grassroots network of members and supporters, and the organization's leaders believe that grassroots activism, rather than professionals and lobbyists, will effect the greatest change in human rights protection.[55] While the membership is a potentially powerful constituency, AI-USA has not always been targeted or effective in its campaigns, a reflection perhaps of the historical emphasis on research over advocacy.[56] The more recent turn toward campaigning at AI-USA has resulted in the development of a more sophisticated lobbying capacity.[57] AI-USA sees the expansion of political capacity and the evolution of the Amnesty agenda in pragmatic, not principled, terms. An expansion of its political actions will not only shape its ultimate effectiveness at achieving its human rights goals, but also help it compete with HRW (Hopgood 2006, 211–12).

The story of advocacy and research at AI-France is quite interesting. Unusually for Amnesty, the national section in France was given substantial research responsibilities as early as 1972, focusing on Francophone Africa. Initially, the French chapter struggled—Amnesty's commitment to being apolitical made little sense in a country where most human rights proponents were also active on the political left—but the group has overcome this problem to achieve some prominence in France.[58] AI-France's members are a fairly homogeneous group who self-identify as members of the political Left but have been wary of linking their human rights work with the antiglobalization movements of many other French human rights INGOs (Duchesne 2003; Poinsot 2004). Perhaps as a result of the relative lack of political opportunities in France for civil society groups,

55. Jane Savitt Tennen, "Broadening Support for Human Rights," *Philanthropy Journal,* April 26, 2006 (http://www.philanthropyjournal.org/archive/112418).

56. Welch 2001, 93–94. Clark suggests that Amnesty is more willing to testify before Congress on human rights conditions than it is to become "mixed up in the partisan calculus of national security." Clark 2001, 132.

57. Personal interview, former AI-USA staffer, April 19, 2006. Advocacy has gone from letter writing to testifying before Congress and direct lobbying. Personal interview, September 11, 2006. See also "The Lobby League: Human Rights," *The Hill,* November 2, 2005.

58. "La section française a vingt ans!" *La Chronique* (1991). On file with author.

AI-France has little involvement or interest in policy work. Like other French NGOs, AI-France has little interaction with government officials.[59] Also, in line with many of the other older European sections, Amnesty France has been particularly concerned over the years with how internal reforms will affect AI's impartiality. In sum, Amnesty's sections prefer different types of advocacy work but all work to realize the benefits of a large membership base.

Finally, FIDH makes different advocacy choices than HRW or AI. Because of its decentralized structure, the organization only engages with political authorities when asked by its national member sections to act. FIDH appears to have a somewhat more cooperative relationship with government officials than other French INGOs, though this appearance may result from its being less vocally insistent on its independence. The organization participates in the National Human Rights Consultative Commission and attends relevant hearings on foreign policy.[60] In the international realm, FIDH maintains a presence at the United Nations, like Human Rights Watch and Amnesty, but FIDH has had a much smaller and sometimes volunteer-only staff in New York and Geneva.[61] Still, these are variations on a theme of limited access, and protest dominates the advocacy work of FIDH, rooted in a domestic understanding of what it means to be a human rights activist. One interviewee active in FIDH and its domestic parent organization, the Ligue des Droits de l'Homme, explained how both groups' identities shaped their advocacy and research:

> The most important thing for you to know about the French League [LDH] is that it is a movement, not an ONG [*organization non-gouvermentale*]. It is made up of people—they work on human rights—and *then* it is an organization. In the association, they want to *faire pression* [lobby] in *France* first, and then internationally.... So I think that LDH is *people*. It is not an organization or an ONG that does research, gathers information, and does expert witnessing. And the FIDH is a league of different associations in different

---

59. Personal interview, Amnesty France staffer, February 22, 2007.

60. Personal interview, FIDH staffer, February 20, 2007.

61. FIDH set up a Geneva office in the early 1990s with a volunteer in charge; the position became paid in 1994. A volunteer ran the New York office until it was closed in 1999; it reopened in 2006 with paid staff (Martens 2006, 25).

countries and the different affiliated associations have the same identity—
we are a movement *en masse,* not a group created for expertise. Mainly these
associations are made of people who have engaged in action inside their
country.[62]

Political work by the leading international human rights group in France
is about expressing a movement identity rather than developing expertise.

Explaining Advocacy and Research Strategies

Advocacy strategies at human rights INGOs are determined by at least
three main factors. External events like the onset of political crises or wars
shape the global human rights agenda and drive human rights organizations to pay attention to similar issues or pressure the relevant players. The
political opportunities that human rights INGOs face are also important,
as are the assumptions actors make about the most effective mechanisms
for change. These last two are deeply tied to an INGO's national origin.
In terms of political opportunities, charities in the United States, Britain,
and France have varied levels of political access. In the fragmented political system in the United States, charities have fairly good access to some
government offices, but achieving widespread change is difficult. In Britain, the relative centralization of power, as well as the openness of government to consultation with civil society groups, creates potentially sizable
opportunities for charities to affect change. In France, charities are afforded almost no meaningful opportunities for participation in policymaking, particularly foreign policymaking.

These political opportunities shape different notions of appropriate political activity in each country. Human Rights Watch has long used insider
lobbying of the U.S. government as the primary mechanism by which it
hopes to influence policy. Note that as the American section of Amnesty
has tried to increase its profile in the United States, it has also expanded its
lobbying capacity on Capitol Hill. Within the fragmented American political system, these INGOs may make progress in particular State Department offices or with certain congress members, but high-level access and
meetings are rare, and the human rights lobby may be entirely shut out on

---

62. Personal interview, LDH, February 7, 2007.

many issues. In Britain, Amnesty UK also employs insider strategies, taking advantage of the relatively good access that civil society groups have to government, but it complements this lobbying with grassroots campaigns and public activism, symbolically visible at the organization's Human Rights Action Center in London. Grassroots activism has a higher chance of success, as the British public is heavily engaged in foreign affairs and the relative centralization of the British government may make pressure from the outside more effective. Finally, in a country where real opportunities for participation in the policy process are effectively absent, FIDH, like its humanitarian counterparts in France, uses protest strategies like open letters to officials printed in newspapers and public demonstrations against poverty, but does little insider lobbying.

These strategies are not just reflections of political opportunities but also reflections of fundamentally different beliefs about what is the most effective mechanism for change. At Human Rights Watch, the targeting of the U.S. government reflects a belief that the United States is uniquely positioned to affect human rights conditions worldwide. At Amnesty, the multimethod approach reflects a belief that a combination of both grassroots activism of ordinary people and top-down political change is necessary to improve human rights. At FIDH, the weak confederation empowers grassroots volunteer activists in the field, while the central FIDH staff works in solidarity with those activists. Thus, human rights groups all tend to use shaming strategies, but the audience for each organization is different. HRW does not aim to mobilize general public opinion through public education and grassroots campaigns like Amnesty or FIDH but rather speaks to the American policymaking community.

These strategic differences in advocacy are critical to a more complete understanding of the "transnational advocacy networks" that have received enormous attention in the INGO literature (Keck and Sikkink 1998). Because organizations bring different orientations to these networks, we might better understand why the networks only include certain players and why effective networking may be relatively rare. Amnesty, Human Rights Watch, and FIDH may each organization have a distinct capacity and willingness to participate in transnational campaigns. These strategic differences also suggest that the very process of constructing durable campaigns is challenging given diverse goals and understandings. Human rights campaigns with a grassroots focus are unlikely to attract Human

Rights Watch. Campaigners seeking to work with Amnesty will encounter slow and thorough deliberation over whether an issue is an Amnesty issue. While FIDH is willing to make provocative public statements, it has limited organizational capacity. Overall, effective transnational campaigns may be the exception rather than the rule.

Issue Selection

Given the limited resources of INGOs, they have to make choices about which issues they will cover. Two choices are particularly important. First, one of the largest divisions within the global human rights community is over the relative importance of civil and political rights versus ESC rights. All three organizations studied here are from Western countries with strong domestic human rights traditions that emphasize the freedoms *from* state interference that constitute the "first generation" of global human rights, and Human Rights Watch, Amnesty, and FIDH have displayed different levels of enthusiasm about the "second generation" of rights. Second, human rights groups must decide whether and how to address human rights violations at home as well as abroad. The three organizations appear to engage in a comparable amount of domestic human rights work (though Human Rights Watch has seen a big change in the past decade), but the justification for working on human rights at home is different at each INGO.

Historically, HRW has understood civil and political rights as those rights that absolutely must be protected without derogation, while ESC rights were thought of as goals to be progressively realized through gradual development and change. In a discussion of this issue, Ken Roth has pointed out that civil and political rights have also historically been the focus of Western governments' foreign policy; by contrast, Soviet bloc countries emphasized ESC rights during the Cold War (Roth 2004, 64). This position has been reflected in HRW's work. Former director Neier has gone so far as to argue that while civil and political rights limit political power and uphold human dignity, "the concept of economic and social rights is profoundly undemocratic" (Neier 2003, xxx).

Human Rights Watch has received criticism for its neglect of economic and social injustices that may arguably impact the lives of victims in larger ways than civil liberty considerations. In response, HRW claimed to expand the scope of its work in 1996 to include investigations of violations of economic and social rights. This new rights language framed reports on discrimination against HIV-positive patients as well as limitations on organized labor.[63] Still, some argue that this is simply a repackaging of work that HRW would be doing anyway.[64] Today, Roth suggests, the organization's work on economic and social rights must remain limited because its preferred strategy of shaming governments is ill suited to addressing rights violations in this area.[65] For a shaming strategy to work, argues Roth, the violation must be clear, but so must the remedy, and it is often difficult to argue that a lack of housing or a decent standard of living is the fault of a single actor that has the capacity to address the violation. In sum, HRW directors Neier and Roth have offered different justifications for the organization's focus on civil and political rights, but the outcome is the same. Like the largest domestic NGOs in the United States, HRW largely focuses on civil liberties issues in its international investigations.

Like Human Rights Watch, Amnesty traditionally worked in the area of civil and political rights, though for a long time the range of Amnesty issues was even narrower than at HRW because of the organization's concern with protecting its mandate. For at least the past two decades, Amnesty has felt external and internal pressure to include ESC rights in its mission; Amnesty members from the global South argue that it must recognize both the indivisibility of all human rights and the importance of these issues outside the developed world. Some were concerned that an expansion to ESC rights would threaten Amnesty's focus and expertise, but it has moved forward and embraced the "full spectrum" of human rights (Bell and Carens 2004, 309–11). Unlike at Human Rights Watch, where leaders focus on the practical concerns of how the group's research methodology can be tailored to addressing ESC rights violations, the discussion at Amnesty covered both practical and principled concerns (Goering 2007;

---

63. This policy initially was limited to only economic, social and cultural violations that involved civil and political rights violations. Later, the policy of HRW was expanded (Brown 2001, 77).

64. Interview, Human Rights First staff member, September 7, 2006.

65. The argument is that it is hard to assign responsibility to a single violator or offer a precise remedy for violations of economic, social and cultural rights. For a debate, see Roth 2007 and Chandhoke 2007.

Nelson and Dorsey 2008). In 2001, Amnesty's statute was altered to expand its mission to include addressing all human rights violations, and since then Amnesty has focused on building its capacity for monitoring and reporting violations of economic and social rights. In 2008, Amnesty launched a six-year "Demand Dignity" campaign, which focuses on poverty as a violation of economic and social rights.[66] The effects of this ongoing campaign cannot yet be discerned, but Amnesty's practice has not yet caught up with its rhetoric. Based on his analysis of Amnesty's premier publication, its annual report, Hopgood (2010) argues that Amnesty's stated commitment to the full spectrum of human rights is little evident in the 2009 edition that launched the "Demand Dignity" campaign. Resistance to continued work on ESC issues comes largely from those Western Amnesty chapters that also have the largest membership.

Unlike Amnesty or Human Rights Watch, FIDH does not issue an annual report on the state of human rights worldwide, as its central research capacity is more limited. Even with this more limited capacity, however, FIDH has developed a strong program on economic and social rights violations, particularly as reflected in its program on globalization (Landman and Abraham 2004). Like other human rights groups worldwide, FIDH was driven to acknowledge the indivisibility of all human rights in the mid-1990s, but it followed these words with a substantive commitment to economic and social rights at a meeting in Dakar in 1997.[67] The economic and social rights program grew into a larger focus on globalization, and the globalization program's present aim is to establish "the pre-eminence of human rights over international trade" by placing limits on both states and corporations.[68] This concern with and critique of globalization echoes many of the *altermondialistes* in France. FIDH's program on globalization constitutes the most robust work on economic and social rights done by any of the three leading INGOs profiled here.

Regarding the balance of domestic and international work, FIDH has long stood out as integrating the two, but both HRW and AI have moved

---

66. http://www.amnesty.org/en/economic-social-and-cultural-rights (accessed January 29, 2008).

67. For an early and bold example, see Antoine Bernard, "One and indivisible," *UNESCO Courier* 47 (March 1994), Academic OneFile.

68. "2004–06 Outlook," www.fidh.org (accessed March 8, 2006; copy on file with author).

toward more domestic human rights work over the past several decades. The United States' global power has led it to receive attention from Human Rights Watch that is arguably disproportionate to the severity of the country's domestic human rights abuses, but conditions there were not a major focus of HRW until recently. From 1991 to 1995, the organization published sixteen reports on the United States (accounting for 4% of total reporting), mainly focused on civil liberties, prison conditions, and human rights violations along the United States–Mexico border.[69] That number had almost tripled by 2006–10. The forty-five reports on the United States during this period still focused on prisons and immigration, but a full quarter of the reports focused on antiterrorism and the treatment of Guantanamo Bay prisoners; 9% of all reports during the period were on the United States. The greater attention of HRW to violations in the United States has largely been driven by the changes in American foreign policy after September 2001. In May 2007, Kenneth Roth noted "a real shift that we've seen in the environment for the defense of human rights over the last 5, 6 years.... Traditionally there is no more important partner in that effort than the U.S. government...so it has been a problem for us that the Bush administration has chosen to fight terrorism by in large part ignoring the constraints in international human rights law."[70] Changes in the foreign policy orientation of its home country government and major pressure point have driven HRW to shift its focus from abroad.

Amnesty International has also seen a change in the balance between domestic and international human rights work. From the very beginning, the International Secretariat was established to separate out the British section from the international movement. In accordance with Amnesty's central concern to maintain its credibility as an apolitical organization, one of the mechanisms by which it did so was an awkwardly named "Work on Own Country" rule, which prevented AI members from working on human rights conditions in their home countries in order to maintain "a

69. Between January 1991 and January 2011, HRW published 117 reports on the United States, out of 1,803 publications. Author's count, based on two searches of HRW publications on their website, one on 1/24/2011 and one on 2/13/2008.

70. *Global Human Rights Leadership: Who Will Fill the Void Left by the US?* Director's Lecture Series on Contemporary International Affairs, Brown University Watson Institute, May 1, 2007. Available at http://www.watsoninstitute.org/events_detail.cfm?id=936.

spirit of international solidarity" (Winston 2001, 32). The rule came under fire in the 1990s from both Amnesty members in the global South, who faced severe human rights crises in their own countries, and chapters in the North, which possessed large membership bases that offered real opportunities to create political change at home. In 2001, the rule was loosened substantially, and Amnesty sections can now engage in work on domestic human rights conditions in consultation with the International Secretariat as well as Amnesty's International Executive Committee.

While we can generally say that the rule change has shifted the balance of Amnesty sections' work toward more domestic issues, this is truer for some sections than for others. Consider a recent review of Amnesty's "Stop Violence Against Women" campaign, which ran from 2004 to 2010. Out of the sixty-four reports that came out of the campaign, eleven were produced by national sections researching conditions in their own countries. Amnesty's report on the campaign found that locally based research that was linked to local campaigns had brought about real change in the United States, Ireland, Britain, and several Nordic countries, but most sections in the South "were not able to undertake work on own country... research, did not shape the overall research agenda in their countries and often did not participate in the research" and they "lacked resources to develop campaign materials themselves" (Wallace and Smith 2010, 8). The research generated by this campaign suggests that the rule change may lead to more and more effective research and campaigning in the global North; the danger is that this will come at the expense of human rights reporting around the globe.

The fact that the secretariat's headquarters are in Britain does appear to have affected the content of AI reporting, resulting in a disproportionate emphasis on that country. Using data from Ron et al. (2005) on Amnesty's background reports and press releases from 1986 to 2000, we can examine the country focus on Amnesty's reporting. During this period, Britain was the subject of 103 press releases and 149 background reports; in fact, it was the sixth most frequent subject of Amnesty press releases.[71] Ron et al. explain Britain's frequent presence in AI reports as a function of state power, which they measure by size of the economy,

---

71. Ron et al. 2005, 568. Britain accounted for 3.21% of all press releases and 1.47% of all background reports during this period.

number of military personnel, and population size. Yet France, which is almost identical to Britain in all three measures, was the subject of only five press releases and eighty background reports from 1986 to 2000.[72] Is national origin a better explanation? Having AI-UK in the same country as the International Secretariat definitely makes a difference. When asked about the relationship between the secretariat and Amnesty UK, one staffer responded: "The truth is, we just bump into them frequently. My experience was that the relationship raised as many positives as it did negatives. It is easier to discuss stuff with them [the IS] because they're right down the street, but it could also be harder, because my colleagues at the IS read my quotes in the newspaper, and it was much more important to be directly on message. The secretary general doesn't wake up and listen to national Kenyan radio; the fact that she and others wake up hearing the news that we are putting out made my job a bit harder."[73] Consistent with Amnesty's vision of itself as a global movement, however, the staffer prefaced this by saying that the close relationship between AI-UK and the secretariat is not inconsistent with Amnesty's global reach. Even if Amnesty has the greatest global reach of any INGO profiled here, however, its British roots pull the secretariat's attention toward human rights conditions at home.

FIDH is almost a mirror image of Amnesty—an organization founded on the idea of bringing together people around the world who are all working on human rights conditions in their own countries. Recall the quote from the LDH member in the above discussion of advocacy: all of FIDH's member sections claim to be mass movements that work at home first, then abroad. Interestingly, however, given the close ties between the LDH and FIDH, reporting on France is not as intensive as one might expect. From 1996 to 2007, FIDH issued fifty-six research reports or press releases on France, making the country the fourth most frequent subject of FIDH statements, behind only Tunisia, Russia, and Algeria.[74] Still, a total of 1,433 reports and press releases was issued during this period, meaning

---

72. State power also doesn't work perfectly for a United States vs. UK comparison. The United States has five times the population and over six times the number of military personnel, yet AI issued only a few more press releases on the United States (136) and only 2.3 times as many background reports (349).

73. Personal interview, November 7, 2006.

74. Tally as of January 26, 2008, based on *interventions* and *rapports* by country, www.fidh.org.

that these France-focused documents accounted for only 4% of FIDH's work during this period—a similar number to HRW reporting on the United States in the 1990s. Many of the reports were produced in concert with the LDH.

In other words, both FIDH and HRW report on conditions in their home countries at similar rates (with recent changes at HRW), but the rationale is quite different. For Human Rights Watch, it is concern that neglect of human rights problems in the United States could damage the organization's credibility; for FIDH, working on human rights at home is inseparable from what it means to work on human rights globally. Without overstating the difference, it appears that one is a more practical consideration, the other is more principled. This has meant that FIDH supporters do not understand the traditional separation of domestic and international human rights work at Amnesty. For example, the president of the LDH has chastised Amnesty France for failing to speak about the *sans-papiers* in France or about the rise of ultraright racist sentiments.[75]

Explaining the Selection of Issues

Out of the universe of injustices that exist, human rights INGOs all have choose to work on particular violations. Ron et al. (2005) revealed that leading human rights INGOs, particularly Amnesty and HRW, tend to report on similar countries and often focus on powerful states in their reporting. Likewise, the three organizations under consideration here all have their roots in civil and political rights. Despite these similarities in country reporting and historical focus, there are two important areas in which we can see substantial variation in issue selection by HRW, Amnesty, and FIDH: incorporation of ESC rights as well as the international-domestic balance of publications. These choices are informed by broader social understandings in each INGO's home country of what it means to engage in global human rights work.

Northern human rights INGOs have been criticized for ignoring economic and social rights concerns that directly, and often primarily, affect people in the less-developed world. But not all Northern human rights groups have the same approach to such issues. FIDH (and other French

---

75. Yves Hardy, *La Chronique d'Amnesty* (February 2000): 24.

INGOs discussed below) have been very active on the issues of globalization and poverty. This enthusiasm for and incorporation of economic and social rights into programming is much weaker among British and American INGOs. The failure to tackle rights violations in issue areas like housing, health, or income may in part reflect the free-market orientation of the British and American political systems. Staff at HRW and Amnesty may be sympathetic to criticisms that their adoption of these "second generation" rights has been slow, but the issues may be nonstarters with their domestic constituencies.

Regarding the domestic-international balance, if we look at the numbers of reports that each organization issues on its home country, HRW, FIDH, and Amnesty do not look very different, though a comparison with Amnesty is difficult as it reports on a much higher number of countries. Yet the justification for reporting on human rights at home is different among the three INGOs. Human Rights Watch has historically used the global power of the United States as leverage in promoting human rights protection abroad; the post-2001 global war on terror has challenged America's claim to the moral high ground, and HRW has responded by focusing on abuses by its prime target, the U.S. government. In France, by contrast, human rights work at home is understood as both a complement to and perhaps a necessary precondition for effective international rights promotion. As the discussion of other British human rights groups below reveals, there isn't a clear discernable national pattern of how British INGOs address human rights conditions in Britain. In interviews, personnel at the Amnesty secretariat were singularly unresponsive to the question about the domestic-international balance, as they refuse to recognize themselves as having any home country. The smaller human rights groups in Britain tend to strictly separate their work from domestic issues; when asked about domestic human rights groups, several staffers at these smaller groups pointed to organizations like Liberty (a British civil liberties group) as the place where that kind of work is done.[76] For at least a decade, Amnesty's national sections have been granted more authority to do domestic human rights work, but only the most resource-rich sections have been able to take advantage of this opportunity.

---

76. Interview, Interights staffer, October 24, 2006; interview, Article 19 staffer, October 25, 2006.

From the Individual INGO to National Patterns

The comparative cases of three leading human rights INGOs offered above enrich our understanding of what specific organizations actually do. The cases reveal that the organizational landscape in the human rights sector remains varied, though national and international pressures exert somewhat different pressures on human rights groups than on their humanitarian counterparts. But national patterns do exist for human rights INGOs, as our "mini cases" will confirm. Altogether, the influence of nationality is less clear-cut for human rights INGOs compared to humanitarian relief groups, given the dominance of a single, unusual organization like Amnesty International and the global influence of the American foundation sector. Still, the national origin explanation accounts for differences in how human rights organizations both select strategies and understand the nature of human rights work.

Other American Human Rights INGOs

How does Human Rights Watch compare to other human rights INGOs in the United States? There is striking similarity among American human rights INGOs, though not perfect homogeneity. The cases of Human Rights First (HRF) and Global Rights clearly demonstrate that an American "model" of human rights activism exists. Human Rights First was established in 1975 as a public interest law firm, the Lawyers Committee for Human Rights, dedicated to international human rights work. Soon thereafter, it began domestic programs, particularly in asylum law.[77] One interviewee estimated that the domestic/international program balance is today around 50/50, whereas it used to be 20/80 before the events of September 11, 2001.[78] This puts Human Rights First somewhere between the domestic American Civil Liberties Union and HRW. A decade ago, it was stated that the organization "issues no World Report, does not identify itself as an international NGO and, except in special circumstances, deliberately chooses to avoid monitoring abuses in other countries, leaving that

---

77. Tolley 1990–91, 623.
78. Personal interview, HRF staffer, March 23, 2006.

to Amnesty International and Human Rights Watch" (Korey 1998, 508). Today, HRF identifies itself as an international human rights organization, but as at Human Rights Watch, the government's reaction to the September 2001 terrorist attacks has resulted in an expansion of the group's domestic human rights work. After 2001, HRF established a program on U.S. law and security that has grown substantially. Today, the organization has offices in New York and Washington, a staff of sixty-five, and a budget of $10 million—more than double its budget a decade earlier, but still a quarter of the size of Human Rights Watch.[79]

Human Rights First shares many structural and strategic features with Human Rights Watch. It is highly professionalized. Most staff members have degrees in law or international affairs, and the few volunteers mainly assist with administrative tasks. Like Human Rights Watch, HRF refuses government funding and is heavily dependent on foundations, which account for over half its income.[80] When asked about the relationship between government funding and advocacy, one staffer contrasted HRF with European human rights organizations: "The European human rights community is very weak. Because they are so used to working with government, they have a hard time speaking out. Most of them would go out of business if the government wasn't funding them, and this has limited their ability to challenge government programs."[81] Whether or not this is true is perhaps less important than the typically American perception at HRF that accepting government funds damages an organization's ability to be critical.

While advocacy is a key facet of HRF's work, it primarily uses an insider approach that concentrates on reaching well-placed elites. For example, one staffer described a conflict between the fundraising and programs offices over the letters that the organization frequently sends to the president or Congress. The programs office preferred to write letters of concern that were then forwarded to an "eminent person" for signature; the fundraising office protested that Human Rights First should also sign these letters to

---

79. HRF had a staff of forty-two and a budget of $3.4 million in 1996 (Korey 1998, 508).

80. Figures only available for 2003–4 (55.4%) and 2005–6 (53.3%). *HRF Annual Reports.* Grants from the Ford Foundation alone have accounted for 16% of total revenue. *Ford Foundation Annual Reports* (2000–2006).

81. Personal interview, HRF staffer, September 7, 2006.

increase its public profile. Ultimately, however, the organization felt that the insider approach "limits our fundraising power but it increases our influence."[82] As at HRW, Human Rights First does not see a connection between a high public profile and greater political influence.

Another interesting American human rights INGO, Global Rights, was founded in 1978 as the International Human Rights Law Group by a group of lawyers and government officials interested in international human rights litigation and treaty construction (Tolley 1990–91, 624). It is a small organization, with an average budget around $6 million, a United States–based staff of twenty-four, and perhaps twice that many people working abroad.[83] Global Rights has a much more local orientation than the other two American groups. Operating on the assumption that "over the long term, local NGOs, progressive lawyers, and other dynamic local professionals must decisively challenge their own government's human rights policies" (Bromley 2001, 141), organization has emphasized technical training and litigation in the field.[84]

In many ways, Global Rights is the exception that proves the rule in the American human rights community. It remains a small organization that has taken a different path from that many of the larger and more visible human rights INGOs. United States–based advocacy has not been a priority for the organization, which some in the organization feel has limited its domestic profile.[85] Like other American human rights groups, Global Rights focuses on litigation for policy change, but does so internationally through its "Advocacy Bridge" program that brings Southern activists to Geneva for training in international law and policy work. In fundraising, Global Rights stands out as perhaps the only American human rights INGO to accept significant support from government agencies, most notably USAID.[86] Some staffers, particularly those who have come from other

---

82. Personal interview, HRF staffer, February 16, 2006.

83. Average budget, 2000–2008. Global Rights, *Annual Reports* (various years).

84. Interview, Global Rights staffer, May 3, 2006; Wilson and Rasmussen 2001.

85. Personal Interview, Global Rights staffer, May 3, 2006. The organization spent no money on lobbying from 1998 to 2009 (IRS Form 990s).

86. According to figures from one source, Global Rights used to receive 90% of its funding from USAID. Personal interview, Global Rights staffer, May 18, 2006. Calculating the INGO's income is difficult because of its small size; a single grant can make a huge difference. Generally, Global Rights's reliance on U.S. government funding has declined over the past decade (from 52% in 1999 to 24% in 2009), and this has been replaced by grants from foreign governments and

American human rights organizations, express concerns about the strings attached to USAID funds and the effects of accepting government funds on the reputation of Global Rights.[87]

Despite this micro-level advocacy approach and reliance on USAID, the organization resembles other American human rights INGOs in terms of professionalization and ties to foundations. Though small, Global Rights is a professionalized organization with strict internal guidelines for program selection.[88] The staff is largely made up of professionals with advanced law degrees; the only volunteers are to be found in the internship program, which is targeted at law students. Like Human Rights Watch, Global Rights got started with grants from the Ford Foundation (Tolley 1990–91, 622), and foundations are a major source of income, accounting for an average 35% of revenue in 2001–4.[89]

The three cases of American human rights INGOs reveal national patterns. Human rights work is understood in the United States as a technically demanding task that is reserved for professionals. This work takes place not throughout the country, but instead in the financial and political centers of New York and Washington. Consider this description of the American human rights sector from Larry Cox, formerly of the Ford Foundation and now executive director of AI-USA: "Twenty years ago, when you went to a meeting at a human rights group, you saw all kinds of people. But these days, you usually find that most of the people there are either lawyers or human rights professionals. To me, the human rights movement has not been successful in capturing the imagination of a broad group of people—the way . . . a strong civil-society group like the National Rifle Association has done" (Rieff 1999, 40). The lack of volunteer opportunities at these organizations, as well as the lack of grassroots campaigning, may contribute to what Cox sees as a failure of human rights INGOs.

---

international organizations. Together, income from all these official sources accounted for three-quarters of the INGO's income in 2010. IRS Form 990s (various years); Global Rights, *Audited Financial Statements 2009 and 2010.*

87. Personal interview, Global Rights staff member, May 18, 2006; personal interview, Global Rights staff member, March 16, 2006.

88. Personal interview, Global Rights staffer, May 3, 2006.

89. *Global Rights Audited Financial Statements* (2001–4, on file with author). The Ford Foundation in particular reports large grants to Global Rights, accounting for an average 7.6% of total revenue from 2001 to 2006. *Ford Annual Reports* (various years), www.fordfound.org.

In fact, the grassroots activism of the NRA (and, as we will see, of Amnesty USA) may be the exception in the United States, given the professionalization of interest representation there. In their advocacy work, American human rights INGOs prioritize insider strategies in order to achieve policy change.

In their financing, these organizations regularly turn to a small group of private foundations to support this technical work. American human rights INGOs fear that accepting government funds threatens their political independence; appropriate action for advocacy INGOs is thus the rejection of government funds, and Global Rights, which does accept government funds, does little advocacy work. In the United States, human rights work is understood as a demanding task for well-connected professionals. As we will see, this model gets carried abroad via American foundations, whose financial support has been critical to the well-being of many British human rights groups beyond Amnesty.

Other British Human Rights INGOs

Making generalizations about the British human rights community is difficult, because of the dominant presence of Amnesty. Still, Amnesty is not the only British human rights INGO; many of the other organizations are small groups that focus on narrow issue areas. These organizations are specialized and technically proficient, but many fail, or perhaps never attempt, to capture the attention of the broader public. Instead, they turn to two reliable sources of funding—the British government and the foundation sector, particularly American foundations. These practices can be found at Interights and Article 19.

Interights, or the International Centre for the Legal Protection of Human Rights, was founded in 1983 as a human rights organization focused on international litigation. Today it remains small, with a budget of $2.5 million and a staff of about twenty.[90] Interights is heavily dependent on both American foundations and the British government. From 2002 to 2004, its top donors were the Ford Foundation, the Foreign and Commonwealth

---

90. Up from $1.05 million in 1999. *Interights Statement of Financial Activities for the year ending 31 March 2006; Extract from Central Register of Charities No. 292357* (www.charity-commission.gov.uk, accessed February 1, 2011).

Office, and the Open Society Institute, which together made up half of the group's income.[91] As one Interights staffer described it, the foundations "have specialists on human rights who know more about human rights than I do!"[92] Until May 2005, Interights actually had no professional fundraiser, as the management of a few large grants was undertaken by the program officers. Like its American counterparts, Interights has only a small handful of volunteers, while many London law firms provide pro bono legal services.

Despite the fact that it doesn't conduct campaigns, Interights has "a close relationship with the government," manifested in its participation in Foreign Office meetings and in panel discussions on issues like the death penalty.[93] One Interights staffer made a point to say that the organization is not a British NGO but an international one; still, the interviewee later said there are important differences between UK- and United States-based INGOs: "The whole attitude towards international law generally is different—U.S. NGOs are conscious that international law has less resonance in the American system. On economic, social, and cultural rights, there are differences about how people see the role of the state—the average citizen here is much more likely to accept that the state has obligations in terms of social security and the provision of health care....I think you will find that the UK domestic human rights agenda is much closer to the European agenda than the American one."[94] A systematic examination of Interights casework is beyond the scope of this project, but this quote suggests a fundamentally different understanding of human rights work shaped by a distinct vision of state-society relations.

The second British human rights INGO, Article 19, was founded in 1987 from the estate of an American philanthropist who envisioned an international organization committed to protecting freedom of expression.[95] Like Interights, it remains a small organization, with a budget of

---

91. These three donors accounted for an average 28%, 13%, and 8%, respectively, of Interights's total income. Charity Commission, *Central Register of Charities No. 292357.*

92. Personal interview, Interights staffer, November 7, 2006.

93. Personal interview, Interights staffer, October 24, 2006.

94. Personal interview, Interights staffer, October 24, 2006.

95. "Working to Nourish Democracy Where Minds Are Being Starved," *New York Times,* August 16, 1992.

$3.6 million and staff of less than twenty.[96] Article 19's primary strategies include research and publication, advocacy, and litigation, and it largely focuses on Africa and Europe, with a few projects in Britain on refugees and antiterrorism.[97] In its work on freedom of expression, staff report that its British presence makes a substantive difference, since international freedom of expression standards are less absolutist that those that exist in the United States.[98]

Article 19 and Interights are very much alike: Article 19 has no professional fundraiser on staff, and gets almost half its income from the British government and a handful of foundations. From 2002 to 2004, major donors included the Open Society Institute, the Foreign and Commonwealth Office, and the Swedish government's development agency SIDA.[99] Like other British groups, Article 19 participates in the regular consultations offered by British officials: "We've been involved in one or two consultations with DFID....[Our] priority is actually to strengthen this relationship. With the Foreign Office, we have well-established collaboration [in many working groups]. We usually have one meeting a year with the minister of foreign affairs [*sic*] and the director for human rights, and this is an opportunity to raise concerns. The meeting is initiated by them....The government is quite consultation-oriented..."[100] The access that small INGOs like Article 19 and Interights have to senior ministers in Britain is impressive (particularly in contrast to the French human rights groups discussed below); notice, though, that consultation is initiated at the behest of the state.

In spite of Amnesty's dominance, a few basic similarities do exist across the British human rights INGO sector. Though Amnesty does not accept

---

96. Article 19, *Statement of Financial Activities* (2008); Charity Commission (UK), *Central Register of Charities No. 327421* (accessed February 1, 2011).

97. Landman and Abraham 2004, 32. A 2004 count of Article 19's total publications found a total of 142 for Africa, 107 for Europe, 51 for Asia, 32 for the Middle East/North Africa, and 2 for Latin America. The organization used to have an office in Johannesburg, but coordination was difficult and the office closed down in 2004.

98. Personal interview, Article 19 staffer, November 9, 2006.

99. These accounted for 21%, 14%, and 12%, respectively, of the organization's income. Article 19 has worked to overcome some poor accounting practices. After 2002–4, funding from the Open Society Institute declined steeply but has been replaced by funding from the Ford Foundation.

100. Personal interview, Article 19 staffer, November 9, 2006.

government money, Amnesty UK, like other British NGOs, benefits from a relatively friendly government that creates opportunities for NGO input. Yet Interights and Article 19 are not as fiercely insistent on their independence from government as Amnesty and the American human rights groups. Amnesty's use of both insider and outsider advocacy strategies actually is closer to the style of British humanitarian INGOs which believe that confrontational campaigning today will not restrict their access to government tomorrow. If we turn to issue selection, Article 19 and Interights look more like their American counterparts. All are deeply committed to civil and political rights achieved through shaming strategies or litigation. Still, the global reach of American foundation support for human rights organizations, combined with Amnesty's many unusual features, makes it difficult to define the contours of a distinctively British human rights community.

Other French Human Rights INGOs

In France, many organizations work on the issue of human rights that might not be recognized as distinctively human rights NGOs in Britain or the United States. The division between this sector and others (including those like humanitarianism or antiglobalization) is less marked in France. Two cases illustrate this point. Reporters sans frontières (RSF) was founded as part of a larger *sansfrontiérisme* movement but evolved into a more traditional human rights INGO focused on free speech. At ATD Quart-Monde, poverty is approached through the lens of human rights rather than through the development lens used at many other organizations.

Reporters sans frontières was founded in 1985 by journalist Robert Menard and Médecins Sans Frontières president Rony Brauman to promote an "alternative journalism"—a critique of the sensationalism in the media's coverage of international emergencies. Soon, however, this *sans frontières* organization began to focus exclusively on freedom of the press issues, resulting in a split between Menard and Brauman.[101] Today, RSF's international secretariat houses fifteen employees based in Paris, and the organization has another dozen or so employees worldwide. The

---

101. Laurent Maduit, "La saga Reporters sans frontières," *Le Monde,* January 21, 2005.

organization is small, with an average budget of around $4 million.[102] Despite its small size, RSF is well known in France and Europe, though virtually unknown in the United States. The organization may be most noted for its public protest of Chinese human rights practices at the Olympic torch-lighting ceremony in March 2008. RSF researcher (and soon-to-be new executive director) Jean-François Julliard unfurled a flag depicting the Olympic rings as handcuffs behind the podium during the opening speeches of the lighting ceremony, while Menard (who was sitting in the audience) unfurled the same flag and shouted "Shame on China!"[103]

In terms of fundraising, RSF, like FIDH, does not receive many charitable gifts from individual donors. The majority of its income (58%) actually comes from newsstand sales of photo albums, which are popular with the French public. Another 16% of its income is provided by the French government and European intergovernmental organizations, while private foundations and companies provide 20%.[104] Like other human rights INGOs worldwide, RSF gets regular support from foundations, including the Open Society Institute and the Fondation de France. On the subject of professionalization, there is little specific information about how many volunteers are involved with the organization, but anecdotal evidence suggests that many of the reporters of RSF are not compensated for their time.

The strategic choices of RSF are influenced by its French roots. In its campaigns for the protection of specific journalists, RSF finds that the coverage of French journalists is an effective way to raise public awareness, as in the case of the late Brice Fleutiaux, who was held hostage in Chechnya for eight months.[105] Like most human rights organizations, RSF relies on a strategy of awareness-raising, publishing an annual report on the state of press freedom worldwide and issuing alerts for journalists in danger or captivity. These campaigns do not focus on insider strategies and

---

102. Average 2002–6. RSF, *Comptes de Reporters sans frontières* (various years).

103. "Pro-Tibet Protesters Strike as the Olympic Flame Is Lit," *The Guardian,* March 25, 2008: 19.

104. Averages, 2002–6. RSF changed its accounting procedures in 2004; before then, official and private funds were all lumped into one category. Thus, the 16% figure for "official" funding is a conservative estimate, while the figure on private companies and foundations is for 2004–6 (and may have been a bit lower over the entire five-year period). Unfortunately, there is no breakdown of French government support versus European Union support.

105. Observatoire L'action humanitaire, "Reporters sans frontières" (www.observatoire-humanitaire.org), last updated September 9, 2010.

policy-directed advocacy, but instead usually involve letters of protest to heads of state and general publicity meant to create political pressure.[106] Consider this description of RSF's strategies by Menard: "The essential difference between Reporters without Borders and other human rights organizations is that we work with the media. We believe that they can make a difference by putting pressure on public opinion, and by extension, on the various governments that jail journalists.... The only way to communicate with everyone concerned is through the press. So our *obsession* is to mobilize public opinion" (Heller and Vienne 2003, 63, emphasis added). This method of awareness-raising—taken to its extreme in the Olympics protest—is a perfect embodiment of an outsider advocacy strategy aimed at mobilizing political pressure from the grassroots.

A second French human rights group that offers an interesting comparison to FIDH is ATD Quart-Monde, founded in 1957 by a priest, Joseph Wresinski, who was concerned with the plight of the impoverished. The organization, which is a fairly prominent INGO in France, explicitly treats poverty as a human rights violation, and does some development work alongside its human rights advocacy.[107] ATD Quart-Monde's approach to extreme poverty and human rights, informed by the personal experiences and philosophy of Wresinski (who himself grew up poor), has received attention at both the World Bank and the United Nations. ATD Quart-Monde has been particularly active at the United Nations: for example, it was a driving force behind the UN's declaration of October 17 as "International Day for the Eradication of Poverty." Wresinski testified before the UN Human Rights Commission in 1987 on economic and social rights—long before they reentered the public discussion of global human rights—and the World Bank has published discussion papers on the organization's approach to extreme poverty (Wodon 2001).

The internationalization process began at ATD Quart-Monde in 1974, and today there are fifteen national chapters worldwide. The French

---

106. For examples, see "China: Reporters Without Borders Representatives Stage Protest in Beijing," *BBC Monitoring World Media,* August 7, 2007.

107. In 1994, it was the fifteenth largest NGO in France, but by 2001 was only in the top half of NGOs included in a survey by the government's Development Cooperation Commission. Désir 1994; Commission Coóperation Développement 2003.

chapter dominates the international organization, accounting for about two-thirds of its income. As with RSF and FIDH, human rights work at home is important to ATD Quart-Monde: work in France accounts for about a third of spending on all program activities.[108] The structure of ATD Quart-Monde reflects its social movement ethos—whereas it has 33 employees in France, it has 390 "permanent volunteers" doing fieldwork, 75 of whom are stationed in France.[109] Like other volunteers in France, these individuals benefit from a monthly stipend, social security contributions, and a housing allowance. Many of those that the organization has helped later stay on as members or volunteers, embodying the group's commitment to solidarity with the poor. ATD Quart-Monde, like the French humanitarian INGOs, has been successful in attracting private donors, who account for 52% of its income, while grants from foundations and governments account for another 23% of income.[110] Grants from French authorities accounted for about 3% of the organization's income in 2003 and 2005, much of which came from local rather than national agencies. Like the other human rights organizations in France, ATD Quart-Monde gets some, though very little, support from its home government.

The main strategic emphasis of ATD Quart-Monde has been to raise awareness in developed countries about poverty worldwide. Still, about a quarter of its resources are directed to work in the developing world, where it aims to work in solidarity with the world's poor. In order to learn about the conditions of poverty, ATD Quart-Monde volunteers engage in participant observation rather than academic research, arguing that the former is most effective for finding concrete actions that best address the aspirations of those living in extreme poverty (Wodon 2001, 5–6). ATD Quart-Monde specifically rejects the idea that outsider activists or researchers can know the best solutions for alleviating poverty (Wresinki

---

108. In 2004, the international movement's income was €14 million. In 2005, the French section's income was €10 million. In the same year, actions in France accounted for €4 million. Cour des comptes, "La Fondation Aide à toute détresse," press release, February 20, 2007; *Comptes financiers,* September 2006.

109. 2004 figures. *Rapport d'observations définitives de la Cour des comptes sur les comptes d'emploi pour 2002 à 2004 des ressources collectées auprès du public par la Fondation Aide à Toute Détresse,* February 22, 2007, 2.

110. Average, 2003–6. *Cour des comptes* 2007, 17; "Lettre ATD Quart Monde aux Amis Donateurs," November 2007, 2–3 (on file with author); Commission Coóperation Développement, *Argent et organizations solidarité internationale* (various years).

2006, 13–15). In sum, ATD Quart-Monde has been a leader, both in France and internationally, in pushing for the recognition of ESC rights by acting in solidarity with impoverished communities.

The French international human rights sector is smaller and less well-defined than in Britain or the United States. Not only are French human rights INGOs more involved in domestic work, but human rights work often happens at organizations involved in multiple issue areas, including development assistance. French human rights INGOs have little access to government, and largely rely on outsider strategies like demonstrations and letters of protest to express their political positions. Financially, given a dearth of government funding and low levels of private charitable giving, French human rights INGOs cobble together many sources of support, and they remain small by international standards. There are also clear differences in issue selection; in a country with a strong antiglobalization movement and a large welfare state, French INGOs are much more willing than their British or American counterparts to work on economic and social rights. Finally, although organizations like FIDH and RSF have become more professionalized, the volunteer ethic remains stronger in the French human rights community than in Britain or the United States.

The international human rights sector is smaller and more globalized than the humanitarian sector, but if we look at actual organizational practices, there is no cohesive global, or even Northern, human rights sector. The financial power of American foundations has created some convergence in organizational practice, as evidenced at the two British organizations Interights and Article 19, though it is difficult to make any generalizations about a sector dominated by Amnesty International, an organization with many unique features whose global expenditures are seven times as large as those of the organization with the next highest budget, Human Rights Watch. Still, national origin has played an important role in determining some of the core practices of Amnesty, Human Rights Watch, and FIDH. Table 4 offers a summary of these organizational practices.

The basic patterns in professionalization and advocacy that were evident among humanitarian organizations show themselves in the human rights sector as well. National patterns are discernible but less clearly evident in fundraising. Amnesty and the American INGOs avoid government funds, unlike the French groups and the smaller British INGOs.

TABLE 4. Comparing three human rights INGOs

	Human rights watch	Amnesty international	FIDH
Size	$42m budget (2008) 200 staff	$294m budget (2008) 450 staff at IS	$6.3m budget (2008) 40 staff
Internationalization	8 country offices 76% of staff in USA	80 national members 52% of IS staff British	141 national members IS staff mostly French
Centralization	High	High	Low
Funding	100 % private—few large wealthy donors Foundations, corporations 37%	100% private—many small private donors Foundations ~ 0%	Private 20% Many other funders: foundations, EU, French government
Professionalization	No volunteers Emphasis on efficiency	~100 volunteers at IS Led by members Tension between efficiency and voluntarism	Professional staff serves volunteers Largely voluntarist
Advocacy	Insider lobbying U.S. focus	IS claims apolitical status Sections follow national advocacy patterns	Protest politics Driven by demands of member sections
Research	High priority, timely; to serve advocacy	Traditional priority; now happens alongside campaigns	Lower priority; done per request of member sections
Issue Selection	Low ESC rights Increased US focus since Sept 2001	Moderate ESC rights Some UK focus	High ESC rights France priority

One factor that might explain these fundraising strategies is the choice made at each organization about how to actually do human rights work. The "naming and shaming" strategy of Amnesty and HRW may keep them from accepting funds from the very governments they criticize; grassroots education, litigation, and media campaigns may not necessitate such a fiercely independent stance. This potential link is a fruitful area for further research.

On choice of issues, FIDH has done the most substantial program work on ESC rights, while Amnesty and particularly Human Rights Watch have been slower to create substantive programming in this area. In terms of the balance of domestic and international programming, the three groups may today engage in similar levels of domestic human rights work, but the justification is different in each case. FIDH argues that human rights at home are on principle indivisible from human rights work abroad; HRW's domestic programs are a reaction to a major turn in 2001 in the foreign policy of its key target, the U.S. government. Both practice areas reveal that leading human rights INGOs have fundamentally distinct identities: Human Rights Watch sees itself as a group of pragmatic professionals, whereas Amnesty and FIDH view their roles as being principled embodiments of a more or less global human rights ethos.

Given the importance of Amnesty to the human rights sector and the organization's status as perhaps the most transnationalized of all INGOs, I conclude with a few words about the importance of national origin to this organization. First, Amnesty has, since its creation, consciously attempted to create a universal identity that transcends national boundaries. Still, in its advocacy work—which has been the focus of most of the scholarship on Amnesty—the organization closely resembles its British humanitarian counterparts. National origin may not be able to explain all, or even most, of Amnesty's unusual and important features, but it does have a strong effect on one of the most celebrated aspects of Amnesty's work.

Second, the importance of national origin for Amnesty's practices may grow rather than shrink over time. Recall that in the humanitarian sector, uniformity among national sections wasn't always a recipe for success— think of CARE's weak financial and political position in France, for example. The largely uniform sections of Amnesty seem to have had great success in all three of the countries discussed here. As others have argued, this may relate to Amnesty's particularly narrow mandate, which drew upon a concept—the prisoner of conscience—that had widespread appeal and spoke to a diverse (though largely Western) audience. As Amnesty moves into issue areas like ESC rights, or allows national sections more autonomy, the organization may be more affected by battles among these sections, which operate in environments with different varieties of human rights activism. In sum, we may see the effects of national origin on Amnesty practices strengthen over time as its global decision-making structures become less centralized.

4

Reconciling Global and Local

Against those who would argue that INGOs have developed shared practices and norms through participation a global community of humanitarian or human right activism, the preceding case studies have revealed marked divergence in the core strategies and structures of some of the largest and most transnationally active organizations. National origin plays a critical role in determining how INGOs raise funds, embrace professionalism, engage in advocacy, relate to governments, and choose issues. In short, national origin determines how INGOs approach the work of human rights activism and humanitarian relief. Globalization may have increased the frequency of interaction among these organizations, but it has not transformed INGOs into members of a global sector or global civil society.

In this final chapter, a side-by-side comparison of the INGOs studied earlier will show that national origin shapes organizational practices in different ways, according to the particularities of the sectors in which the INGOs operate, but that the organizations respond to those pressures through practices and norms established in their home countries.

Ultimately, a complete account of the role of national origin must also explore how national origin interacts with other factors that shape organizational practice. In the introduction, I suggested that pressures from the global environment, leadership, and competition among organizations might also shape organizational strategies and structures. One way to understand the relative importance of national origin is to look at a particular event where human rights and humanitarian INGOs were all active—the U.S.-led invasion of Iraq in 2003. As we will see, the six INGOs largely followed national patterns.

The conflict in Iraq offers at least three advantages for understanding varieties of activism. First, the broad facts of the Iraq conflict were well understood by all parties: Saddam was a nasty ruler, and President Bush was launching a precedent-setting preemptive war. Second, because the United States was a belligerent, even human rights and humanitarian groups that wanted to stay out of politics had a hard time doing so. The politicization of aid required some form of INGO advocacy and a reexamination of INGO relationships with government authorities. The political stakes may have been particularly high for American-based INGOs, but generally, no organization had the option of sitting on the sidelines and each was forced to express a position more or less consistent with past organizational practice. Finally, if the proponents of global convergence are right and INGOs are increasingly shedding the baggage of their national origin, it should be in more recent settings that we should find evidence of that growing similarity. The Iraq invasion is not necessarily representative of all humanitarian or human rights crises, but it is neither the first nor the last time that the United States has been a belligerent in a conflict.

Finally, the story of this book may not be one that humanitarian and human rights practitioners want to hear, and their ultimate goal—to create meaningful and positive change in the lives of individuals worldwide—is a laudable one. In conclusion, therefore, I explore the issues of stability and change at INGOs and offer recommendations to practitioners hoping to overcome national differences to create globally powerful organizations.

National Origin across the Sectoral Divide

Long before INGOs aspired to be global activists, they were national NGOs that had an international focus. In its home environment, each organization faced a particular set of regulations, a certain pool of material resources, an established pattern of relating to government officials, and a unique constellation of social networks. These national environments encourage American INGOs to be cooperative professionals, lead British INGOs to act like "Establishment radicals," and push French INGOs to be principled protestors. Throughout the six major cases of this study and the dozen supplementary cases, national patterns are readily apparent in two important areas of organizational practice—advocacy and professionalization. In other areas of organizational practice, the effects of national origin interact with the particular demands of humanitarian or human rights work.

American, British, and French INGOs approach the task of advocacy in very different ways. American organizations regularly turn to insider lobbying strategies and largely reject grassroots activism. True, legal regulations prevent American charities from using government funds for advocacy or from prioritizing political activity, but the law is not the only mechanism at work. American INGOs do not see themselves as fundamentally political actors. Instead, they have a pragmatic focus on getting the job done efficiently; in the words of the director of Human Rights Watch, "it is far from clear" to American INGOs that "constituency building" would be worthwhile (Roth 2007, 177).

By contrast, British INGOs invest heavily in advocacy; Oxfam and Amnesty are recognized in their respective fields as worldwide leaders in raising awareness and driving policy change. British INGOs benefit from a centralized government willing to engage them but seemingly uninterested in co-opting them. Unlike the Americans, the British see both a pragmatic and a principled value in advocacy. Practically, the root of a problem like poverty may well lie with donor governments and international institutions, so it just makes sense, they argue, for British INGOs to engage with these actors. Yet there is a principle at work as well—British INGOs see themselves as part of a broader social movement where individuals work voluntarily to change the society around them.

French INGOs largely engage in protest politics. Advocacy is understood as an important facet of charitable activity, exhibited both in the wide use of the term *témoignage* among many INGOs and in the lack of legal restrictions on political activities by charities. Nevertheless, INGOs rarely directly engage the state by making specific policy recommendations, in part because of the limited political opportunities that they face. Instead, in the words of MSF's Rony Brauman (2004, 408), French INGOs serve as "alarm bells" for states, alerting institutional authorities to their failures and demanding that states take responsibility. These protest strategies reflect the general nature of state-society relations in France, based on an understanding that the state has both the capacity and the authority to address societal problems.

There are also stark national patterns in the areas of professionalization and management. The American groups are highly professionalized INGOs with well-compensated staff and little space for volunteers or community members. For these INGOs, charitable work is understood as the preserve of technical specialists and experts. One important factor driving this charitable model is the high level of pressure within the American system for charities to demonstrate their efficiency. In Britain and France, INGOs have increased the size of their salaried staff without displacing volunteers, who not only contribute valuable time but also inform the identity of the organization concerned. Both Oxfam and Amnesty have a large cadre of professional staff but both also offer multiple and meaningful avenues for the public to participate in their substantive work. The volunteer ethic appears even stronger among French INGOs than among British ones, although this may be a result of the ability of the wealthier British organizations to hire more staff. MSF France and FIDH are the most professionalized INGOs in their respective sectors, but salaries remain low by international standards and volunteers lead the field activities of these organizations. This is not simply a matter of resource availability, however; recall the unusual objection of CARE France staffers to their own salaries (relatively high by French standards). The identity of French INGOs is a voluntary one, and professional staffers at French INGOs understand their role as subordinate to this voluntary ethic.

When it comes to fundraising strategies, there are notable differences between human rights and humanitarian INGOs. The leading human rights INGOs are less willing than humanitarian INGOs to accept large amounts of government funding, whereas the role of American private foundations in the creation of human rights INGOs worldwide can hardly be overstated. Still, a few interesting observations can be made about national fundraising patterns in both sectors. Charities in the United States enjoy an abundance of financial support; across the board, American groups are larger than their British and French counterparts.[1] American INGOs target their fundraising efforts at sources of support that offer the most bang for the buck, keeping fundraising costs down and overhead low, again in service to efficiency goals. In Britain, the largest INGOs rely instead on many modest private donations, consistent with British habits of charitable giving.[2] At Amnesty and Oxfam, and throughout the relief and development sector, British INGOs rely primarily on a public interested in international affairs, making frequent but small and spontaneous donations. In France, there is a comparative lack of both public and private resources for charities. Most INGOs rely on private sources of support, since the French government offers very little funding at all. In addition, French INGOs looking to expand their financial base have gone international, either seeking funds at the European Union or establishing chapters abroad. The growth of INGOs like MSF and RSF has only been possible through this international expansion that has allowed access to donors in other countries.

Finally, while the nature of charitable work may vary across the two sectors, national origin still plays a highly significant role. In the humanitarian relief field, there are notable differences in the ways that INGOs relate to government, ranging from close partnership (American INGOs) to limited cooperation (British INGOs) to antagonism (French INGOs). In the human rights sector, American, British, and French INGOs differ in how they incorporate domestic human rights issues into their work and how they prioritize work on the group of "second generation" rights related to economic, social, and cultural issues.

I do not claim, however, that only nationality determines each of an INGO's choices. Instead, norms and habits originating in the home environments of INGOs serve as a lens through which they survey their options. The weakness of advocacy among American humanitarian groups cannot explain the fact that Peter Bell, a major proponent of advocacy, took the helm at CARE in the mid-1990s. What the national origin argument

---

1. Amnesty International is an exception, inasmuch as worldwide income of AI is even larger than that of Human Rights Watch. Still, as noted earlier, AI-USA is significantly larger than either the British or the French section, and in fact is Amnesty's largest section worldwide.

2. This trend is less evident among small human rights INGOs with little fundraising capacity.

does explain is how that change introduced by an individual creative agent was interpreted and incorporated into CARE strategies. The results are evident in CARE's contemporary campaigns. In 2011, CARE's "Help Her Learn" campaign offered an unobjectionable and nonpartisan statement about the importance of girls, who "need our attention because they face a systematic denial of their right to education, and the repercussions could not be more serious."[3] This is a message sure to alienate no one but unlikely to attract many fervent supporters. It is a far cry from Oxfam's "Robin Hood Tax" campaign, in which Oxfam declares: "It's simply not fair for poor people to pay the price of mistakes made by rich bankers."[4] Oxfam names names and identifies solutions; CARE simply raises awareness and places no public blame. This advocacy is more than CARE used to do, but it remains within the bounds of appropriate action by an American charity.

The cases presented here not only help explain the origins of the strategies of the major INGOs discussed but also offer analysts the ability to predict organizational practices at other American, British, and French INGOs. If the "varieties of activism" are so powerful that they continue to affect the core practices of the most transnationally active INGOs, these strategies and structures should be even more evident among INGOs that are more firmly based in these three countries. The "mini-cases" offer strong support for this contention. In sum, this book offers testable hypotheses for INGO scholars interested in understanding how these key nodes within transnational advocacy networks actually work.

Varieties of Activism in Iraq

The United States-led invasion of Iraq in March 2003 was a moment of deep confusion and conflict for humanitarians and human rights activists. They had been active for decades documenting the abuses of the regime and providing assistance when possible, and they were aware that

---

3. http://www.care.org/campaigns/2009/powerwithin.asp (accessed March 13, 2010).

4. http://www.oxfam.org.uk/get_involved/campaign/actions/robinhood.html (accessed April 1, 2011).

"Saddam Hussein is as bad as they come."[5] At the same time, INGOs had witnessed the injurious effects of United States–led sanctions on the Iraqi people (Sponeck 2006). Many INGOs were thus deeply troubled by President Bush's declaration at the United Nations on September 12, 2002 that the Iraqi people had "suffered too long in silent captivity," making regime change in Iraq "a great moral cause, and a great strategic goal."[6] Members of the United States–led coalition against Saddam explicitly used evidence of human rights violations and humanitarian abuses to make the case for regime change. In a background report accompanying Bush's UN speech, the administration cited Saddam's violence against civilians, torture of innocents, and harassment of humanitarian workers. In December 2002, the British Foreign Office released a dossier detailing rape, torture, and killings by the Iraqi regime.[7] After the invasion in late March 2003 failed to uncover massive weapons caches, humanitarian and human rights concerns became the primary rationale for the war.

On the heels of Afghanistan, the invasion of Iraq dominated the agenda in both the humanitarian and the human rights sectors. The issue of humanitarian intervention was already a divisive one in the INGO community; as one 2001 report bluntly put it, the crucial dilemma was that of "killing for human rights" (Mahoney 2001, 2). An examination of INGO actions from the fall of 2002 to the summer of 2003 demonstrates that each INGO's national origin played a critical role in shaping the organization's response.

Human Rights INGOs and Iraq

While the human rights stakes in Iraq were clear, there was important variation in the issues chosen, the political positions taken, and the recommendations offered by the major human rights INGOs. Through

---

5. Human Rights Watch, *Annual Report 2003* (January 2003): xxx. Saddam's government maintained very tight restrictions on humanitarian actors and repeatedly denied entrance to human rights groups, so few INGOs had a presence on the ground.

6. "President's Remarks at the United Nations General Assembly," White House press release, September 12, 2002.

7. *A Decade of Deception and Defiance,* White House background paper, September 12, 2002; *Saddam Hussein: Crimes and Human Rights Abuses,* Foreign and Commonwealth Office report, November 2002.

the 1990s, the "report mill" of Human Rights Watch had amply documented the brutality of the Iraqi regime, particularly its abuses of the Kurdish population in northern Iraq, yet the organization was relatively silent on Iraq through late summer and early fall of 2002.[8] By December, staffers were speaking out, pointing to the moral and logistical challenges of an intervention. In response to the dossier released by the British government, the director of HRW's international justice program pointed to the Foreign Office's unreceptive response to HRW's attempts to bring Saddam to justice in 1994; meanwhile, a HRW researcher suggested to the *New York Times* that a history of forced relocation in Iraq made for a potentially explosive refugee situation after an invasion.[9] In a formal policy paper on Iraq in mid-December, HRW pushed for the prosecution of Saddam Hussein and other senior officials but took no position on the use of force or the goal of regime change.[10] Instead, HRW called for the creation of an international tribunal to bring senior Iraqi officials to justice—a recommendation it would repeat over the coming months.

Immediately before and after the invasion, HRW focused its efforts on documenting rights violations and making targeted and practical policy recommendations to the U.S. government. Between January and mid-March, HRW released three reports on rights violations by the Iraqi regime that covered the repression of the Marsh Arabs, the use of executions, and the forcible expulsion of ethnic minorities. Meanwhile, in its reports and meetings with government officials, HRW was drawing attention to the likely "profound humanitarian consequences" of military action and urging potential combatants to uphold their obligations under

---

8. A search of both major newspapers and the group's news archive shows no statement on Iraq, save a late November press release. "US Needs to Screen Iraqi Opposition Allies," November 20, 2002, available at http://www.hrw.org/en/news/2002/11/20/us-needs-screen-iraqi-opposition-allies.

9. "Media and Political Salvo Hits Activists," *The Guardian,* December 3, 2002: 11; "Uprooted Iraqis See War as Path to Lost Homes," *New York Times,* December 5, 2002.

10. Human Rights Watch, *Justice for Iraq: A Policy Paper* (December 2002). Although HRW had previously recommended intervention in northern Iraq, Somalia, Bosnia, and Rwanda to protect civilians, it argued in January 2004 that an invasion of Iraq was not justified, as the slaughter of civilians was not imminent and the humanitarian rationale was clearly subordinate to other goals. "War in Iraq: Not a Humanitarian Intervention," *Human Rights Watch Annual Report 2004* (January 2004).

international humanitarian law.[11] When war was imminent, the organization focused on possible human rights violations in its conduct, including the use of human shields by the regime and cluster munitions by the coalition.[12] In the months after the invasion, HRW emphasized the need to restore law and order, offered a proposal for managing Iraqi oil, and asked that President Bush establish an international tribunal for senior Iraqi leaders.[13] The INGO did not come out in opposition to the war until its annual report was released in January 2004. In the run-up to the invasion, it used its contacts in the U.S. government to push narrow and actionable items on the human rights agenda, and its documentation of abuses by the Saddam regime provided ammunition for the supporters of the invasion.

The approach of Amnesty International looked similar on paper, but was actually much more antagonistic toward the U.S. government. AI has long taken a formal "no-position position" on violence and the use of force generally, but many Amnesty members and staffers are pacifists and were opposed to the war.[14] After Bush's September UN speech, Amnesty immediately took issue with threatening force in the name of the Iraqi people, calling it a "cold and calculated manipulation of the work of human rights activists."[15] In a letter to the UN Security Council several weeks later, AI secretary general Irene Khan pointed out that the UN had been created to "preserve peace" as well as protect human rights.[16] Amnesty was de facto opposed to the war.

---

11. "A Lonely Fight for Human Rights," *Toronto Star,* December 29, 2002; Human Rights Watch, *Iraqi Refugees, Asylum Seekers, and Displaced Persons* (February 2003); Human Rights Watch, *International Humanitarian Law Issues in a Potential War in Iraq* (February 20, 2003); Human Rights Watch, "Open Letter to the United Nations Security Council," February 24, 2003.

12. "Human Shields Take Stand in Baghdad," *Washington Post,* February 25, 2003; *Cluster Munitions a Foreseeable Hazard in Iraq, HRW Briefing Paper* (March 18, 2003).

13. "Iraqi Civilians Face Security Vacuum," HRW press release, April 9, 2003; *Considerations for the Management of Oil in Iraq, HRW Background Briefing,* April 2003; "Investigate Civilian Deaths in Iraq Military Operations," HRW press release, June 18, 2003; "Letter to President Bush: No Amnesty for Abuses by Former Iraqi Leaders," HRW press release, June 27, 2003.

14. Hopgood 2006, 198–99; Mahoney 2001, 6. Systematic studies of AI membership are few. One of AI France shows that 53% of members identify themselves politically as on the left or extreme left; another 29% identify as center-left (Duchesne 2003, 29).

15. "Iraq/USA: Not in the Name of Human Rights," AI press release, September 12, 2002 (AI Index MDE 14/009/2002); Irene Khan, "Who Cares about the People? Iraq II," *International Herald Tribune,* September 25, 2002.

16. "Iraq: Secretary General Asks UN to Ensure that Force is the Last Resort," AI press release, September 24, 2002 (AI Index MDE 14/010/2002).

Through the winter, Amnesty repeatedly stated that war could provoke a "massive humanitarian and human rights disaster," arguing at one point that "sacrificing the human rights of people for the sake of geopolitics is unacceptable."[17] While HRW focused on bringing Saddam to justice in an international tribunal, Amnesty spent the early months of 2003 calling for the deployment of international human rights monitors to Iraq to assess the possible impact of war.[18] Irene Khan claimed that though Iraqis faced an uncertain fate, the "only certainty is that if war comes, some of them will die."[19] In mid-February, Amnesty used its Urgent Action network to ask its worldwide membership to write to the Security Council to "avoid a human rights disaster of unprecedented gravity," and local Amnesty chapters later organized peace vigils as the bombing began.[20]

After the invasion, Amnesty continued its provocative criticisms of the U.S. government. Like HRW, Amnesty drew attention to the humanitarian obligations of occupying powers, but it used much more challenging language, suggesting that both sides might have committed "war crimes" and accusing the United States and Britain of working harder to protect oil wells than to protect the Iraqi people.[21] A formal July 2003 memorandum on law and order in Iraq returned to Amnesty's traditional tactics of careful documentation, drawing upon reports from Amnesty staff in Iraq since late April.[22] Yet its opposition to the war, rather than research on Iraq, shaped Amnesty's public pronouncements. The 2004 annual report described the U.S. administration's security agenda as "bankrupt of vision and bereft of principle," while the 2005 report claimed that the U.S. military prison at Guantánamo was "the gulag of our times."

---

17. "US Prepared to Act Alone," *International Herald Tribune,* January 27, 2003; "Iraq: Secretary General Challenges Powell," AI press release, January 26, 2003 (AI Index MDE 14/002/2003).

18. "United Nations/Iraq: Security Council Scared to Face Up to the Human Toll of Conflict in Iraq," AI press release, February 11, 2003 (AI Index MDE 14/017/2003).

19. Irene Khan, "Security for Whom? A Human Rights Response," *Amnesty International Report 2003* (May 2003), 5.

20. "Fear for Safety: the People of Iraq and Surrounding Countries," AI Urgent Action appeal, February 11, 2003 (AI Index MDE 14/006/2003); "War in the Gulf," *The Guardian,* March 21, 2003.

21. "In Iraq, A Battle for the Moral High Ground," *Christian Science Monitor,* April 1, 2003; "The Iraq Conflict: US Said to Care More about Iraqi Oil than Its People," *The Independent,* April 17, 2003.

22. Amnesty International, *Iraq: Memorandum on Concerns Relating to Law and Order,* July 2003 (AI Index MDE 14/157/2003)

The French group FIDH shared concerns about the massive human rights violations under the Saddam Hussein regime, but in contrast to both HRW and Amnesty, it had no qualms about opposing the war from the beginning. As early as December 2001, FIDH declared that the embargo against Iraq was itself a systematic violation of human rights. In a statement titled *No to America's War,* released on December 10, 2002—International Human Rights Day—FIDH argued that "under no circumstances" would an invasion help the Iraq population break free of repression.[23] FIDH did report on rights violations under the Saddam regime: for example, a co-authored report in January 2003 documented "silent ethnic cleansing" in Iraq and recommended the creation of an international criminal tribunal.[24] Generally, though, FIDH's protest strategy was in full force. The founding member of FIDH, the French Ligue des Droits de l'Homme, called on the French president to block the war through a veto at the Security Council and organized at least four demonstrations against the war between October 2002 and May 2003.[25]

As the fighting began in March, the stance of FIDH was clearly anti-war. The international secretariat and member organizations "vigorously condemn[ed]" the unilateral use of force as "illegal and illegitimate."[26] With two other European human rights INGOs, FIDH argued that the use of force was an act of international aggression.[27] In the months following the invasion, FIDH joined HRW and Amnesty in pushing for an international tribunal at which to try former Iraqi leaders rather than the establishment of a court within Iraq (the strategy preferred by the Americans).[28]

Overall, discomfort with the Iraqi invasion forced human rights activists to reassess their political strategies while creating divisions among and within organizations. In a December 2002 editorial, Bill Keller of the *New York Times* accused Amnesty of being indignant and squeamish

---

23. "No to America's War," FIDH press release, December 10, 2002.

24. *Iraq: Continuous and Silent Ethnic Cleansing,* FIDH and AIJ report, January 2003.

25. "La guerre contre l'Irak ne doit pas avoir lieu," LDH press release, October 7, 2002; "Non à la guerre en Irak!" LDH press release, March 14, 2003; "La LDH avec les organisations syndicales le 1er mai," LDH press release, April 30, 2003.

26. "An Appeal by the FIDH for Uniting for Peace and Justice for the Victims of the Iraqi Regime," FIDH press release, March 18, 2003; "Human Rights Federation Head Warns Iraq War Countries of World Court Role," *BBC Summary of World Broadcasts,* March 27, 2003.

27. "The Invasion of Iraq: Joint NGO Appeal," FIDH press release, March 27, 2003.

28. FIDH, "Open Letter to Members of the Security Council," May 13, 2003.

about the use of force, while lauding the general decision of Human Rights Watch to support military intervention.[29] Others who believed in the justifiability of the war chastised all human rights groups, including Human Rights Watch, for emphasizing the potential abuses in an uncertain postwar Iraq rather than the concrete and known heinous rights violations under Saddam (Cushman 2005). Still others were troubled by the implications of the arguments offered by human rights groups. For David Rieff, the argument that powerful governments are inconsistent in their protection of human rights (made explicitly by Amnesty and HRW) implies "a plea for endless colonial wars... and that scares me to death."[30]

The Iraq war also created divisions within human rights organizations, particularly Amnesty, which must juggle the demands of different national sections as well as the sometimes conflicting pressures from membership and staff. For example, when pressed to defend Amnesty's unwillingness to speak up about whether war is ever justified, the director of Amnesty Canada was forced to admit that the INGO would have taken no position on Britain's 1939 declaration of war against Nazi Germany.[31] Meanwhile, the director of Amnesty's American branch has since publicly expressed his personal belief that military action is not only appropriate but imperative in the face of massive crimes against humanity, a position clearly echoing that of Human Rights Watch.[32]

Thus, the three human rights INGOs acted in ways consistent with past practice and reflecting the central role of national origin. Human Rights Watch was unwilling to support the invasion as humanitarian, but it did not go so far as to condemn the war. Rather than alienate American policymakers, HRW pragmatically and publicly noted the awful nature of Saddam's regime and offered ample documentation of its disregard for human rights. Meanwhile, FIDH and Amnesty played up the negative

---

29. "The Selective Conscience," *New York Times,* December 14, 2002.

30. "Conversations with History: David Rieff," UC Berkeley Institute for International Studies video, March 2003.

31. "The Activist's Dilemma: What to Do about Iraq?" *The Globe and Mail* [Canada], December 4, 2002.

32. Bill Schulz (2003, 145) argued that if Saddam Hussein's brutality "did not at least arguably warrant military intervention of some sort, the debate over that concept fails to be an interesting one."

consequences of the sanctions regime and highlighted the likely rights violations in case of war, reflecting popular sentiment in both France and Britain. FIDH offered a principled protest against the war, characterizing the American unilateral action as aggression, while Amnesty tried to walk a fine line between being apolitical and acting in accordance with its membership in Europe opposed to the war. Amnesty's increasing emphasis on campaigning over research is evident in Iraq, but as predicted in the last chapter, that revealed tensions between different AI sections, particularly the American and British ones. The starkest difference between the political tactics of HRW and Amnesty may have been evident in each group's discussion of Iraqi oil—while HRW offered practical suggestions for managing oil revenues, Amnesty accused the Americans of putting economic considerations before human ones.

Humanitarian INGOs in Iraq

In many crises, humanitarian INGOs can claim an advantage over official donor agencies in the provision of humanitarian aid by pointing to deep local ties and a long-standing local presence. This was not the case in Iraq. Restrictions under the Baathist regime had kept most INGOs and donor agencies out of southern and central Iraq, and this fact, combined with the American military's explicit goal to "win hearts and minds," created substantially less space in Iraq for humanitarian INGOs than in many other conflicts. CARE, Oxfam, and MSF responded to this situation in very different ways according to their national origins.

CARE was unusual among INGOs in that it had been in Iraq since 1991, though under tight restrictions. As a result, it was uniquely positioned to shape the debate over the invasion, but it did not undertake a large advocacy role, instead prioritizing its programs in the field. The Iraq situation was difficult for CARE, as its historically close ties to the U.S. government clashed with its desire to protect its independence and the safety of its staff. Early on, CARE anticipated a large role in postwar Iraq, but it withdrew totally following the tragic kidnapping and murder in October 2004 of field office director Margaret Hassan.

In the months leading up to the war, CARE focused on delivering aid while advocacy remained a low priority. As early as May 2002, the CARE Iraq office and CARE Australia had begun contingency planning for war, but the first major CARE meeting on Iraq did not occur until December (CARE International 2003a, 2). Through the early months of 2003, CARE joined other INGOs in predicting likely devastation for the Iraqi people and pushing for unimpeded access for humanitarians. For example, director Hassan spent a week at the UN in January briefing the Security Council and UN agencies, arguing that the humanitarian situation had already reached "near catastrophic levels" and that a new war would make things vastly worse.[33] Hassan's UN visit was important, but CARE's focus remained on aid delivery; according to a September 2003 internal review, there was "no single advocacy strategy for Iraq" (CARE International 2003b, 23, 33).

The question of cooperation with the U.S. government was deeply troubling for CARE. Several times, USAID invited major INGOs to apply for funding for humanitarian response and community development, and although many other American INGOs agreed to participate, CARE decided to reject the funding.[34] According to internal CARE documents, this was a last-minute decision that was "painful" for many staffers, and the board of CARE International later clarified the organization's policy: CARE would not take money from belligerents prior to or during a war, but would accept funding afterward.[35] Later, CARE and the U.S. Office of Foreign Disaster Assistance entered into a cooperative agreement to provide assistance in the areas of health and water and sanitation, and the $10 million provided by OFDA accounted for 45% of CARE's Iraq office budget.[36] Beyond funding, the different national chapters of CARE met regularly with their government counterparts throughout the spring to discuss logistics and planning.[37] The exception to this was CARE France, which was "somewhat sidelined by press, government and the NGO community because of its image as an Anglo-Saxon NGO" (CARE

---

33. "Concern over Optics Clogs Aid Flow for Iraq," *Globe and Mail,* February 1, 2003.

34. Nick Pelham, "Aid Groups Face Dilemma," *Christian Science Monitor,* February 12, 2003; "Humanitarian Groups Spurn Iraq," *Wall Street Journal,* May 29, 2003.

35. CARE International 2003b, iv. See also "Aid Groups Will Refuse Cash for Iraq," *Toronto Star,* March 11, 2003.

36. Author's calculations based on figures in CARE International 2003b, Annex 3.

37. Clare Short, "Written Ministerial Statement by the Secretary of State," House of Commons International Development Committee, *Government Response to the Committee's Fourth Report of Session 2002–03,* HC 561, March 24, 2003.

International 2003b, 11). In delivering aid, CARE, like many other humanitarian INGOs, refused to accept protection from the military forces of the coalition.[38]

Consistent with its high level of professionalization, CARE invested many resources in ensuring staff safety. While all humanitarians are of course cognizant of the personal risks of humanitarian action, the safety of personnel is "an overriding consideration in all that CARE does."[39] For example, when several humanitarian INGOs were asked in a House of Commons hearing if there was an ideological basis for objecting to receiving military assistance with the provision of humanitarian aid, CARE instead highlighted the practical implications for the safety of workers in the field.[40] When the bombing began, CARE decided not to evacuate its international staff from Baghdad—the trade-off for the organization was that security concerns kept its advocacy staff from speaking publicly about its work in Iraq (CARE International 2003a, 2–5). Through the spring and summer of 2003, CARE was the only INGO in Iraq with a dedicated security adviser on its staff (CARE International 2003b, 18).

Like CARE, Oxfam focused on addressing what appeared to be a pending humanitarian disaster, but clearly expressed its opposition to the war. Oxfam had been active in Iraq in the early 1990s but did not have a presence in Baghdad in 2002.[41] In the month after Bush's UN speech, Oxfam argued that war would likely create a humanitarian catastrophe. After a visit by staffers to Iraq at the end of October, Oxfam claimed that it "is not true to assume that the suffering of Iraqi civilians...could not get any worse...[a military attack] could do just that."[42] Oxfam GB director Barbara Stocking made the same argument in an *International Herald Tribune*

---

38. "Relief Crisis Unfolds as Iraq War Progresses," *The Lancet,* March 29, 2003.

39. CARE International 2009, 3. This is according to guidelines on cooperation with the military developed in the wake of Iraq.

40. See comments by Raja Jarrah (CARE UK) in "Preparing for the Humanitarian Consequences of Possible Military Action Against Iraq, Volume I," House of Commons, Select Committee on International Development, *Fourth Report of Session 2002–03* (London: The Stationary Office Limited, March 12, 2003), 20.

41. Rita Bhatia, "NGO Opportunities, Options, and Constraints Regarding Iraq," *Sanctions on Iraq: Background, Consequences, Strategies* (Cambridge, UK: Campaign Against Sanctions on Iraq, 2000): 55–56.

42. *Oxfam: Iraq Assessment Visit Oct 2002,* Oxfam report, October 31, 2002.

op-ed piece in December.[43] To back up this policy position, Oxfam released
several briefing papers on the humanitarian crisis among Iraqi civilians.[44]
Oxfam continued its vocal opposition to the war up until the bombing
began, and different Oxfam chapters worldwide, including Oxfam America, organized antiwar marches and vigils.[45] In a brief released right before
the invasion, Oxfam highlighted the obligation of the occupying force to
provide for the civilian population, arguing that if the environment proved
too dangerous for civilian agencies, "military forces must be prepared to
provide assistance."[46]

Once the war began, Oxfam focused on delivering aid, particularly in
water supply and sanitation and in public health, but continued its policy
work.[47] In research reports released in the spring, Oxfam advanced several concrete policy recommendations, including the transfer of authority within Iraq to the United Nations and cancellation of Iraq's external
debt.[48] In typical fashion, Oxfam did not shy away from provocative criticism of policymakers. For example, when British forces delivered food aid
to the southern port city of Umm Qasr, an Oxfam media officer said, "a
few boxes chucked out of the back of an Army truck may look good, but
it is not the same as organized distribution to the 16 million in Iraq who
needed it before the war even began."[49] As one Oxfam policy advisor explained, "Oxfam's stance at the beginning of the Iraq war was not neutral,"
but "our humanitarian response remains independent and impartial," fo-

43. "Iraqis' Suffering Can Be Made Worse—Don't Go to War," *International Herald Tribune,*
December 27, 2002. Compare this to CARE's language: "Despite our firm conviction that war is
not inevitable, and our strenuous advocacy for a diplomatic solution, we reluctantly accept that a
war is very likely to take place. We do not condone this war.... However, we have a responsibility
to the population we have been serving all these years." CARE, House of Commons Select Committee on International Development Minutes of Evidence, *Memorandum Submitted by CARE International,* February 11, 2003.
44. *Protecting Iraq's Civilians, Oxfam Briefing Paper 40* (February 2003); *Iraq's Reconstruction
and the Role of the United Nations, Oxfam Briefing Note* (April 2003).
45. "Oxfam Holds Candlelight Vigil in Hong Kong to Protest Iraq War," *BBC Summary of
World Broadcasts,* February 12, 2003; "Dialing Up Anti-War Protests," www.time.com, February
26, 2003 (accessed January 14, 2010); "Virtual Protesters Bombard Washington," www.guardian.
co.uk, February 26, 2003 (accessed January 14, 2010).
46. *Iraq: Humanitarian-Military Relations, Oxfam Briefing Paper 41* (March 2003): 3.
47. Oxfam, "Iraq Crisis Update," May 2, 2003 (available at www.reliefweb.int).
48. *Iraq's Reconstruction and the Role of the United Nations, Oxfam Briefing Note* (April 2003);
A Fresh Start for Iraq, Oxfam Briefing Paper 48 (May 2003).
49. "Don't Use This for Propaganda, Warns Oxfam," *Daily Telegraph,* March 29, 2003.

cused on the delivery of aid to those in need.[50] The deterioration in secu-rity conditions in August 2003 led Oxfam to remove its international staff while continuing to fund local partners on the ground.[51]

Likewise, Oxfam continued to accept government funds for non-Iraqi programs but refused funding from belligerent states for its efforts in Iraq. A spokesman argued that this was "highly unusual" for the organization but said Oxfam wanted to avoid being seen as "an instrument of British foreign policy."[52] Unlike CARE, which accepted U.S. government financing after the invasion, Oxfam continued to refuse funding "from countries that have troops in the country."[53] Additionally, Oxfam and other British INGOs were ambivalent about raising private funds for Iraq, for fear that soliciting large sums would signal their support for the war. The Disasters Emergency Committee, the national fundraising consortium of a dozen INGOs includ-ing Oxfam, announced that it would raise funds and operate only under the banner of the United Nations (Graham 2003, 40). In the United States, Oxfam America used the subscriber list of the liberal group MoveOn.org to raise more than half a million dollars in 2003 for relief efforts in Iraq.[54]

Consistent with the advocacy strategy described in chapter 2, Oxfam's provocative statements were accompanied by visits by the INGO with gov-ernment officials in London and Washington. In the weeks before the war, Oxfam participated in meetings with American and British donor agen-cies to share information and discuss postwar plans.[55] Unlike in the United States, where NGOs were intentionally excluded from prewar planning, general planning by the British government for postwar Iraq was weak until early March, when DFID began to consider postwar humanitarian needs with the assistance of British INGOs.[56]

---

50. Jo Nickolls, "Limits to Neutrality in Iraq," *Humanitarian Exchange Magazine* 25 (Decem-ber 2003), 9.

51. In April 2004, Oxfam closed its office in Nassiriyah that had operated with local staff. Oxfam International and NGO Coordination Committee in Iraq, *Rising to the Humanitarian Challenge in Iraq, Oxfam Briefing Paper105* (July 2007): 23.

52. "Charities Boycott Grants in War Protest," *Daily Telegraph,* March 12, 2003.

53. *Rising to the Humanitarian Challenge in Iraq, Oxfam Briefing Paper 105,* 27.

54. "Americans Open Their Wallets for Iraqis," *Christian Science Monitor,* April 17, 2003.

55. Short, "Written Ministerial Statement by the Secretary of State"; Oxfam, "Right Now: Oxfam on Iraq," January 8, 2003 (available at www.reliefweb.int).

56. James K. Bishop, "War In Afghanistan and Iraq," *The Liaison* [Annual Newsletter of the Center for Excellence in Disaster Management and Humanitarian Assistance, U.S. Pacific

Unsurprisingly, the MSF approach to Iraq stood out among humanitarian INGOs. MSF had been active in northern and southern Iraq after the Gulf War but had been unable to establish a presence in the country since 1993. In January 2003, MSF issued a statement that echoed the sentiments of many other INGOs: MSF described its difficulty in reaching Iraqis in the past and calling for access to victims in case of a war.[57] But MSF was unique in its political stance, as described by the director of MSF USA in 2004:

> As many U.S.-based NGOS were discussing possible cooperation with a potential belligerent [in early 2003], other NGOs, mainly in Europe, implicitly and explicitly opposed the war. A consortium of French NGOs, for example, questioned the necessity of going to war given the possibilities for the peaceful disarmament of Iraq...
>
> The positions of both U.S.- and European-based NGOs were remarkable because while they generally reflected public opinion in the United States and Europe respectively, then also contradicted the accepted principles of humanitarian action [of neutrality and impartiality]....For that reason, MSF adhered to its longstanding position...and did not speak out on the "rightness" or "wrongness" of this or any other war (Torrente 2004, 11–12).

MSF carefully guarded this neutrality; for example, when MSF founder Bernard Kouchner publicly expressed the view that "Saddam must go," the organization took pains to explain that Kouchner had had no involvement with MSF since 1979 and that his views in no way reflected those of MSF.[58]

Instead of opposing or supporting the war, MSF worked to get into Iraq quickly and visibly. The president of MSF International, Morten Rostrup, and five other MSF staff drove into Baghdad a few days before the

---

Command] (2004); "Transcript of Maj Gen Tim Cross Hearing," *Iraq Inquiry Committee* [UK] *Hearings,* December 7, 2009; letter from Clare Short to Tony Blair, "Iraq: Humanitarian Planning and the Role of the UN," February 14, 2003 (available at http://www.iraqinquiry.org.uk/media/44223/140203short-blair.pdf, accessed February 24, 2010).

57. Nicolas de Torrente, "Humanitarian Concerns about a Possible War on Iraq," MSF press release, January 30, 2003.

58. "Why One French Voice Says 'Saddam must go,'" *International Herald Tribune,* February 25, 2003; "Letters to the Editor," *The Australian,* March 20, 2003.

bombing began. Rostrup later said this was not a "typical" MSF mission but that he believed it was worth the risk to provide medical assistance.[59] Several weeks later, MSF alerted coalition forces that they would be driving two trucks of emergency medical supplies on the dangerous road from Amman, Jordan, to Baghdad.[60] Risky actions of this kind did not come without costs; two MSF volunteers were kidnapped on April 2 and held for eight days by Iraqi police.[61] When asked whether MSF's critics were right to condemn the organization as "cowboys," Rostrup responded that MSF knew the risks but felt that an independent organization needed to be in Iraq.[62] MSF later described these actions as "a powerful expression of solidarity, person to person, without discrimination and devoid of any ulterior motive."[63]

There had actually been a heated debate at a March 28th board meeting in Paris over what, exactly, the rationale was for installing an MSF team in Baghdad (Fassin 2007). Many at the meeting questioned the efficacy of sending just a half-dozen people whose contribution would be modest at best; others pointed to the principles of the MSF charter that required providing assistance to victims of armed conflict. Even though the need to save lives was the official justification for MSF's insertion into Baghdad, the *de facto* reason was a principled one—it allowed MSF to place themselves "on the side of the victims" (Fassin 2007, 517). Consistent with the evidence from Chapter 2, principle drove practice at this French INGO.

In relation to government authorities, MSF continued its longstanding practices of refusing government funding while highlighting the responsibilities of states to care for civilians. MSF-USA director Nicholas de Torrente testified before the UN Security Council in early April, highlighting the constraints felt by relief agencies and criticizing the American attempt to use humanitarian aid to win "hearts and minds." The provision of relief by belligerents was not humanitarian action, according to MSF, "but part of a belligerent's obligations under the Geneva Conventions," and MSF

---

59. BBC News, "Putting Profit Before Health," *HARDtalk,* June 4, 2003.

60. "French Medical Supplies Cross Border with Jordan on Long Journey to Baghdad," *The Independent,* March 27, 2003.

61. "Freed Aid Workers Tell of Prison Torture," *Independent on Sunday,* April 13, 2003.

62. HARDtalk, June 4, 2003.

63. Nicolas de Torrente, "Humanitarian Concerns in Iraq," testimony given at the UN Security Council, April 9, 2003 (available at www.reliefweb.net).

repeatedly criticized the United States for failing to live up to its obligations as an occupying power (Brauman and Salignon 2004; Torrente 2004,
15–16). Because of its refusal to cooperate with American authorities, MSF
was initially frustrated by coalition forces, who instructed local hospital
personnel and the Ministry of Health to not accept any private emergency
assistance until Baghdad was deemed secure (Salignon 2003, 58). While
MSF was willing to ignore these instructions, many other NGOs were not,
as they feared that defiance would lead to a future loss of funding.[64] Still,
fierce independence did not protect MSF from the deteriorating security
situation, and MSF closed its mission in Iraq in October 2004.

In Iraq, humanitarian groups worldwide were concerned with the
politicization of aid as part of the coalition strategy to "win hearts and
minds." Despite this universal concern, the three INGOs responded in
quite different ways. CARE took the unprecedented step of refusing U.S.
government money during the conflict, but it sought to reestablish that
relationship once the fighting was over. As usual, the "Establishment radicals" at Oxfam had a coherent advocacy strategy and policy position, and
the organization's opposition to the war slowed private fundraising and
steered it away from government money. Today, CARE's website is nearly
devoid of information on Iraq, an attempt perhaps to bury painful memo-
ries, while Oxfam continues to work with partners there, including the
umbrella organization of local and international NGOs, the NGO Coordination Committee in Iraq. And while MSF stands out among French
NGOs for its unwillingness to officially oppose the war, its need to see aid
as not just assistance but as "de facto protest," standing in solidarity with
the victims of war, echoes the voluntarist spirit of the French associative
sector.[65]

Lessons from Iraq

The organizations discussed here represent just a handful of the INGOs
that responded to the Iraq conflict. Many INGOs had to rethink their

---

64. "In an Iraqi Hospital Which Ran Out of Oxygen, Hope Is in Short Supply," *Daily Telegraph,* April 14, 2003.

65. Austen Davies, *Thoughts on Conditions and Conditionalities, Terms of Engagement: HPG
Report,* no. 6 (July 2000): 27.

practices in Iraq, from the American umbrella group InterAction, which was unusually tough in its criticism of the U.S. government, to the International Save the Children Alliance, whose American and British sections were sharply divided over fundraising and advocacy.[66] Yet while the attempted co-optation of the language of humanitarians and rights activists by the American-led coalition may have been particularly egregious in Iraq, it is nothing new. In fact, the humanitarian rationale has been and likely will be increasingly used as justification for war.[67]

The Iraq conflict brings the INGO practices of fundraising, advocacy, and professionalization into sharp relief, and the short discussion here suggests the power of national origin in the field as well as at home. Broad national patterns among INGOs held true in the run-up to the war. The American groups were challenged to rethink their cooperative stance with government, but both CARE and HRW avoided a direct challenge to the basic premise of the U.S. government policy of regime change, focusing their considerable professional capacities instead on the pragmatic considerations of how to get aid to Iraqis (CARE) and how to run Iraq after the war (HRW). Meanwhile, the "Establishment radicals" at the British INGOs opposed the British and American war effort (though only de facto at Amnesty), but the largest British humanitarian groups still met with UK government officials in the weeks before the war and offered concrete policy proposals for a postwar Iraq. Finally, the tendency toward principled and vocal protest among French INGOs was quite evident at FIDH and MSF, though MSF's more classic vision of humanitarianism kept it from joining most other French INGOs in staunchly opposing the invasion.

One important weakness of the Iraq case is that it offers little opportunity to explore the relationship between home offices and field offices within INGOs. Because few INGOs had a presence in central and southern Iraq before April 2003, we cannot explore how plans formulated in headquarters translated into actual practice in Baghdad. The one exception is CARE, whose Iraq country office had long worked in coordination with CARE Australia. Interestingly, CARE Iraq received funding from

---

66. Sunga 2007; Kevin Maguire, "How British Charity Was Silenced on Iraq," *The Guardian,* November 28, 2003.

67. For a description and critique of this trend, see Mamdani 2008.

the U.S. government for the first time in 2003, and the international CARE offices were initially concerned with the country office's ability to meet the stringent reporting requirements of USAID. Subsequent country visits by representatives from CARE USA and CARE Australia were meant to "build capacity"—in other words, to bring CARE Iraq's practices in line with the CARE confederation's emphasis on being efficient and effective (CARE International2003b, 15). In Iraq, therefore, the sudden prominence of the country brought the practices of the field office closer to the center of gravity within CARE International—CARE USA. Beyond the Iraq case, the particular interactions between home and field office will vary by organization based on the centralization of decision making; these interactions deserve much more attention as cases where national cultures and organizational practices intersect.

This look at how human rights and humanitarian INGOs responded to the American-led invasion of Iraq, like the opening discussion of humanitarian agencies in Haiti, starkly reveals that while INGOs may all respond to the same global events and crises, the ways in which they respond vary substantially. In Iraq, with the world's most powerful state an active belligerent, the questions of where to get money, how to relate to government authorities, and whether and how to engage in political action became critical points of contention within and among INGOs. CARE took the painful and unprecedented step of rejecting U.S. government funding during the invasion but quickly returned to cooperation with American authorities. Amnesty had to reconcile its long-standing aim of being seen as apolitical with the strong antiwar sentiments of its members. MSF's desire to get into Baghdad early and independently meant that few Iraqis actually received any assistance from it. The examples of Haiti and Iraq suggest that the "varieties of activism" approach may offer a powerful explanation for differences among INGOs in other situations.

The Strength of National Roots

Despite two decades of globalization, and the establishment by most INGOs of global umbrella structures meant to make these organizations more cosmopolitan, large and prominent INGOs are still substantially different from each another because they are products of different national environments. These "varieties of activism" shape the practices of an organization's headquarters in the developed world and, as demonstrated in Haiti and Iraq, the practices of the organization as it moves abroad. To continue the metaphor suggested by Tarrow's description of transnational activists as "rooted cosmopolitans," the national roots of these organizations are strong in the face of the winds of globalization.

Proponents of the idea that globalization will make INGOs more similar to each other may argue that change is coming but not yet evident. I am suspicious of this ultimately unfalsifiable argument. Still, even if convergence in organizational practice is on the horizon, this book offers precise information about the various national starting points that differentiate INGOs and it suggests that the success of any particular strategy may depend on the national setting. For example, if the protest politics of French INGOs become the global model upon which INGOs converge, it is unlikely that they will have much success in achieving policy change in the American arena, where institutions and practices are much more amenable to insider lobbying.

Of course, the national environments examined here are not static but change over time, as evidenced by the growing strength of civil society organizations in France over the twentieth century. In addition, policymakers look to the experiences of other countries in governing their civil society sectors when considering policy change. Still, this change is slow and governed by preexisting nationally rooted social practices and norms. Thus, in spite of British charity officials' interest in an "American-style" tax regime for encouraging private donations when the reform of British charity law was under way, the change has not resulted in substantial growth in the overall size of charitable giving in the UK. Local changes in rules and procedures are unlikely to produce radical changes in the underlying national vision of how charitable organizations should act. This study has focused on tangible and easily measurable factors like regulations, material resources, and staff levels, but it is the underlying differences in how Americans, British, and French understand appropriate charitable action that drive the variation in INGO practice.

Two examples help illustrate the importance of these underlying norms. First, consider the fact that the oversight of political activities by charities in Britain and the United States seems to have produced effects opposite from what would be expected if we consider the regulatory structure alone. Despite several prominent investigations and sanctions on the part of the active watchdog Charity Commission in Britain, Oxfam continues with aggressive advocacy work, suggesting that the organization views political activism as perfectly appropriate and necessary. In the United States, by contrast, oversight by the Internal Revenue Service is weak, yet charities like CARE remain deeply wary of confrontational political activity. The threat of penalties from regulatory institutions does not account for different INGO practices.

As a second example, consider the relationship between human rights INGOS and the American foundation sector. These foundations have, to a substantial degree, shaped the organizational landscape of the global human rights movement, which would seem to support the resource dependency hypothesis that the preferences of organizations are primarily shaped by their financial supporters. Article 19, Interights, Human Rights Watch, Human Rights First, and perhaps Reporters sans frontières may be more alike than not in the areas of professionalization and management, and all receive significant support from a small group of donors. Yet these practices first emerged in the United States as shared understandings among donors and human rights groups about the appropriate mechanism for pursuing human rights protection. The idea of human rights monitoring and reporting—today the hallmark of American groups like Human Rights Watch—was developed with the support of, but not at the behest of, HRW's major donor, the Ford Foundation. Thus, while practices may be diffused to international human rights groups via the mechanisms suggested by resource dependency, those practices may reflect a deeper consensus regarding the appropriate ways in which INGOs should promote the cause of human rights.

All of this may be terribly depressing to activists and aid workers looking to overcome what appear to be barriers to effective non-state international action. But the lack of collaboration within both the human rights and the humanitarian sectors is not news to practitioners: a 2009 review of international humanitarian action finds "little consistent or collective working across the whole humanitarian sector," while a recent book on rights advocacy highlights some tactical convergence among INGOs but admits that this does not seem to signal a "merging and blurring of identities and methods."[68] These groups are not completely incapable of cooperation—the prominent examples of successful transnational campaigns discussed in the introduction demonstrate this—but if we are going to understand why specific campaigns succeed or fail, we need to understand the particular stakes at each of the potential members of these transnational efforts.

Ultimately, the fundamental problem may be one of perspective: rather than viewing nationally grounded practices as restrictions on the growth of transnational activism, we might reimagine them as supports and nourishment. The deep roots of Oxfam in Britain, of Human Rights Watch in the United States, and of Médecins Sans Frontières in France are *assets* for transnational activists looking to change British, American, or French policy or practice. One lesson from recent campaigns against globalization may be that it is much easier to identify a shared set of undesirable outcomes than it is to identify and achieve concrete solutions. Real action requires money, organization, political access, and friends, and these things do not exist in a cosmopolitan ether but in particular states and societies. INGOs that are part of global confederations are uniquely capable of recognizing the limits of any one state policy or social practice and of using their national roots to push for global good.

Beyond rethinking the role of national origin, the case studies I have outlined suggest that the initial decisions of the founders of nongovernmental organizations are crucial: to build a strong transnational organization, you need to start with an intentionally transnational organization. Amnesty International was founded in just this way, and although divisions among different national chapters may still create headaches for Amnesty leaders, the centralization and relative insulation of the International Secretariat make for a much more cosmopolitan organization than the international secretariats of either Oxfam or CARE. Of course, setting down roots in many countries is difficult, given the varied understandings of charitable action described here. An additional recommendation might be that a narrow issue focus is more likely to attract adherents in many countries than a multi-issue approach that will oblige an organization to

---

68. Active Learning Network for Accountability and Performance in Humanitarian Action, *Eighth Review of Humanitarian Action* (London: ODI, July 2009): 3; Nelson and Dorsey 2008, 177.

choose priorities. The concept of the "prisoner of conscience" was easily identifiable and had broad appeal through the Western world. In sum, rather than try to homogenize national organizations into a global one, the proponents of global civil society would be better served by trying to graft a narrow vision onto several organized groups with strong national roots.

International nongovernmental organizations are powerful actors in world politics and fascinating objects of study. The existing literature on INGOs has done an excellent job of demonstrating their significance while arguing for the importance of identity and interest in the field of international relations. INGOs do affect state policy, but state-level factors—including regulations, material resources, political opportunities, and social networks—also affect INGOs. Thus, while activists may have global interests and may seek to have transnational identities, their practices are firmly national. From the Parisian offices of Action contre la Faim to the headquarters of Amnesty UK in London to the CARE advocacy office in Washington, INGOs raise money, engage policymakers, and understand the very nature of their work in very different ways. This book has only scratched the surface of the different "varieties of activism" in the United States, Britain, and France, but hopefully it will begin an important conversation about how both global and domestic forces interact to shape the field upon which nonstate actors operate. There is no global civil society of shared norms and practices. But the fragmented and dynamic reality of transnational associational life is equally fascinating.

Appendix A

CASE SELECTION

These few pages give a more detailed elaboration of my case selection method, regarding both the choice of countries and of particular INGOs and also the extent to which the selection allows for testing alternative explanations of INGO practices.

Selecting Countries and Organizations

Research into the role of national origin for INGOs involves two related questions: *Does* national origin matter, and if so, *how* does it matter? The first question speaks directly to the claims of global civil society proponents, while the second question involves a more complex picture of the role of various national-level factors. Answering the first question would suggest the selection of very different countries—the United States and Japan, for example. Yet early research revealed that the answer to the first question was fairly clear; for example, Kim Reimann and Robert

Pekkanen offer clear evidence that Japanese INGOs are quite different from American INGOs.[1] Many of my early interviews revealed that practitioners themselves thought that the national origin of INGOs mattered in some sense.

Thus, this book aims to answer the second and more difficult question of *how* national origin matters. The "least-likely" method of case selection suggests looking at very similar countries. According to the Union of International Associations, the United States, Britain, and France are among the top four hosts of INGO headquarters.[2] All three are also rich Western industrialized democracies with the wealth and freedoms that make them amenable to civil society organizations. A demonstration of significant differences among INGOs from these three countries thus offers great insight into the transnational INGO sector as a whole. The comparison between the United States and Britain is particularly useful for examining whether national origin matters, as the shared cultural heritage and political traditions of the two countries make it least likely that observable differences among INGOs from each country exist. Of course, this is not the only paired country comparison that would be useful for examining the role of national origin—France and Belgium would also make for an interesting comparison, though choosing organizations in Belgium is complicated by the presence of European Union offices, which draw in many INGOs whose origins are not Belgian. Ultimately, I chose three countries that are fairly similar in global perspective.

The next question thus became: Among all of the French, British, and American INGOs, how to choose particular cases? Looking to other studies of INGOs and multinational corporations offers little guidance. A leading American study of the largest humanitarian NGOs (Lindenberg and Bryant 2001) included those organizations willing and able to attend a series of conferences. Many of the major studies of human rights NGOs are essentially biographies of these organizations and focus more

---

1. Kim D. Reimann, "Building Global Civil Society from the Outside In?" in *The State of Civil Society in Japan,* ed. Frank Schwartz and Susan Pharr (Cambridge University Press, 2003); Robert Pekkanen, *Japan's Dual Civil Society: Members without Advocates* (Stanford University Press, 2006).

2. A ranking of countries based on the number of INGO headquarters puts the US first, UK second, Belgium third, and France fourth. See Union of International Associations, *Yearbook of International Organizations* (2003), fig. 2.1.8.

on deep description than on explicit and careful comparison with other NGOs (Welch 2001; Korey 1998; Tolley 1990–91; though see Hopgood 2006). The "varieties of capitalism" literature has few examples of a case-study methodology; most studies used broad survey-type approaches to study corporations, though several focus more narrowly on specific sectors or issues (Doremus et al. 1998; Berger and Dore 1996, esp. chaps. 4 and 10; Harzing and Sorge 2003). One important insight that came out of this review was that INGOs working in different issue areas or sectors face very different tasks, and my study needed to take into account these sectoral effects.

Ultimately, the critical case research design suggests focusing on those cases where it is least likely that one would observe national origin effects. Thus, I chose organizations that have a broad global reach, with many offices in both the developed and developing world. It would not be very surprising to find national effects for a British INGO with just one or two offices abroad, but the expectation is that the effects of national origin should be much less strong for those organizations that have created vast global structures. At the same time, the analysis of the offices of the major INGOs in foreign host countries provides additional "least-likely" scenarios, and the dozen "mini-cases" provide confirmation that the practices of smaller INGOs are also strongly affected by their national origins.

Case Selection and Alternative Explanations

The multitiered case selection across two different sectors allows for the simultaneous exploration of the effects of both the national origin and the charitable sector of the organizations studied. In addition, this research design offers insight into the process by which organizational practices are exported to different national settings. Still, there are at least two possible objections to the case selection.

First, there are possible generational effects on organizations. One might argue that INGOs established more recently are less likely to be affected by national patterns, as coming of age in an era of globalization has made these organizations more responsive to global pressures. In other words, perhaps younger INGOs are actually the least likely of all to be affected by their national origins. Yet there are empirical and theoretical reasons for not looking at these INGOs. First, anecdotal evidence suggests that younger organizations are not necessarily less rooted in national environments. For example, International Relief and Development, an American humanitarian INGO, was established in 1998, but is heavily reliant on American sources of funding and uses fundraising and advocacy strategies closely in line with those of other American INGOs.[3] Second, because younger organizations tend to be smaller, a study of younger INGOs would reveal much less about the human rights sector or the humanitarian relief sector as a whole.[4] In addition, there is good reason for thinking that the INGOs that are leaders today are likely to be leaders tomorrow. For example, American and British grant-making agencies tend to favor larger INGOs, making it harder for other organizations to challenge the preeminence of the major groups. Finally, different charitable sectors have expanded at different times; while the interwar and post–World War II period saw the establishment of many leading humanitarian INGOs, the human rights sector saw an explosion of INGOs in the late 1970s. All combined, these factors make it difficult to control for organizational age in any particular sector. Instead, this study focuses on those INGOs that, according to practitioners and scholars alike, are dominant in their fields. Still, as the cases demonstrate (particularly of MSF and the human rights INGOs), organizational age may be an important factor for some INGOs.

A second possible objection is that the case studies are rather static, looking only at recent practices of the INGOs concerned. In order to discover whether INGOs today are truly increasingly uniform as a result of globalization, we would need reliable data on their activities over several decades. Unfortunately, they generally do a poor job of breaking down and reporting their activities in regular fashion. INGOs have gotten better over time (perhaps, convergence proponents might argue, as a reflection

---

3. According to the organization's 2005 IRS 990 form, out of a total revenue of $85 million, half came from the U.S. government, and nothing was spent on lobbying.

4. Among the largest American INGOs with a global reach in the sectors of human rights, international relief, and general relief and development, the average age of founding is 1963 (n = 41). The decade with the most frequent number of foundings was the 1970s (10 American INGOs). In total, 73% of the largest American INGOs were established before the 1980s. Data kindly provided by Janelle Kerlin, from Reid and Kerlin 2006.

of worldwide professionalization of the sector), but the dearth of reliable figures on their activities before the mid-1990s makes it difficult to assess whether they are more alike today than they were two or three decades ago. A few organizational histories describe INGO core strategies over time, and several used for this study—including Maggie Black's (1991) profile of Oxfam and Eugene Linden's (1976) study of CARE—reveal substantial continuity in past and present practice at these two INGOs, despite the significant expansion of their global reach.

Appendix B

Interviews Conducted

The list below identifies the organizations and agencies at which I conducted interviews. Most of the over seventy interviews were conducted between February 2006 and May 2007 in the United States, Britain, and France. These semistructured interviews averaged an hour in length and offered invaluable background to the public information produced by each INGO. A special effort was made to select interview subjects who had experience at more than one charity or INGO, who might be able to offer a broader perspective on strategies and structures within their organization. Most subjects agreed to being identified simply as "staff member" of the INGO, and all were assured anonymity. A few subjects elected to have their name used, and they are identified in the text. The list is not exhaustive, as some subjects asked that no organization identity be given.

Humanitarian INGOs

Primary Cases

CARE France
CARE International
CARE UK
CARE USA
MSF France
MSF UK
MSF USA
Oxfam America
Oxfam France
Oxfam GB

Other American Humanitarian INGOs

International Rescue Committee
Mercy Corps
Save the Children USA

Other British Humanitarian INGOs

Action Against Hunger UK
Christian Aid
Salvation Army UK
Save the Children UK

Other French Humanitarian INGOs

Action contre la Faim
Médecins du Monde
Oxfam France

Human Rights Organizations

Primary Cases

Amnesty France
Amnesty International (Secretariat)
Amnesty UK

Amnesty USA
FIDH
Human Rights Watch

Other American Human Rights INGOs

Global Rights
Human Rights First
Physicians for Human Rights

Other British Human Rights INGOs

Anti-Slavery International
Article 19
Interights

Other French Human Rights INGOs

Ligue des Droits de l'Homme

Other Organizations

United States

Department of State
InterAction
Open Society Institute

Britain

Foreign and Commonwealth Office
HAP (Humanitarian Accountability Partnership) International
Overseas Development Institute

France

CEDETIM (Center for International Solidarity Studies and Initiatives)
Coordination SUD
Groupe URD (Urgence Réhabilitation Développement)

References

ALNAP [Active Learning Network for Accountability and Performance in Humanitarian Action]. 2010. *The State of the Humanitarian System.* London: Overseas Development Institute, January.

Alvey, Norman. 1995. *From Chantry to Oxfam: A Short History of Charity and Charity Legislation.* Chichester: Phillimore for British Association for Local History.

Aksartova, Sada. 2003. "In Search of Legitimacy: Peace Grant Making of US Philanthropic Foundations, 1988–1996." *Nonprofit and Voluntary Sector Quarterly* 32 (March): 25–46.

Amos-Wilson, Pauline. 1996. "Management Training in UK NGOs." *Journal of European Industrial Training* 20 (1): 15–19.

Anderson, Ian. 2000. "Northern NGO Advocacy." *Development in Practice* 10 (3–4): 445–52.

Anheier, Helmut, and Siobhan Daly. 2005. "Philanthropic Foundations: A New Global Force?" *Global Civil Society 2004/5.* London: SAGE Publications.

Anheier, Helmut, Marlies Glasius, and Mary Kaldor. 2001. *Global Civil Society 2001.* Oxford: Oxford University Press.

Appleton, Andrew. 2006. "Associational Life in Contemporary France." In *Developments in French Politics 3,* edited by Alistair Cole et al., 54–69. London: Palgrave.

Archambault, Edith. 1996. *The Nonprofit Sector in France.* New York: St. Martin's Press.

———. 2001. "France." In *Foundations in Europe,* edited by Andreas Schluter et al., 121–22. London: Directory of Social Change.

Archambault, Edith, Marie Gariazzo, Helmut K. Anheier, and Lester M. Salamon. 1999. "France: from Jacobin Tradition to Decentralization." In *Global Civil Society: Dimensions of the Nonprofit Sector,* edited by Lester Salamon et al., 81–97. Bloomfield: Kumarian Press.

Barman, Emily. 2002. "Asserting Difference: The Strategic Response of Nonprofit Organizations to Competition." *Social Forces* 80 (June): 1191–222.

Barnett, Michael. 2005. "Humanitarianism Transformed." *Perspectives on Politics* 3 (4): 723–40.

———. 2009. "Evolution without Progress? Humanitarianism in a World of Hurt." *International Organization* 63 (Fall): 621–63.

Barrett, Christopher, and Daniel Maxwell. 2005. *Food Aid after Fifty Years: Recasting Its Role.* London: Routledge.

Beckford, James. 1991. "Great Britain: Voluntarism and Sectional Interests." In *Between States and Markets,* edited by Robert Wuthnow, 30–63. Princeton: Princeton University Press.

Bell, Daniel, and Joseph Carens. 2004. "The Ethical Dilemmas of International Human Rights and Humanitarian NGOs." *Human Rights Quarterly* 26 (2): 300–329.

Benthall, Jonathan. 1993. *Disasters, Relief and the Media.* London: IB Taurus.

Berger, Suzanne, and Ronald Dore, eds. 1996. *National Diversity and Global Capitalism.* Ithaca: Cornell University Press.

Berkovitch, Nitza, and Neve Gordon. 2008. "The Political Economy of Transnational Regimes: The Case of Human Rights." *International Studies Quarterly* 52 (4): 881–904.

Biberson, Philippe, and François Jean. 1999. "The Challenges of Globalization of International Relief and Development." *Nonprofit Sector and Voluntary Quarterly* 28 (supplement):104–8.

Black, Maggie. 1992. *A Cause for Our Times: Oxfam, The First 50 Years.* New York: Oxford University Press.

Bob, Clifford. 2005. *The Marketing of Rebellion.* New York: Cambridge University Press.

Boli, John, and George M. Thomas. 1999. *Constructing World Culture: International Nongovernmental Organizations since 1875.* Stanford: Stanford University Press.

Boris, Elizabeth, and Jeff Krehely. "Civic Participation and Advocacy." In *The State of Nonprofit America,* edited by Lester Salamon, 299–330. Washington, D.C.: Brookings, 2002.

Bortolotti, Dan. 2004. *Hope in Hell: Inside the World of Doctors Without Borders.* Richmond Hill, Ontario: Firefly Books.

Brauman, Rony. 1996. *Humanitaire—le dilemme.* Paris: Editions Textuel, 1996.

———. 2004. "From Philanthropy to Humanitarianism." *South Atlantic Quarterly* 103 (2–3): 397–417.

———. 2006. "Préface." In *Critique de la raison humanitaire.* Edited by Karl Blanchet and Boris Martin, 5–12. Paris: Le cavalier bleu.

Brauman, Rony, and Pierre Salignon. 2004. "Iraq: In Search of a 'Humanitarian Crisis.'" In *In the Shadow of "Just Wars,"* edited by Fabrice Weissman, 269–85. Ithaca: Cornell University Press.

Brinkerhoff, Derick W., and Jennifer Brinkerhoff. 2004. "Partnership between International Donors and Nongovernmental Development Organizations." *International Review of Administrative Sciences* 70 (2): 253–70.

Bromley, Mark K. 2001. "The International Human Rights Law Group," In *NGOs and Human Rights: Promise and Performance,* edited by Claude E. Welch Jr., 141–50. Philadelphia: University of Pennsylvania Press.

Brown, Widney. 2001. "Human Rights Watch: An Overview." In *NGOs and Human Rights: Promise and Performance,* edited by Claude E. Welch, Jr., 72–84. Philadelphia: University of Pennsylvania Press.

Bryant, Coralie, and François Rubio. 2006. "ONG américaines et françaises: Différences dans les discources et les pratiques." *Tocqueville Review* 27 (1): 77–95.

Bryer, David, and Edmund Cairns. 1998. "For Better? For Worse? Humanitarian Aid in Conflict." In *From Conflict to Peace in a Changing World,* edited by Deborah Eade, 27–37. *Oxfam Working Papers.* Oxford: Oxfam.

Bryer, David, and John Magrath. 1999. "New Dimensions of Global Advocacy." *Nonprofit and Voluntary Sector Quarterly* 28 (supplement): 168–77.

Buchanan, Tom. 2002. "The Truth Will Set You Free: The Making of Amnesty International." *Journal of Contemporary History* 37 (4): 575–97.

Burnell, Peter. 1992. "Charity Law and Pressure Politics in Britain: After the Oxfam Inquiry." *Voluntas* 3 (3): 311–34.

Campbell, Wallace. 1990. *The History of CARE.* New York: Praeger.

CARE International. 2003a. *Final Report: Baseline for CARE International's Response to a Humanitarian Crisis in the Iraq Conflict: Real-Time Evaluation (RTE) #1.* April 24.

CARE International. 2003b. *Final Report: CARE International's Humanitarian Response to the Iraq Conflict, Real-Time Evaluation (RTE) #2.* September.

CARE International. 2009. *Policy Framework for CARE International's Relations with Military Forces.* June.

Carmichael, William. 2001. "The Role of the Ford Foundation." In *NGOs and Human Rights: Promise and Performance,* edited by Claude E. Welch Jr., 248–60. Philadelphia: University of Pennsylvania Press.

Carpenter, Charli. 2007. "Studying Issue (Non)-adoption in Transnational Advocacy Networks." *International Organization* 61 (Summer): 643–67.

———. 2010. *Forgetting Bosnia's War Children: Human Rights Agenda-Setting and Transnational Politics.* New York: Columbia University Press.

Chabbott, Collette. 1999. "Development INGOs." In *Constructing World Culture: International Nongovernmental Organizations since 1875,* edited by John Boli and George M. Thomas, 222–48. Stanford: Stanford University Press.

Chandhoke, Neera. 2007. "Thinking Through Economic and Social Rights." in *Ethics in Action: The Ethical Challenges of International Human Rights Organizations,* edited by Daniel Bell and Jean-Marc Coicaud, 181–97. New York: Cambridge University Press.

Charities Aid Foundation. 1994. *International Giving and Volunteering.* London: CAF.
———. 2006. *International Comparisons of Charitable Giving.* London: CAF. November.
Chaves, Mark, Joseph Galaskiewicz, and Laura Stephens. 2004. "Does Government Funding Suppress Nonprofits' Political Activity?" *American Sociological Review* 69 (April): 292–316.
Child, Curtis, and Kristen Grønbjerg. 2007. "Nonprofit Advocacy Organizations: Their Characteristics and Activities," *Social Science Quarterly* 88 (1): 259–81.
Christiansen, Lars, and Keith Dowding. 1994. "Pluralism or State Autonomy? The Case of Amnesty International (British Section)." *Political Studies* 42 (March): 15–24.
Clark, Ann Marie. 2001. *Diplomacy of Conscience.* Princeton: Princeton University Press.
Clark, John. 2003. *Worlds Apart: Civil Society and the Battle for Ethical Globalization.* Bloomfield: Kumarian Press.
Clarke, Michael. 1988. "The Policy-making Process." In *British Foreign Policy,* edited by Michael Smith et al., 71–95. New York: Routledge.
Cohen, Samy. 2006. *The Resilience of the State: Democracy and the Challenge of Globalization.* Boulder: Lynne Rienner.
Commins, Steven. 1997. "World Vision International and Donors: Too Close for Comfort?" In *NGOs, States, and Donors: Too Close for Comfort?* edited by David Hulme and Michael Edwards, 140–55. New York: St. Martin's Press.
Commissariat Général du Plan. 2002. *L'État et les ONG: Pour un partenariat efficace.* Paris: La Documentation Française.
Commission Coopération Développement. 2003. *Argent et Organisations Solidarité Internationale 2000/2001.* Paris: Ministère des Affaires étrangères, September.
———. 2005. *Argent et Organisations Solidarité Internationale 2002/2003.* Paris: Ministère des Affaires étrangères, September.
Congressional Research Service. 2006. *Restructuring US Foreign Aid: The Role of the Director of Foreign Assistance.* Washington June 16.
Cooley, Alexander, and James Ron. 2002. "The NGO Scramble: Organizational Insecurity and the Political Economy of Transnational Action." *International Security* 27 (Summer): 5–39.
Council on Foundations. 2006. "Country Information: France." *US International Grantmaking.* November.
Cumming, Gordon. 2008. "French NGOs in the Global Era: Professionalization 'Without Borders'?" *Voluntas* 19 (4): 372–94.
———. 2009. *French NGOs in the Global Era.* New York: Palgrave Macmillan.
Cushman, Thomas. 2005. "The Human Rights Case for the War in Iraq." In *Human Rights in the "War on Terror,"* edited by R. A. Wilson, 78–107. New York: Cambridge University Press.
Darcy, James, and Charles-Antoine Hoffman. 2003. *According to Need? Humanitarian Practice Group Report 15.* London: Overseas Development Institute. September.
Desforges, Luke. 2004. "The Formation of Global Citizenship." *Political Geography* 23 (June): 548–69.
Désir, Harlem. 1994. *La Situation et la devenir des associations à but humanitaire.* Paris: Conseil Économique et Social.

Devone, Ralph. 1990. "CARE Plans a New Strategic Package." *Management Review* 79 (12): 64.

DiMaggio, Paul, and Walter Powell. 1983. "The Iron Cage Revisited: Institutional Isomorphism and Collective Rationality in Organizational Fields." *American Sociological Review* 48 (2): 147–60.

Donini, Antonio. 2010. "The Far Side: The Meta-functions of Humanitarianism in a Globalized World," *Disasters* 34 (supplement 2): S220–S237.

Donnelly, Jack. 1999. "Social Construction of International Human Rights." In *Human Rights in Global Politics,* edited by Tim Dunne and Nicholas Wheeler, 71–102. Cambridge University Press, 1999.

———. 2007. *International Human Rights.* 3d ed. Boulder: Westview Press.

Doremus, Paul, William Keller, Louis Pauly, and Simon Reich. 1998. *The Myth of the Global Corporation.* Princeton: Princeton University Press.

Dreano, Bernard. 2004. "In Paris, the Global Place Is No More Saint Germain des Prés." In *Exploring Civil Society: Political and Cultural Contexts,* edited by Marlies Glasius et al., 82–88. New York: Routledge.

Doucin, Michel. 2002. "Société civile internationale et diplomatie." In *Les diplomates: Négocier dans un monde chaotique,* edited by Samy Cohen, 85–99. Paris: Autrement.

Duchesne, Sophie. 2003. "Don et recherche de soi, l'altruisme en question aux Restaurants du Coeur et à Amnesty International." *Cahier du CEVIPOF no. 33.*

Dudai, Ron. 2007. "A to Z of Abuses: 'State of the Art' in Global Human Rights Monitoring." *Development and Change* 38 (6): 1255–65.

Dunne, Tim, and Nicolas Wheeler. 1999. *Human Rights in Global Politics.* New York: Cambridge University Press.

Ebrahim, Alnoor. 2005. *NGOs and Organizational Change: Discourse, Reporting and Learning.* New York: Cambridge University Press.

Edwards, Michael. 1993. "'Does the Doormat Influence the Boot?' Critical Thoughts on UK NGOs and International Advocacy." *Development in Practice* 3 (October):163–75.

Edwards, Michael, and David Hulme. 1995. *Nongovernmental Organizations: Performance and Accountability.* London: Earthscan.

Fack, Gabrielle, and Camille Landais. 2010. "Are Tax Incentives for Charitable Giving Efficient? Evidence from France." *American Economic Journal: Economic Policy* 2 (May): 117–41.

Fagnou, Emmanuel. 2004a. "Panorama des ONG françaises: Acteurs majeurs de la solidarité internationale." In *Les ONG dans la tempête mondiale: Nouveaux débats, nouveaux chantiers pour un monde solidaire,* 57–66. Paris: Coordination SUD.

———. 2004b. *Présentation du secteur des ONGs françaises.* Paris: Coordination SUD. September.

Fassin, Didier. 2007. "Humanitarianism as a Politics of Life." *Public Culture* 19 (Fall): 499–520.

Finnemore, Martha. 1996a. *National Interests and International Society.* Ithaca: Cornell University Press.

———. 1996b. "Norms, Culture and World Politics: Insights from Sociology's Institutionalism." *International Organization* 50 (2): 325–47.

Forman, Shepard, and Abby Stoddard. 2002. "International Assistance." In *The State of Nonprofit America,* edited by Lester Salamon, 24–74. Washington: Brookings Institution, 254–58.

Forsythe, David. 2005. *The Humanitarians: The International Committee of the Red Cross.* New York: Cambridge University Press.

Fowler, Alan. 1991. "Building Partnerships between Northern and Southern Development NGOs." *Development in Practice* 1 (Spring): 5–18.

Frumkin, Peter. 1998. "The Long Recoil from Regulation: Private Philanthropic Foundations and the Tax Reform Act of 1969." *American Review of Public Administration* 28 (3): 266–86.

Frumkin, Peter, and Mark Kim. 2001. "Strategic Positioning and the Financing of Nonprofit Organizations." *Public Administration Review* 61 (May–June): 266–75.

General Accounting Office. 2002. *Foreign Assistance: USAID Relies Heavily on Nongovernmental Organizations, but Better Data Needed to Evaluate Approaches.* Report to the Chairman, Subcommittee on National Security, Veterans Affairs, and International Relations, Committee on Government Reform, House of Representatives. GAO-02-471. Washington: GAO, April.

Gnaerig, Burkhard, and Charles MacCormack. 1999. "The Challenges of Globalization: Save the Children." *Nonprofit and Voluntary Sector Quarterly* 28 (supplement): 140–46.

Goering, Curt. 2007. "Amnesty International and Economic, Social and Cultural Rights." In *Ethics in Action: The Ethical Challenges of International Human Rights Organizations,* edited by Daniel Bell and Jean-Marc Coicaud, 204–17. New York: Cambridge University Press.

Goodman, Ryan, and Derek Jinks. 2004. "How to Influence States: Socialization and International Human Rights Law." *Duke Law Journal* 54 (3): 621–703.

Graham, Clare. 2003. "Iraq: Dilemmas in Contingency Planning." *Forced Migration Review* 17 (May): 38–40.

Grønbjerg, Kristin. 1998. "Markets, Politics, and Charity." In *Private Action and the Public Good,* edited by Walter Powell and Elisabeth Clemens, 137–50. New Haven: Yale University Press.

Grønbjerg, Kristen, and Lester Salamon. 2002. "Devolution, Marketization, and the Changing Shape of Government-Nonprofit Relations." In *The State of Nonprofit America,* edited by Lester Salamon, 447–70. Washington: Brookings Institution: 447–70.

Guillén, Mauro. 2001. "Is Globalization Civilizing, Destructive, or Feeble?" *Annual Review of Sociology* 27: 235–60.

Halfpenny, Peter, and Margaret Reid. 2002. "Research on the Voluntary Sector: An Overview." *Policy and Politics* 30 (4): 533–50.

Hall, Peter. 1986. *Governing the Economy.* New York: Oxford University Press.

———. 1999. "Social Capital in Britain." *British Journal of Political Science* 29 (3): 417–61.

Hall, Peter, and David Soskice, eds. 2001. *Varieties of Capitalism: The Institutional Foundations of Comparative Advantage.* New York: Oxford University Press.

Hall, Peter Dobkin, and Colin Burke. 2002. "Historical Statistics of the United States Chapter on Voluntary, Nonprofit, and Religious Entities and Activities."

Harvard University Hauser Center for Nonprofit Organizations Working Paper #14. November.

Hammack, David. 2002. "Nonprofit Organizations in American History." *American Behavioral Scientist* 45 (11): 1638–74.

Hammack, David, and Steven Heydemann. 2009. *Globalization, Philanthropy, and Civil Society*. Bloomington: Indiana University Press.

Harzing, Anne-Wil, and Arndt Sorge. 2003. "The Relative Impact of Country of Origin and Universal Contingencies on Internationalization Strategies and Corporate Control in Multinational Enterprises." *Organization Studies* 24 (2): 187–214.

Hatton, Jean-Marie. 2007. *Note sur la structuration progressive des OSI dans leur relation avec les pouvoirs publics*. Paris: Coordination SUD. May.

Heller, Stephen, and Veronique Vienne. 2003. *Citizen Designer: Perspectives on Design Responsibility*. New York: Allworth Press, 2003.

Henry, Kevin. 1999. "CARE International: Evolving to Meet the Challenges of the 21st Century." *Nonprofit and Voluntary Sector Quarterly* 28 (Supplement): 109–20.

Hopgood, Stephen. 2006. *Keepers of the Flame: Amnesty International*. Ithaca: Cornell University Press.

———. 2009. "Moral Authority, Modernity, and the Politics of the Sacred." *European Journal of International Relations* 15 (2): 229–55.

———. 2010. "Review Essay: Dignity and Ennui." *Journal of Human Rights Practice* 2 (1): 151–65.

Hoffman, Peter, and Thomas Weiss. 2006. *Sword & Salve: Confronting New Wars and Humanitarian Crises*. Lanham: Rowman & Littlefield.

Hudson, Alan. 2002. "Advocacy by UK-Based Development INGOs." *Nonprofit and Voluntary Sector Quarterly* 31 (3): 402–18.

Hudson Institute. 2006. *Index of Global Philanthropy*. Washington: Hudson Institute.

Hwang, Hokyu, and Walter Powell. 2009. "The Rationalization of Charity: The Influences of Professionalism in the Nonprofit Sector." *Administrative Science Quarterly* 54 (2): 268–98.

Ignatieff, Michael, ed. 2005. *American Exceptionalism and Human Rights*. Princeton: Princeton University Press.

Irvine, William. 2007. *Between Justice and Politics: The Ligue des Droits de l'Homme, 1898–1945*. Stanford: Stanford University Press.

Johnson, Larry. 1993. "Management: World Vision's New Weapon," *Fund Raising Management* 24 (4): 22–26.

Joint Committee on Taxation. 2005. *Historical Development and Present Law of the Federal Tax Exemption for Charities and Other Tax-Exempt Organizations*. JCX-29-05. April 19.

Johnson, Erica, and Aseem Prakash. 2007. "NGO Research Program: A Collective Action Perspective." *Policy Sciences* 40 (3): 221–40.

Jordan, Lisa, and Peter Van Tuijl. 2000. "Political Responsibility in Transnational NGO Advocacy." *World Development* 28 (12): 2051–65.

Karl, Barry D. 1998. "Volunteers and Professionals: Many Histories, Many Meanings." In *Private Action and the Public Good*, edited by Walter Powell and Elisabeth Clemens, 245–57. New Haven: Yale University Press.

Keck, Margaret, and Kathryn Sikkink. 1998. *Activists beyond Borders: Advocacy Networks in International Politics.* Ithaca: Cornell University Press.

Kendall, Jeremy. 2000. "The Mainstreaming of the Third Sector into Public Policy in England in the Late 1990s: Whys and Wherefores." *Policy and Politics* 28 (4): 541–62.

Kendall, Jeremy, and Stephen Almond. 1999. "United Kingdom." In *Global Civil Society: Dimensions of the Nonprofit Sector,* edited by Lester Salamon et al., 179–99. Bloomfield: Kumarian Press.

Khagram, Sanjeev, et al. 2002. *World Politics: Transnational Social Movements, Networks and Norms.* Minneapolis: University of Minnesota.

Koch, Dirk-Jan, Axel Dreher, Peter Nunnencamp, and Rainer Thiele. 2009. "Keeping a Low Profile: What Determines the Allocation of Aid by Non-Governmental Organizations?" *World Development* 37 (5): 902–18.

Korey, William. 1998. *NGOs and the Universal Declaration of Human Rights.* New York: St. Martin's Press.

———. 2007. *Taking on the World's Repressive Regimes.* New York: Palgrave.

Laber, Jeri. 2002. *The Courage of Strangers: Coming of Age in the Human Rights Movement.* New York: PublicAffairs.

Lancaster, Carol. 2007. *Foreign Aid: Diplomacy, Development, Domestic Politics.* Chicago: University of Chicago Press.

Landman, Todd, and Meghna Abraham. 2004. *Human Rights Organization Assessment and Performance Evaluation.* The Hague: Ministry of Foreign Affairs.

Lamont, Michèle. 1992. *Money, Morals, and Manners.* Chicago: University of Chicago Press.

Lévêque, Philippe. 2004. "After 20 years, CARE France Aims for More Recognition." *iCARE News* 36 (April).

Levy, Jonah. 1999. *Tocqueville's Revenge.* Cambridge, Mass.: Harvard University Press.

Lewis, David. 2008. "Crossing the Boundaries between 'Third Sector' and State." *Third World Quarterly* 29 (1): 125–41.

Leyton, Elliott, and Greg Locke. 1998. *Touched by Fire: Doctors Without Borders in a Third World Crisis.* Toronto: McClelland and Stewart.

Light, Paul. 2000. *Making Nonprofits Work.* Washington: Brookings Institution.

Linden, Eugene. 1976. *The Alms Race.* New York: Random House.

Lindenberg, Marc. 2001. "Are We the Cutting Edge or the Blunt Edge?" *Nonprofit Management and Leadership* 11 (Spring): 247–70.

Lindenberg, Marc, and Coralie Bryant. 2001. *Going Global: Transforming Relief and Development NGOs.* Bloomfield: Kumarian Press.

Lipset, Seymour Martin. 1996. *American Exceptionalism: A Double-Edged Sword.* New York: Norton.

Loya, Thomas, and John Boli. 1999. "Standardization in the World Polity." In *Constructing World Culture: International Nongovernmental Organizations Since 1875,* edited by John Boli and George M. Thomas, 169–97. Stanford: Stanford University Press.

Madsen, Mikael. 2004. "France, the UK, and the 'Boomerang' of the Internationalization of Human Rights." In *Human Rights Brought Home,* edited by Simon Halliday and Patrick Schmidt, 57–86. Portland: Hart.

Mahoney, Liam. 2001. "Military Intervention in Human Rights Crises." International Council on Human Rights Policy Working Paper. www.ichrp.org/files/papers/49/115. March.

Mamdani, Mahmood. 2008. "The New Humanitarian Order." *The Nation*, September 10.

March, James, and Johan Olsen. 1998. "The Institutional Dynamics of International Political Orders." *International Organization* 52 (Autumn): 943–69.

Martens, Kerstin. 2006. "Professionalized Representation of Human Rights NGOs to the United Nations." *International Journal of Human Rights* 10 (1): 19–30.

McAdam, Doug, and W. Richard Scott. 2005. "Organizations and Movements." In *Social Movements and Organization Theory,* edited by Gerald Davis et al., 4–40. New York: Cambridge University Press.

McCleary, Rachel. 2009. *Global Compassion: Private Voluntary Organizations and U.S. Foreign Policy since 1939.* New York: Oxford University Press.

McCleary, Rachel, and Robert Barro. 2008. "Private Voluntary Organizations Engaged in International Assistance, 1939–2004." *Nonprofit and Voluntary Sector Quarterly* 37 (3): 512–36.

Mertus, Julie. 2009. *Human Rights Matters: Local Politics and National Human Rights Institutions.* Stanford: Stanford University Press.

Meunier, Sophie. 2000. "The French Exception: A Growing Movement against Globalization in France." *Foreign Affairs* 79 (July–August): 104–16.

Meyer, John, and Bryan Rowan. 1977. "Institutionalized Organizations: Formal structure as Myth and Ceremony." *American Journal of Sociology* 83 (2): 340–63.

Meyer, Megan. 2004. "Organizational Identity, Political Contexts, and SMO Action." *Social Movement Studies* 3 (2): 167–97.

Minear, Larry. 2002. *The Humanitarian Enterprise: Dilemmas and Discoveries.* Bloomfield: Kumarian, 2002.

Minear, Larry, and Thomas Weiss. 1995. *Mercy under Fire: War and the Global Humanitarian Community.* Boulder: Westview Press.

Ministère des Affaires étrangères. 2003. *For Democratic Governance: French Development Cooperation Policy Steering Document.* Paris.

——. 2004. *Part de l'APD versée aux ONG françaises en 2003.* Paris.

Moog, Sandra. 2009. "Exporting Associational Logics into the Amazon?" In *Globalization, Philanthropy, and Civil Society,* edited by David Hammack and Steven Heydemann, 258–91. Bloomington: Indiana University Press.

Moore, Gwen, Sarah Sobieraj, J. Allen Whitt, Olga Mayorova, and Daniel Beaulieu. 2002. "Elite Interlocks in Three US Sectors: Nonprofit, Corporate, and Government," *Social Science Quarterly* 83 (3): 730–31.

Moyn, Samuel. 2010. *The Last Utopia.* Cambridge, Mass.: Harvard University Press.

Neier, Aryeh. 2003. *Taking Liberties: Four Decades in the Struggle for Rights.* New York: PublicAffairs, 2003.

Nelson, Paul. 2000. "Heroism and Ambiguity: NGO Advocacy in International Policy." *Development in Practice* 10 (August): 478–90.

——. 2004. "New Agendas and New Patterns of INGO Political Action." In *Creating a Better World: Interpreting Global Civil Society,* edited by Rupert Taylor, 116–32. Bloomfield: Kumarian Press.

Nelson, Paul, and Ellen Dorsey. 2008. *New Rights Advocacy.* Washington: Georgetown University Press.

Newman, Caroline. 2001. "France: The Status of Political Activities of Associations and Foundations." *International Journal of Not-for-Profit Law* 3 (March). http://www.icnl.org/knowledge/ijnl/vol3iss3/cr_9.htm#france (accessed October 10, 2008)

OECD [Organization for Economic Cooperation and Development]. 2000. *Results-Based Management in the Development Cooperation Agencies,* Report for the DAC Working Party on Aid Evaluation. Paris: OECD. February.

OECD DAC [Development Assistance Committee]. 1998. *Development Cooperation Review: United States.* Paris: OECD.

OECD DAC. 2000. *DAC Journal 2000: France, New Zealand, Italy* 1 (3).

OECD DAC. 2006a. *United Kingdom: Development Assistance Committee Peer Review.* Paris: OECD.

OECD DAC. 2006b. *The United States: Development Assistance Committee Peer Review.* Paris: OECD.

OECD DAC. 2010. *United Kingdom: Development Assistance Committee Peer Review.* Paris: OECD.

Offenheiser, Raymond, Susan Holcombe, and Nancy Hopkins. 1999. "Grappling with Globalization, Partnership and Learning: A Look inside Oxfam America." *Nonprofit and Voluntary Sector Quarterly* 28 (supplement): 121–39.

O'Flaherty, Michael, and George Ulrich. 2010. "The Professionalization of Human Rights Field Work." *Journal of Human Rights Practice* 2 (January): 1–27.

Orbinski, James. 1999. *Médecins Sans Frontières Nobel Lecture.* Oslo, December 10. http://www.nobelprize.org/nobel_prizes/peace/laureates/1999/msf-lecture.html (accessed March 31, 2011).

Osviovitch, Jay. 1998. "Feeding the Watchdogs." *Buffalo Human Rights Law Review* 4:341–63.

Ott, J. Steven. 2001. "The Blurring and Blending of Sectors." In *The Nature of the Nonprofit Sector.* Boulder: Westview Press.

Paquot, Élizabeth. 2001. *International Solidarity Organizations and Public Authorities in Europe.* Paris: Ministère des Affaires étrangères.

Pfeffer, Jeffrey, and Gerald Salancik. 1978. *The External Control of Organizations.* Stanford: Stanford University Press.

Pieck, Sonja, and Sandra Moog. 2009. "Competing Entanglements in the Struggle to Save the Amazon." *Political Geography* 28 (7): 416–25.

Prakash, Aseem, and Rebecca Szper. 2011. "Charity Watchdogs and the Limits of Information-based Regulation." *Voluntas* 22 (March): 112–41.

Poinsot, Eric. 2004. "Vers une lecture économique et sociale des droits humains: L'évolution d'Amnesty International." *Revue française de science politique* 54 (3): 399–420.

Price, Richard. 1998. "Reversing the Gun Sights: Transnational Civil Society Targets Landmines." *International Organization* 52 (3): 613–44.

Putnam, Robert. 2000. *Bowling Alone.* New York: Simon and Schuster.

Queinnec, Erwan. 2003. "The Ambivalence of the Inherent Nature and Purpose of Humanitarian Organizations: A Research Theme for the Management Sciences." *International Social Science Journal* 55 (177): 501–23.

Rabben, Linda. 2002. *Fierce Legion of Friends.* Brentwood: The Quixote Center.

Randel, Judith, and Tony German. 2002. "Trends in the Financing of Humanitarian Assistance." In *The New Humanitarianisms: A Review of Trends in Global Humanitarian Action, HPG Report 11,* edited by Joanna Macrae, 19–28. London: ODI.

———. 2003. *Global Humanitarian Assistance 2003.* London: Development Initiatives.

Redfield, Peter. 2005. "Doctors, Borders, and Life in Crisis," *Cultural Anthropology* 20 (3): 328–61.

———. 2006. "A Less Modest Witness: Collective Advocacy and Motivated Truth in a Medical Humanitarian Movement." *American Ethnologist* 33 (1): 3–26.

Reid, Elizabeth, and Janelle Kerlin. 2006. *The International Charitable Nonprofit Sector in the United States.* Washington: Urban Institute.

Reimann, Kim. 2006. "A View from the Top: International Politics, Norms, and the Worldwide Growth of NGOs." *International Studies Quarterly* 50 (1): 45–67.

Rieff, David. 1999. "The Precarious Triumph of Human Rights." *New York Times Magazine,* August 8.

———. 2002. *A Bed for the Night: Humanitarianism in Crisis.* New York: Simon and Schuster.

Risse, Thomas. 2002. "Transnational Actors and World Politics." In *The Handbook of International Relations,* edited by Walter Carlsnaes et al., 255–74. Thousand Oaks: Sage.

Risse, Thomas, Steven Ropp, and Kathryn Sikkink. 1999. *The Power of Human Rights: International Norms and Domestic Change.* New York: Cambridge University Press.

Risse-Kappen, Thomas. 1994. "Ideas Do Not Float Freely." *International Organization* 48 (2): 185–214.

Roberts, Susan, John Paul Jones III, and Oliver Frohling. 2005. "NGOs and the Globalization of Managerialism." *World Development* 33 (11): 1845–64.

Ron, James, Howard Ramos, and Kathleen Rogers. 2005. "Transnational Information Politics: NGO Human Rights Reporting, 1986–2000." *International Studies Quarterly* 49 (3): 557–88.

Roth, Kenneth. 2004. "Defending Economic, Social and Cultural Rights." *Human Rights Quarterly* 26 (1): 63–73.

———. 2007. "Defending Economic, Social, and Cultural Rights." In *Ethics in Action: The Ethical Challenges of International Human Rights Nongovernmental Organizations,* edited by Daniel Bell and Jean-Marc Coicaud, 169–80. New York: Cambridge University Press.

Rouillé d'Orfeuil, Henri. 2006. *La diplomatie non gouvernementale.* Paris: Éditions de l'Atelier.

Rucht, Dieter. 1996. "The Impact of National Contexts on Social Movement Structures." In *Comparative Perspectives on Social Movements,* edited by Doug McAdam et al., 185–204. New York: Cambridge University Press.

Ryfman, Philippe. 2006. "Les ONG françaises: Crises de la maturité et mutations." In *Critique de la raison humanitaire,* edited by Karl Blanchet and Boris Martin, 21–32. Paris: Le cavalier bleu.

Salamon, Lester, ed. 1999a. *Global Civil Society: Dimensions of the Nonprofit Sector.* Bloomfield: Kumarian Press.

———. 1999b. "The Nonprofit Sector at a Crossroads: The Case of America." *Voluntas* 10 (1): 5–23.

Salignon, Pierre. 2003. "Guerre en Irak: Les représentations humanitaires en question." *Revue humanitaire 8* (Fall): 43–60.

Sanchez-Salgado, Rosa. 2001a. "L'Européanisation de la société civile." Thesis, Mémoire de DEA de l'Institute d'Études Politiques, Paris.

———. 2001b. "Europeanization of Civil Society?" *Observatori de política exterior europea,* Working Paper no. 16. Barcelona: Institut Universitari d'Estudis Europeus. October.

Saurugger, Sabine. 2007. "Democratic 'Misfit'? Conceptions of Civil Society Participation in France and the European Union." *Political Studies* 55 (2): 384–404.

Schofer, Evan, and Ann Hironaka. 2005. "The Effects of World Society on Environmental Protection Outcomes." *Social Forces* 84 (1): 25–47.

Schofer, Evan, and Marion Fourcade-Gourinchas. 2001. "The Structural Contexts of Civic Engagement: Voluntary Association Membership in Comparative Perspective." *American Sociological Review* 66 (6): 806–28.

Schraeder, Peter, Steven Hook, and Bruce Taylor. 1998. "Clarifying the Foreign Aid Puzzle." *World Politics* 50 (2): 294–323.

Schulz, William. 2003. *Tainted Legacy: 9/11 and the Ruin of Human Rights.* New York: Nation Books.

Scott, Esther. 1995. *Providing Two-Way Feedback: Assessing Headquarters and Field Service Performance at CARE.* Harvard University Kennedy School of Government Case Study in Public Policy and Management 1283. January.

Scott, Esther, and David Brown. 2004. *Oxfam America: Becoming a Global Campaigning Organization.* Harvard University Kennedy School of Government Case Study C16-04-1738.

Scott, W. Richard. 1994. "Institutions and Organizations." In *Institutional Environments and Organizations,* edited by W. Richard Scott and John Meyer, 55–80. Thousand Oaks: Sage.

Sell, Susan K. 2002. "TRIPs and the Access to Medicines Campaign." *Wisconsin International Law Journal* 20:481–522.

Sell, Susan, and Aseem Prakash. 2004. "Using Ideas Strategically: The Contest between Business and NGO Networks in Intellectual Property Rights." *International Studies Quarterly* 48 (1): 143–75.

Sikkink, Kathryn, and Jackie Smith. 2002. "Infrastructures for Change: Transnational Organizations, 1953–1993." In *Restructuring World Politics,* edited by Sanjeev Khagram et al., 24–46. Minneapolis: University of Minnesota Press.

Siméant, Johanna. 2001. "Entrer, rester en humanitaire: Des fondateurs de MSF aux membres actuels des ONGs médicales françaises." *Revue française de science politique* 51 (1): 47–72.

———. 2005. "What Is Going Global? The Internationalization of French NGOs 'Without Borders.'" *Review of International Political Economy* 12 (5): 851–83.

Siméant, Johanna, and Pascal Dauvin. 2002. *Le travail humanitaire: Les acteurs des ONG, du siège au terrain* (Paris: Presses de Sciences Po).

Skocpol, Theda. 2002. "United States: From Membership to Advocacy." In *Democracies in Flux,* edited by Robert Putnam, 103–36. New York: Oxford University Press.

———. 2004. "Voice and Inequality," *Perspectives on Politics* 2 (1): 3–20.

Slim, Hugo. 2006. "Les radicaux de l'establishment: Un aperçu historique des ONGs britanniques." In *Critique de la raison humanitaire,* edited by Karl Blanchet and Boris Martin, 33–48. Paris: Le cavalier bleu.

Smillie, Ian. 1995. *The Alms Bazaar: Altruism under Fire.* London: Intermediate Technology.

Smillie, Ian, and Henny Helmich, eds. 1993. *Non-Governmental Organizations and Governments: Stakeholders for Development.* Paris: Organization for Economic Cooperation and Development.

———, eds. 1999. *Stakeholders: Government-NGO Partnerships for International Development.* London: Earthscan.

Smith, Brian. 1990. *More than Altruism: The Politics of Private Foreign Aid.* Princeton: Princeton University Press.

Smith, David Horton, Burt Baldwin, and William Chittick. 1980. "U.S. National Voluntary Organizations, Transnational Orientations, and Development." *International Journal of Comparative Sociology* 21 (3–4): 163–81.

Smith, Jackie. 2005. "Globalization and Transnational Social Movement Organizations." In *Social Movements and Organization Theory,* edited by Gerald Davis et al., 226–48. New York: Cambridge University Press.

Smith, Jackie, and Joe Bandy, eds. 2005. *Coalitions Across Borders: Transnational Protest and the Neoliberal Order.* Lanham: Rowman & Littlefield.

Smith, Jackie, and Dawn Wiest. 2005. "The Uneven Geography of Global Civil Society." *Social Forces* 84 (2): 621–52.

Sommer, John G. 1977. *Beyond Charity: US Voluntary Aid for a Changing Third World.* Washington: Overseas Development Council.

Sondorp, Egbert. 2006. "Français et Anglo-Saxons: Une approche éthique différente?" In *Critique de la raison humanitaire,* edited by Karl Blanchet and Boris Martin, 49–58. Paris: Le cavalier bleu.

Sorgenfrei, Mia. 2004. *Capacity Building from a French Perspective. Praxis Papers 1.* Oxford: INTRAC [International NGO Training and Research Centre]. July.

Sponeck, Hans von. 2006. *A Different Kind of War: The UN Sanctions Regime in Iraq.* Oxford: Berghahn.

Stoddard, Abby. 2002. *Trends in US Humanitarian Policy. HPG* [Humanitarian Policy Group] *Policy Briefs 3.* London: Overseas Development Institute. April.

———. 2006. *Humanitarian Alert: NGO Information and Its Impact on US Foreign Policy.* Bloomfield: Kumarian.

Strange, Susan. 1996. *The Retreat of the State: The Diffusion of Power in the World Economy.* New York: Cambridge University Press.

Stroup, Sarah. 2010. "National Origin and Transnational Activism." In *Power and Transnational Activism,* edited by Thomas Olesen, 151–70. New York: Routledge.

Sunderland, David. 2004. *The British International Development Sector.* Paris: Coordination SUD. March.

Sunga, Lyal. 2007. "Dilemmas Facing NGOs in Coalition-Occupied Iraq." In *Ethics in Action: The Ethical Challenges of International Human Rights Nongovernmental Organizations,* edited by Daniel Bell and Jean-Marc Coicaud, 99–116. New York: Cambridge University Press.

Tarrow, Sidney. 2005. *The New Transnational Activism.* New York: Cambridge University Press.

——. 2010. "Outsiders Inside and Insiders Outside: Linking Transnational and Domestic Public Action for Human Rights," *Human Rights Review* 11 (2): 171–82.

Tinkelman, Daniel, and Kamini Mankaney. 2007. "When Is Administrative Efficiency Associated with Charitable Donations?" *Nonprofit and Voluntary Sector Quarterly* 36 (1): 41–64.

Tolley, Howard. 1990–91. "Interest Group Litigation to Enforce Human Rights." *Political Science Quarterly* 105 (4): 617–38.

Tonkiss, Fran, and Andrew Passey. 1999. "Trust, Confidence, and Voluntary Organizations: Between Values and Institutions." *Sociology* 33 (2): 257–74.

Torrente, Nicolas de. 2004. "Humanitarian Action under Attack: Reflections on the Iraq War." *Harvard Human Rights Journal* 17 (1): 1–30.

——. 2005. "The Professionalization and Bureaucratization of Humanitarian Action." Draft paper for Social Science Research Council seminar series, "The Transformation of Humanitarian Action." March.

Tvedt, Terje. 1998. *Angels of Mercy or Development Diplomats? NGOs and Foreign Aid.* Oxford: James Currey.

Useem, Michael. 1986. *The Inner Circle.* New York: Oxford University Press.

Veeken, Hans, and Bernard Pecoul. 2000. "Editorial: Drugs for 'Neglected Diseases': A Bitter Pill." *Tropical Medicine and International Health* 5 (5): 309–11.

Versluys, Helen. 2008. "European Union Humanitarian Aid." In *Europe's Global Role,* edited by Jan Orbie, 91–116. Burlington: Ashgate.

Veugelers, Jack, and Michèle Lamont. 1991. "France: Alternative Locations for Public Debate." In *Between States and Markets: The Voluntary Sector in Comparative Perspective,* edited by Robert Wuthnow, 125–56. Princeton: Princeton University Press.

Vogel, Ann. 2006. "Who's Making Global Civil Society: Philanthropy and US Empire in World Society." *British Journal of Sociology* 57 (4): 635–55.

Wallace, Tina. 2003. "Trends in UK NGOs: A Research Note." *Development in Practice* 13 (5): 565.

Wallace, Tina, Sarah Crowther, and Andrew Shepherd. 1997. *Standardizing Development: Influences on UK Policies and Procedures.* Oxford: Worldview Publishing.

Wallace, Tina, and Helen Banos Smith. 2010. *A Synthesis of the Learning from the Stop Violence Against Women Campaign 2004–2010.* AI Index ACT 77/008/2010. London: Amnesty.

Wapner, Paul. 1995. "Politics beyond the State: Environmental Activism and World Civic Politics." *World Politics* 47 (3): 311–40.

Watt, David H. 1991. "United States." In *Between States and Market: The Voluntary Sector in Comparative Perspective.* Princeton: Princeton University Press.

Weiss, Thomas. 1999. "Principles, Politics and Humanitarian Action." *Ethics and International Affairs* 13 (1): 1–22.

Welch, Claude E., Jr., ed. 2001. *NGOs and Human Rights: Promise and Performance.* Philadelphia: University of Pennsylvania Press.

Whaites, Alan. 1999. "Pursuing Partnership: World Vision and the Ideology of Development—a Case Study." *Development in Practice* 9 (4): 410–23.

Wheeler, Nicholas, and Tim Dunne. 1998. "Good International Citizenship: A Third Way for British Foreign Policy." *International Affairs* 74 (4): 847–70.

Williams, Paul. 2004. "Who's Making UK Foreign Policy?" *International Affairs* 80 (5): 909–29.

Wilson, James Q. 1989. *Bureaucracy.* New York: Basic Books.

Wilson, Richard J., and Jennifer Rasmussen. 2001. *Promoting Justice: A Practical Guide to Strategic Human Rights Lawyering.* Washington: International Human Rights Law Group.

Winston, Morton. 2001. "Assessing the Effectiveness of International Human Rights NGOs: Amnesty International." In *NGOs and Human Rights: Promise and Performance.* Philadelphia: University of Pennsylvania Press.

Wodon, Quentin, ed. 2001. *Attacking Extreme Poverty: Learning from the Experience of the International Movement ATD Fourth World. World Bank Technical Papers 502.* Washington: World Bank.

Worms, Jean-Pierre, 2002. "France: Old and New Civil and Social Ties in France." In *Democracies in Flux,* edited by Robert Putnam, 137–88. New York: Oxford University Press: 137–88.

Wresinki, Joseph. 2006. "A Knowledge That Leads to Action." In *Participatory Approaches to Attacking Extreme Poverty,* edited by Quentin Wodon, 13–22. *World Bank Working Papers 77.* Washington: World Bank.

Wright, Karen. 2001. "Generosity vs. Altruism: Philanthropy and Charity in the United States and United Kingdom." *Voluntas* 12 (4): 399–416.

Young, Dennis, Bonnie Koenig, Adil Najam, and Julie Fisher. 1999. "Strategy and Structure in Managing Global Associations." *Voluntas* 10 (4): 323–43.

INDEX

Page numbers followed by *t* refer to tables.